Blood From Your Own Pen

A Practical Guide on Self-Editing and Common Mistakes

For Beginning Authors Who Intend to Survive to Publication

Revised and Updated 2nd Edition

Sam Knight

ORIGINAL DEDICATION

To the authors of the stories included in the anthologies:

Sidekicks: A Speculative Fiction Anthology Supporting MileHiCon

and

Adventures in Zookeeping: A Speculative Fiction Anthology Supporting MileHiCon

Helping you learn helped me learn. As it should be.

And to my wife and children, who tolerate me more than I can comprehend.

2ND EDITION DEDICATION

To the authors who have trusted me with their stories and formatting in the years since the first edition.

And to my wife and children, who still tolerate me more than I can comprehend.

Blood from Your Own Pen

TABLE OF CONTENTS

Revised and Updated 2nd Edition
Introduction

A lot has changed in the five years since I wrote this guide. In the publishing world it always does, but recently it seems to happen faster and faster. I wanted to do a section on marketing and advertising for self-publishers, but that changes so quickly that, in my opinion, you are better off being a part of a social media group, learning and exchanging ideas in real time, as things change, so that you can react and respond in a timely manner.

Many of the places I had mentioned self-publishing had to be updated for this edition, and more and more authors are self-publishing. That was a huge part of the reason for a revised edition. Places go out of business, merge, change the services they offer, or get replaced by the new upstarts claiming to be better. By the time this edition is published, that will likely be true all over again.[1]

And that's okay. Don't let any of that discourage you.

If you picked this book up and read this far, chances are good you are, or want to be, a writer.

As this is my book, and you likely came to it looking for advice, here is the best advice I can give you:

Don't listen to anyone who says you can't.

Don't listen to anyone who says there is only one way (or one right way) to do something.

Don't blindly follow rules (especially ones that say "always" or "never"), but rather follow them until you figure those rules out and understand why they exist. And then:

Break the hell out of them in ways that work for you.

This doesn't merely apply to writing; this applies to life.

If you don't believe in yourself, no one else will. Unfortunately, when you do believe in yourself, a lot of people will waste a lot of your time and energy trying to convince you that you shouldn't.

Don't let them.

You've got this.

Do it.

---

[1] That turned out to be true. As this went to press, KDP announced they would start doing hardback books.

ORIGINAL INTRODUCTION

Hi! I'm Sam Knight, and I have an editing problem. It's not that I can't stop editing; in fact, it's pretty much the opposite. I don't like to do it. Especially when it's my own stuff. I hate editing my own stuff. As do most writers.

I don't consider myself to be a great editor, or even a very good one, and I am not claiming to be an editing guru, so let's just get that out of the way right now. I am neither a grammarian nor a linguist, and I don't want to be.

So, what exactly is all this then?

You see, there are a few things in life that make everything else a lot easier, if only you know them. But they always seem to be hard lessons to learn. Sometimes people won't tell you something because they think you already know. Or they don't care. Or they think it's amusing that you don't know. Or it's not their job. Or they are too embarrassed for you.

Life is full of little things like that. Like knowing that if you close the zipper on your pants by pointing the pull tab on the slider down, it will be much less likely to unzip when you don't want it to. Some people have no idea that some zippers have a little pin lock that fits into the teeth of the zipper and stops the slider from working its way down. See? Life hack.

One I learned the hard way.

Like knowing that you can put soda in a sippy cup—but not one that uses a straw. Because it squirts out at you. Another lesson learned the hard way.

(Okay. Wait. Time-out. I want to take a moment to mention my frustrations coming up with examples for this book. I used my own real-life examples there, but using real examples of other peoples' mistakes is not cool[2]. I'm not going to do it. So, I made up examples throughout every section of this book. And it wasn't easy. It is really difficult to take an example of something you've seen and attempt to make a whole new example of the mistake without leaving it looking a lot like the old example. But I have tried. I didn't want to put anyone on the spot by using actual examples, which would have also required getting permission.

Now let's return to our regularly scheduled Introduction, already in progress. Where were we anyway? Oh, yes! Life hacks and lessons learned the hard way...)

Writing is the same way. Sometimes there are little things you didn't know about that can change everything, and that's why I decided to write this guide. It is a compilation of things that have taken me sixteen years to learn, and I am going to give you the chance to learn it all in sixty minutes[3]! Yay! Talk about a return in time investment!

---

[2] Recently a small publisher was called out for posting lists of stories they rejected and why.

[3] It was pointed out to me, soon after the first edition was published, that sixty

Hmmm… That's a great tag line. I think I'm going to put it on the back cover.

So, am I qualified to be an authority on this? Nope. I refuse to be an authority on anything. It's not worth the headaches of arguing with people about whatever it is they are sure I am wrong about (and probably am).

But here is what I do know:

In 2014, Villainous Press, with Guy Anthony DeMarco, myself, and a handful of writers put together a charity anthology to benefit MileHiCon in Denver, Colorado. The writers offered up their stories, Villainous Press offered up formatting, layout, and publication, and I offered to edit the stories.

It worked out so well, we did it again in 2015.

During the course of editing the stories, I saw many of the writers had made similar mistakes. Many of those mistakes were ones I had seen before and had even made myself, over and over again, until someone (usually from my writers group) finally called me out on it[4].

Some of the mistakes seem obvious, once you realize they are a mistake. Some are eternally confusing (at least to me). Either way, merely being aware of them helps you to prevent making them.

Which is partly what I mean by self-editing. The rest of what I mean is: doing the best you can to fix everything you can yourself, before you send the story on to someone else.

If you have attended any form of writing class or seminar, there are a couple of ideas you have probably heard. Things like "your first million words are crap" and "never edit your own stuff."

Well far be it from me, the self-proclaimed non-expert, to go against what the professionals teach, but…I seem to always have contrary opinions.

First, yeah, your first million words probably are crap. Even when you pay people to teach you how to write, they usually focus on the big things, as they didn't have the time to teach you all the little things. Which means, maybe your first million words didn't have to be crap.

Second, I totally agree that you should never edit yourself for final publication. If you are a self-publisher, editing yourself is a bad, bad, no-no. You will miss all kinds of mistakes you would have caught in someone else's writing. You can't see these errors in your own writing because you are blind to them.

We all suffer from this problem. Please don't think you are immune. There is no cure. You don't develop a resistance[5]. What happens is that your brain fills in the blanks. You see things that aren't there and miss things that are. You

---

minutes was overly optimistic. Sorry if I misled anyone there.

[4] It was pointed out to me that this sounded as if these two anthologies were my entire editing résumé. They were not. They were the 4th and 5th anthologies I had edited (one was never published), not to mention all the other stories I edited in various writers groups or workshops and for friends or clients. Which I just mentioned.

[5] Actually, it seems to get worse over time.

know what you meant to write, so your brain tells you that is what you did, even when you didn't[6].

That having been said, there is no reason not to go over your own stuff a half-dozen times before you give it to someone else to edit. If you have already cleaned out most of the problems, the editor can focus on the things you really need help with—like making it a better story rather than being overwhelmed with correcting your grammar and punctuation. You'll get a lot more bang for your buck from the editor that way. Trust me. An editor can have problems seeing the story if they can't see past the impossible dialog tags you've used every single time someone speaks.

Also, if you are trying to get paid for your stories, a lot of acquisition editors will turn down good stories as soon as they see novice mistakes. Why? Because they don't want to deal with taking the time to argue with a writer about fixing them. Some editors consider this an automatic sign that the author isn't professional enough to be published. It's best to turn in the cleanest manuscript you can, every time, if you want to get paid for being published.

In summary, I don't consider myself an expert. Some of the things I list in this book go against the grain of what some experts advocate. In fact, I break many of my own rules throughout this very guide. I am a big fan of writing stylistically.

I am not trying to teach you how to write, but I am trying to show you some of the mistakes that will get in the way of your writing. When I can, I will try to point out the differences and the arguments for and against something.

I am a believer in poetic license (breaking the standard rules of writing to create an effect), and I feel a writer should tell a story the way they want to. When I edit for someone, I often point out things they did against the norm. If they have a reason, whether I agree with it or not, I let it go. But if it was obviously done because the writer didn't know any better, the reader will see that too, and it ruins the story.

One thing I generally agree with: you have to know the rules before you can break them.

In the pages ahead, you will find lots of rules that can ruin the best of stories. Before you pay an editor to bleed red all over your manuscript with their pen, grab hold of as many of these rules as you can and squeeze them until the metaphorical blood drips from your imaginary fist. Use it to fill your own red pen and then go bleed red on your story first. You will get more benefit, and learn more, from an editor who doesn't have to correct these kinds of mistakes for you.

And it will cost you less in the long run. You will never find anyone else in the writing world whose blood is less precious or expensive than your own.

Ooooh… That was good. I think I'll use that on the back cover too!

---

[6] Not to mention psychological tricks like the internet memes that say, "What I if I told you, you read the first line wrong?"

TL;DR

Just in case you felt the need for a quick summary of this book, perhaps a highlight of what I thought the important things you needed to know were, here you go:

The Little Things Matter.

This guide is full of things to keep in mind the next time you write or edit a story. Merely being aware of them can help you take advantage of using them, or, if they are a mistake, help you avoid them.

If you feel you didn't completely understand something, please take the time to do some research. In the long run, you will be a better writer for knowing.

The whole point of writing is to communicate ideas. If an idea is not communicated clearly, that is the author's fault, not the reader's fault. If an idea was communicated clearly, then it doesn't matter if a "rule" was broken.

When readers "don't get it," it is not usually because the author is a genius, writing something extraordinary and beyond the readers' ken, it is because the author has failed at written communication.

There is knowledge required of a reader to participate in the exchange of ideas via the written word, but the same, and more so, is true of the author. Writing rules exist to assist in this flow of ideas. They are a way to assure we are all "speaking the same language."

While the expectation is readers are trying to comprehend, there is also the expectation that a writer is trying to convey ideas. Unless you are writing in detail about specialized topics, and the reader wasn't the target audience, a lack of communication of ideas is your fault, not the reader's. So, buck up, listen to the advice of others when they tell you something in your writing doesn't work, and fix it instead of thinking you know better than they do.

And remember: We all make mistakes. We all miss things. There will always be one more mistake, one more typo, and one more thing. Don't get overwhelmed by it, and don't let it eat at you.

As soon as I published my book on editing, the first edition of the one now in your hand—which I had personally re-checked dozens of times, and which I had paid not one, but two professional editors to go through, and through which several beta readers had proofread—I started finding mistakes.

A lot of them.

Some of the mistakes were flat out embarrassing. One of them actually a bit mortifying. But, there they were. It happens. There will still be mistakes in this edition. Probably one in this sentence right hear.

When it happens to you, learn to roll with it. Learn to learn from it. Writers have to develop thick enough skins to not only withstand criticisms, but to use them to their advantage. We need them so we can learn, grow, and improve.

And finally, the theme this guide was originally built around:

To get the most benefit from hiring an editor, you should always hand them the best, cleanest (error-free) manuscript you can, letting them focus on all of the little things that can make your story better rather than being overwhelmed by the process of just trying to make your story readable.

WHAT YOU DON'T NEED TO KNOW...
YET.

New writers, especially those who have finally decided to really sit down and write their novel, have a tendency to obsess about things they don't need to be concerned with yet or at all. If you haven't finished writing your novel or story yet, there are a ton of other things that don't matter, and learning them, at that time, is nothing more than a distraction. If you never manage to finish that novel, you will have wasted a lot of time, energy, effort, and stress for no reason, because none of it will ever have mattered.

What does matter is finishing that first story. That's the step most people can't get past. A lot of people try writing. Some start dozens or hundreds of stories but never finish any of them. If you can finish a story, you are ahead of the curve. If you consistently finish stories, you are way ahead.

It doesn't matter how you write your stories. Dictate them, write them out longhand on a yellow legal pad, scribble in shorthand in a journal, type them up on an old Royal typewriter, tap them out on a BlackBerry, use your iPad, or use a desktop computer. What matters is that you do it in a way that is conducive to you writing, and actually finishing, your story.

Until you have finished a story, don't worry about what software you need. Don't worry about formatting margins, spacing, fonts, page numbers, or what kind of printer, paper, and ink you have access to. Don't worry about how many words go on a page, how many pages are in a book, what the text on the back of the book is called, or who to get a quote from to put on the cover. Don't worry the title isn't quite right, what the cover art will be, what genre it is, whether you need an agent, or if it will be released in hardback edition.

Writing is an entire, complex industry, with so many minutiae involved that few people know most, let alone all of it. If you go down that career path, traditional or self-published, it will be a continual learning process for the rest of your life, as things can, do, and will change and grow.

While some of the stuff can be fun to tinker with, like coming up with the perfect pen name, don't let it distract and overwhelm you, or you won't finish that story, and then none of it will have mattered.

YOUR FIRST BIG MISTAKE

"Okay, Sam," you may ask, *"just how do you know what my first big mistake will be?"*

Well, okay, I don't. Not really. But the subtitle of this book is *For Beginning Authors Who Intend to Survive to Publication*, so I am assuming you want to be published. With that in mind, here is the first big mistake new authors tend to make:

They don't follow the guidelines.

Nearly every magazine, anthology, editor, agent, blog, or anywhere else you can submit a story, will have guidelines. Some are short and simple, and some are intentionally difficult. If you don't follow the guidelines, you are telling the person who receives your submission that you are likely a difficult person to work with, and it gives them a pretty good sense that they don't want to work with you.

Some editors, usually at places that pay well and get swamped with submissions, are actually grateful to see someone not follow the guidelines so they can immediately cross that story off their list of things to look at and move on. A lot of editors will publicly deny this practice, and for some it is not true, but don't kid yourself—there are some editors who are looking for any reason to reject your story, and this is the first and easiest reason.

Why would they want a reason to reject your story? Because some editors get hundreds or more submissions every month, and they need to wade through and decide to accept or reject each one. An easy rejection—one that is obviously unprofessional—can be a small blessing for an editor (or their assistant or their slush pile readers) swamped in submissions[7].

So, if the guidelines say to use Times New Roman font, you'd better not be using Comic Sans. Even if you adore Comic Sans and despise Times New Roman. If you want someone to pay you, you need to give them what they want, not what you want. If you absolutely *must* write in the font you love, do so. It's not a big deal to change the font of the story after you write it. Just make sure you actually do change the font to what is required before you submit.

If the guidelines say double-space your submission, then double-space the lines on your submission. If they say to single-space it, use single spaced lines. If they say they want **.rtf** or **.doc** files only, don't send them a **.docx** file. None

---

[7] Or it can be a flat-out unbelievable! As I prepare this edition, my friend and sometimes co-author Kevin J. Anderson is getting ready to release *SLUSHPILE MEMORIES: How NOT to Get Rejected*. I haven't read it yet, but I assume he will include some of the amazing stories of submissions gone wrong I've heard of.

of these are a big deal to change after you finish your story. Modern computers are wonderful for that.

This seems like common sense, but some people (hopefully not you) honestly seem to think that they are the exception, and that it will be all right for them to bend the rules a little[8].

What does that tell the acquisitions editor?

It tells them you are going to be a serious pain in the patookie, and that they don't want to work with you unless you've already sold a million copies of your e-book and will likely sell a million more. (And maybe not even then, if you've proven yourself a problem.)

Which brings me to the other question raised by the title of this section:

"But Sam, I'm going to self-publish. I don't need to follow any guidelines!"

Let me know how that works out for you.

Seriously though, even as a self-published author, you need to follow some rules. If you don't follow the guidelines for publication, you could have your books taken down and your accounts closed. As a self-publisher who has to build up an audience on their own, that can be impossible to recover from. On top of that, if your book is poorly formatted, poorly edited, or *gasp* poorly written, people won't buy from you a second time[9]. They will feel like they wasted their money the first time, and you will have lost your chance at any future sales to them.

"But Sam! What about (redacted to avoid lawsuit)*?*

"That book was horribly written/edited/formatted (circle all that apply)*, and the story sucked! It still sold a bazillion copies and even got made into a movie!"*

Well, all I can say about that is this: if you figure out how to get your book made into a movie, let me know. Life is full of surprises and the truth is often stranger than fiction, but that's not the norm. I don't recommend thinking you'll be the one to buck the status quo—at least not in this way.

---

[8] When I first opened up Knight Writing Press to submissions for anthologies, the second submission I received obviously hadn't read the guidelines. More disappointing, six out of the next ten submissions didn't follow the guidelines either. By the time I closed submissions on that first anthology, the rate of compliance with the guidelines was down to around 11%.

[9] This is less true now, with authors putting out vast quantities of work in short time periods, writing for niche markets, but the advice is sound, and there is no telling when, or if, the trend will reverse.

YOUR SECOND, AND MAYBE BIGGEST, MISTAKE

"Okay, Sam," you may ask again, *"if this is the biggest, why didn't you warn me about it first?"*

Well, if you followed the advice I gave to avoid the First Big Mistake, chances are pretty good you wouldn't make this mistake. But sometimes it happens anyway. So here goes:

You may accidentally enter a contract without realizing it.

I will explain, but first, below are three lines I lifted from the section **Contracts Are Your Safety Nets**, but it is related, and it is so important I decided to put it here as well. Please make sure to read that section also. I really do consider it to be the most important advice in this book:

Always use contracts. Always make sure that you fully understand a contract before you sign it.

If you take only one thing away from this book, let it be those last two sentences.

Now, I added this section because of a disturbing new trend, and I felt the need to emphasize the importance of paying attention to what you are doing, even before you thought you were signing a contract.

Keyword there: thought.

I'm not talking about verbal contracts. While those are nasty, quasi-legal things, and I recommend avoiding them completely, they are not the landmine you're most likely to step on.

In recent years, some rights grabs have become blatant. (That's when publishers (or others) try to obtain rights they don't need or deserve, and probably aren't properly paying for.) And it's not just being done by small publishers or scam artists, but some big businesses as well. While you can't avoid things you don't know about or can't foresee, there is no excuse for not trying to protect yourself.

With that in mind, attempting to protect myself from upsetting people/companies who may feel singled out, I am not going to name names of companies, or even drop big hints. If you want more on these examples, you should be able to find tons of information, or at least other people's opinions of the situations if you do a little digging on your own.

A current (as of this writing) example of something authors couldn't foresee and protect themselves from was something a bit complicated to go much into detail here, but the thumbnail sketch is Company A appears to have bought up multiple other companies' assets but seemed to believe it did not also inherit those other companies' liabilities of continuing to make royalty payments owed to the original authors/creators of said assets, as per those original authors' original contracts.

I am sure future contracts will contain clauses that address this directly, and my understanding is that it is being hashed out in negotiations now, but meanwhile, it's been a big problem for some authors, denying them income they really needed during a pandemic. (This was written during the COVID-19 Pandemic of 2020-2021.) (At least I hope it's confined to 2020-2021…)[10]

While this isn't directly related to those affected authors not paying attention to their contracts, it is something that will have repercussions in the future, and I feel it would behoove budding authors to be abreast of changes in the industry, as they need to watch for clauses, both in favor of the author and in favor of the publisher, that will end up in future contracts because of this.

Company A certainly hasn't been the only company to try to take advantage of any opportunities they can. Wanting something for nothing, or less than should be paid for it, is human nature, so you will run into it everywhere, and you need to be careful. Which brings me to the point of this section:

You know all that gobbledygook legalese no one reads before accepting terms and conditions? Those dense text swamps that every website, app, software, and service make you agree to?

Well, it turns out reading them *is* important after all.

Hidden within those, some websites, social media platforms, and more, state that you grant them the rights to your creations when you click "I accept," or maybe even just by using their platform or service.

Now, it's one thing to sign up for something and think, *yeah, yeah, whatever,* and assume that if something is really over the top, the law will probably find for your side, and you're probably not risking much more than some personal information you don't care about anyway, but when you upload content somewhere, whether you type it in or attach a file, you might be giving your rights to it away.

We've all heard about social media sites using images for facial recognition and whatnot. And a few years back some popular sites had problems with private photos and artwork being "scraped" from their websites and used in merchandizing and advertisements—not cool to find your artwork or family photo is making someone $$$ while you had no say in it and get nothing but humiliation out of it.

As a writer or artist trying to make money from your work, you definitely need to read all the fine print *before* you post your story (or photo or video or artwork) to a website, social media, or whatever, but there is more than the

---

[10] It wasn't.

social media stuff we've become inured to.

Even worse than taking your photos, posts, or whatever, some "publishers" and some websites claim that the mere act of you submitting a story to them is you knowingly entering into a contract with them, wherein you grant them **all of the rights to your story** (or photo, or art, or whatever), **perpetually and irrevocably.** This is usually in their fine print, which may not really look like much of anything but tiny print hidden at the bottom of one webpage in the back, let alone an actual Terms of Service or End User License Agreement.

Don't fall for it.

Even some bigger companies get in on that act. I've seen contracts from Big Publishers that try to get rights they don't need, and I've seen contracts from places that pretended to be publishers but were really selling editing and publishing services, and they still went for the rights grab.

Some will dispute me on this example, but I feel it is a good example for a warning, and I still feel the same way about it as I did a few years ago, when Company B, along with Company C in a joint venture, decided to expand upon a popular Intellectual Property (IP) one of them owned the rights to. They put out a call for authors to submit stories written in that fictional universe, in the form of a contest. Chance of a lifetime! Write a (IP name redacted for my protection) story!

A lot of people submitted. I hope it worked out well for them. I did not submit anything. Because, in the Official Rules, it was stated:

> Each entry will be the sole property of the Sponsors. By competing in the Contest and/or accepting a prize, each entrant (including the prize winner) grants to Sponsors the right to edit, adapt, publish, copy, display, reproduce and otherwise use their entry in connection with this Contest and in any other way, in any and all forms of media now known or hereafter devised, throughout the world, in perpetuity, including publication on *(redacted by me so as not to identify the companies)*. Further, each entrant (including the prize winner) grants to Sponsors the right to use each entry and the winner's name, likeness, and biographical information in advertising, trade and promotional materials, without notice, review or approval, or further compensation or permission, except as set forth herein, and except where prohibited by law. Sponsors are not obligated to use, publish, display or reproduce any entry.

If you read that, you'll see it seems like the companies involved not only grabbed for unlimited perpetual rights to stories any and all authors submitted, even if the authors didn't win, they also went for the rights to use the authors' names and images. All you had to do was send in an entry, and you were screwed.

And there is no limitation on the use of the author's image. What if you eventually became famous and one of the things you were known for was that you were very much against animal abuse, and then they used your name and likeness in advertising hunting safaris, making it look like you approved of it? Yeah, I know that's far-fetched. But guess what. There are no limitations in that agreement, are there?

Oh, wait. Yes, there are. But they are limitations on you, not them.

> By entering, you hereby forever waive, and release Sponsors from any claim, including any claim for injunctive relief, that you may have at any time in the future related to your entry and/or Sponsors use of your entry. UNDER NO CIRCUMSTANCES SHALL THE RELEASED PARTIES BE LIABLE FOR INDIRECT, INCIDENTAL, CONSEQUENTIAL, SPECIAL OR EXEMPLARY DAMAGES, ATTORNEYS' FEES, OR ANY OTHER DAMAGES.

(The capital letters were their emphasis, not mine.) Would that hold up in court if you tried to fight it? I don't know, but it is feasible to consider that had I submitted something, those companies could, without compensating me, at any time, use my name and likeness to advertise and promote anything, related to the IP or not, even though it was not anything I wrote nor had anything to do with.

Think about that.

What if J.K. Rowling or George R.R. Martin had submitted? (Not that they would have. They would have read that fine print and balked or demanded full payment up front, in advance, I am sure.) The thought of the scandal over using their stories without paying, or using their names to advertise something they had nothing to do with, would probably stop those companies from doing it.

But what if it were just little ol' you or me? And what if someday, eventually, we became Big Famous Household Names?

Sam Knight wrote (IP) stories BEFORE he was famous!
Look! See how much Sam Knight loves our new Cheddar Cheese flavored marijuana vape pens! He smokes them in the nude!

See how that could work?

It was a rights grab.

Why not? Free stuff! And I would have given it to them. For free. It was right there in the fine print. The people who submitted stories (I do not know of anyone who actually did, so I couldn't talk to them about this) did give them those rights. And they can't get them back. Which means even if they trademark their likeness, like was done with Elvis and Marilyn, that likeness could go up on any billboard anywhere. For anything. For free.

Now, I have written media tie-ins. I am a member of the International Association of Media Tie-In Writers. I have signed non-disclosure agreements, and I understand these companies are dealing with a franchise here, an intellectual property, and within that there are trademarks and copyrights they need to protect.

So, with all that in mind, I'm cool with the idea that if you write a (fill in the name of an IP) story for them and they don't buy it, you don't get to sell it somewhere else or publish it on your own. I mean, honestly, fanfiction is technically still illegal no matter who feels like it shouldn't be or how many websites are making money off it.

But then again, that is why companies have writers on staff or writers that they hire for projects. That is why writers get a contract and get paid *before* they put all the time and effort into writing a story.

That is what work for hire is. They even called it that at the beginning of the rules to the contest.

> Each entrant hereby acknowledges that their entry is derived from and legally dependent upon the copyright of *(redacted by me so as not to identify the companies)*, and therefore entrant has no legitimate independent rights to either *(redacted by me so as not to identify the companies)* or the entry, and that the entry will be considered a work made for hire for Sponsors, and each entry will be the sole property of the Sponsors.

And those are the kinds of contracts, work for hire, that Company A seemed to have been disregarding in the disputes I mentioned at the start of this section. The difference being a normal word for hire contract pays the author for the work, usually at least partly in advance, and often with royalties after.

And I realize the reasons for their all-inclusive legalese language stuff was that they were protecting themselves from possible future lawsuits, from people saying things like, "*Hey! You stole my idea after I submitted it to your contest!*"

But I feel like this was the opposite of that.

They asked for stories and then claimed *all rights* to them if you submitted one, whether or not they paid your, or you won, or anything. Arguably, you couldn't even do revisions and make it not a (fill in the name of an IP) story and use it somewhere else because they took the rights to edit and adapt and...everything. They didn't even have to say they accepted the story, let alone pay for it. They didn't have to do anything. It just became theirs to do whatever they wanted with if you submitted a story.

They could eventually make it into a movie or TV show and earn millions off of it, while the author who wrote it gets nada.

And on top of that, they took the right to use the names and likenesses of the authors too, because why not?

Not cool.

Now, I do know that there are reasons for those sorts of clauses in contracts (for promotional purposes, to make sure famous authors help promote the stuff they got paid to do), but I can't abide the way they did it. It is supposed to go along with authors being compensated for their work and helping to promote it, not just…stolen.

Please realize that any and all companies involved in these kinds of things would likely argue that what I have said was not what they intended, and that I have misinterpreted what was written. It was all just contract jargon the lawyers make them use and it is intended only to allow them to CTA. (Cover their asses, not yours.)

Okay. Sure. My bad. I'm not a lawyer. Maybe all intentions were altruistic and preventative, a way to give new writers a chance at something big.

The problem is that what is written in a contract is what a contract is. It doesn't matter who claims it wasn't supposed to mean this or be interpreted as that, or who claims that it really means this instead, or who whispers promises and reassurances to you on the side not to worry because (fill in the blank) would never happen. (See **Contracts Are Your Safety Nets** for more.)

In the end, people and companies cannot be trusted not to take advantage of opportunities. It's human nature. Those who can benefit from what a contract *actually* says, can and will enforce it in that way if they choose to do so.

And they have deeper pockets and more lawyers than you do.

So, to avoid your second, and maybe biggest mistake:

ALWAYS READ THE TERMS OF SERVICE BEFORE YOU SUBMIT ANYTHING ANYWHERE

In fact, I recommend you do research and see what other authors have to say before you even "sign up" or "log in" to any website, social media, or whatever. I have seen places hide their terms of service behind the login page, which could mean they don't really want you to see it, or it could mean they are tricking you into agreeing to it before you get to see it.[11]

Signing up with a company that does something like that is just asking for trouble, if you ask me.

Sorry for getting on a soapbox. This sort of thing really bothers me. Protect yourself.

---

[11] This was the biggest problem I had getting information for the section on TurnKey publishers.

I'M (X) YEARS OLD…

Some of the more common questions I have been asked, and heard other authors asked about writing, have to do with age being an obstacle to becoming a writer.

Younger writers worry they are too young to ____(fill in the blank)____.

Older writers worry they are too old to ____(fill in the blank)____.

Writing has no age requirements or restrictions. If you want to write, then write. Easy-peasy.

Just because some people may think you don't know about something does not invalidate your point of view or diminish what you have to say. If you want to express yourself, then express yourself.

If you think people won't be interested in something you want to write, but you want to write it anyway, that's okay. They don't have to read it. But maybe others will want to. Not to mention you get to do something you wanted to do.

Publishers don't care how old you are, they are only interested in books they think they can sell. Your age is not a factor in their decision-making process. Your writing is. The salability of the story is.

If you're going to self-publish, you don't need to care if some readers don't want to read what you wrote. Maybe other readers will. You did.

The only time age becomes a problem is:

1) If you let it.

2) If you are too young to legally sign contracts. (Or too young to legally set up accounts, if you want to self-publish.)

The solution to 1) is easy: don't let it.

The solution to 2) is almost as easy: have a parent or legal guardian help sign contacts on your behalf and/or help you set up accounts you may need. As with **Pen Names**, real publishers are used to dealing with this. It is not an issue.

If you do have a parent or legal guardian sign on your behalf, make sure *you* stay on top of everything. Just because they are signing doesn't mean they will know the business—that's *your* job. And so is knowing and understanding the contract. It affects you. It may affect you the rest of your life. Read the section **Contracts Are Your Safety Nets**.

TYPES OF EDITORS

After outlining the draft for this guide and seeing my list of things editors do and don't like to see in submissions, it occurred to me that many new writers (and even a few who have been around for a while) have no idea how many different types of editors there are, or what they do, so here is a quick overview to help you get a grasp of the situation.

Please understand that many editors do a variety of tasks, so an individual editor may do more than one of the things on this list, and different places may use different terms for the jobs the editors do. Editors in the media tend to have different titles and duties than editors in the entertainment publishing industry.

As someone trying to get published, the first kind editor you are likely to think of is an **acquisitions editor**. This is the person who will decide whether to purchase or publish your story. This decision is usually based on the editor's interest in the type of story you have written. (There is no point in submitting your romance story to the acquisitions editor for a horror magazine!) Also, if this editor is responsible for other editorial jobs, they may be quick to reject or turn down poorly written or poorly formatted manuscripts because they don't want to deal with future problems. If it gives them a headache thinking about what they will have to deal with, chances are it goes into the rejection pile.

And that is the reason why you need the other types of editors first!

Most people think a **proofreader** is an editor, but they are not. They are only what the name implies: someone who reads the manuscript looking for errors. They don't edit anything; they just find typos and mistakes. They don't even (usually) correct them. They point them out for the author or copy editor to correct. Many writers make the mistake of having someone proofread their story before handing their story over to an editor. The proofreader should be the last one to read the story, as the other kinds of editors will suggest changes and the proofreader will (hopefully) catch any mistakes introduced after those changes.

The **content editor** (sometimes called *developmental editor* or other things —more on that in a moment) is generally the one who should be hired by a writer first (before you try to sell it to an acquisitions editor). Sometimes they call themselves "story doctors," but sometimes people who call themselves story doctors are not content editors. This editor will read your story and offer suggestions to help make it better. They may be minor suggestions, such as not using a name too similar to that of a real person or cutting out an unnecessary scene that slows the story down. They could also be major suggestions, such as re-writing the whole book from the point of view of the dog to make an otherwise commonplace story interesting, or maybe your story about Cuban refugees landing in the United States should be set in Florida instead of Utah, as Utah doesn't have any oceanfront for the boats to come ashore. Either way, the content editor will help with the overarching aspects of your story such as staying true to your characters, your narrative voice, and your genre.

This is the kind of editor this book was meant to supplement. If you deal with your own typos and grammar/punctuation/dialog/misplaced modifier problems before you send your story to the content editor, then they can concentrate on your story instead of trying to figure out what the words you wrote were supposed to mean.

Some people confuse the content editor with a different kind of **developmental editor**, and it's easy to see why, as they seem to do similar things. But while a content editor is trying to help make your story better, a developmental editor is more of a person who helps you figure out what your story is going to be before (or maybe while) you write it. Most fiction writers won't need a developmental editor, but that doesn't mean they can't be extremely helpful to a fiction writer. Think of the developmental editor as a project manager. If you are working for someone, the developmental editor will help tell you what to do and keep you on track. They can help with themes, character arcs, morals, and more. Sometimes an agent acts as a developmental editor for their author, but that is rare. (Like maybe helping come up with ideas for what to do in the fourth book in a series.)

After an acquisitions editor decides they want your story, other editors get involved in fixing it. (Or the acquisitions editor puts on their other editing hat and gets to work on it for real!) Here the lines blur a bit more. Some publishing houses use a **content editor** (or they may call them something like a *substantive editor* or *structural editor*), who, just like the content editor you hired before you sold your story, will try to help you fix any problems with the story and turn it into exactly what the publisher wants.

They may also use a **copy editor**, who finally does the job many writers always thought for sure someone else would do for them: fixing punctuation, spelling, and generally correcting anything messy the writer did. (These editors are used much more rarely in today's publishing world, so you need to have things the best you can already.) They also make sure grammar is done according to the house rules or house style of the publisher (things like spaces before and after ellipsis, or use of the Oxford comma). This assures books released by the publisher all use punctuation and spelling the same way.

The **line editor**, so called because they go through the story line by line and try to fix or maintain the consistency of the writing style and word usage of the story, can also include the jobs of the copy and developmental editors.

In today's publishing world, many of the larger publishers are now only accepting submissions that appear as though a professional editor already went over it (they don't necessarily admit that, but that doesn't make it not true), so many writers hire editors before they submit a manuscript. Conversely, many self-publishers don't bother with editors, editing, or even proofreading.

I can't tell you what to do, but in my opinion, everyone needs to have an editor go over their stuff before it is sent out into the world.

Remember, to get the most out of an editor, you should always hand them the best, cleanest (error-free) manuscript you can, so they can focus on what they're good at, not on what you're bad at.

THOUGHTS ON GETTING PUBLISHED

Getting published is a big topic. One that entire books are routinely written about. I can't even pretend to cover it faithfully or completely, so I won't even try. But I can try to give you a push in the right direction.

In years past, a lot of people thought there were right and wrong ways to be published. Self-publishing was called vanity publishing, and places that would help you do that were called vanity presses, and it was frowned upon to the point where some authors were ostracized from their writing communities because of it. They were considered to have gone around the gatekeepers; they didn't pay their dues or earn their way properly, which meant whatever it was they wrote must be crap and not worth reading.

In your journey as a writer, you may find a few holdovers from that era. Not many, not likely, but maybe.

Fortunately, a lot of things have changed since then, and I mention it only so that you can recognize those biases if you stumble across them. Ignore them and move on. They're as outdated as cuneiform tablets.

Before we start in on considering what is a right or a wrong way to get published, I would like you to take a moment and consider the idea of publication the same way you think of sports. I don't mean think of it as football, or baseball, or basketball. I mean think of it as sports in general. All sports.

When it comes to sports, we can all do *something*. If we can't play football professionally in the NFL, then maybe we can play baseball in high school, or we can play basketball at the local rec center with intermural sports, or soccer in the park with our friends, or kickball in our backyard with neighbors, or paddleball in the house with siblings. Maybe we can Yo-Yo, or jump rope, or hopscotch.

My point is, there is a wide variety of things we can do, and they come in many different forms and skill levels and are held in different levels of esteem, which varies widely between individuals.

Some of us are much better than others at spitting watermelon seeds, but only a few of us can win the prize at the State Fair for it—and that contest attracts only a certain audience, but that doesn't mean the contest, or the contestants, are any the less for their skills or participation. That contest was for the people it was for, and it was valid regardless of who may think it worthless or frivolous.

Some of us can't jump a rope to save our lives, but others can win gold medals in the World Jump Rope Championship, and some of us can't learn the rules to checkers, but others can win the World Chess Championship. Those contests may attract only certain, limited audiences, but those kinds of contests are still valid. They still matter to the people they matter to.

Let's add another point onto that. Quickly looked up online, so don't trust the generalized numbers, but they illustrate my point: the average NFL player earns over $800,000 a year, and the average NBA player over $8 million. Obviously, a lot more people are interested in those contests than in the Calaveras County Jumping Frog Jubilee. World-wide interest has created a market and increased (perceived) value for football and basketball, but that does not mean those sports are more worthwhile than other sports. They are merely more worthwhile to a certain set of people, which just happens to be a much larger set.

How do you think earning a living as a professional football or basketball player compares to trying to live off the prize money from Jump Rope Championships or Chess Tournaments? Or what about the Olympics, where a *lot* of money exchanges hands, but not much of it goes to the athletes themselves? Or the Jumping Frog Jubilee? People travel from all over the world just to participate in that, but they certainly won't make a living out of it.

Getting published is a lot like this.

You can have a steady job, but no one knows who you are or maybe even what you do. You can be recognized as the best at what you do, but you earn little to nothing. You can become the kind of superstar everyone recognizes, and earn a hundred times more than your peers, but maybe you don't really deserve the fame because your peers, and many who aren't, are actually better than you.

Or maybe you only wrote in high school, because you had to, and your creative writing teacher entered your story into a contest, and you got published in a book you never even saw a copy of.

My point is, it is a great, big world out there, and it is up to you to decide what you want to do, what you want to get out of it, how to approach it, and when, or if, to give up on, or change, that goal. You need to set your own goals and accomplish what you want, not what other people say you should or shouldn't. Sometimes that means doing what you've seen others do. Sometimes that means making your own way and creating something entirely new.

It is okay to set new goals for yourself, to change your goals, to move the goalposts. Maybe you achieved one goal too easily, or maybe you learned about new obstacles along the way you hadn't known of, and you need a set of steps, a set of smaller goals, to climb to get there. If you set the bar, you can move the bar yourself; you don't need others to do it for you. It's your goal, not theirs.

You can print five copies of your story off your computer, staple them together, and hand them out to your family. Or you can pay a printer to make twenty copies of your book and give them out as presents. Or you can self-publish a book and hope someone outside of your family will buy a copy. You can have articles published in the school newspaper or in Newsweek. You can sell your story to a magazine, put it up on a website, or sell it to an anthology. All are valid ways to be published. You can choose any of them, all of them, or more.

One of the first things you need to figure out, before you decide how to get published, is what it is that *you* want to get out of being published.

Is having your story available for people to find online enough for you? Many writers are perfectly happy with websites that let them post stories where readers can find them and comment. Some authors are happy to write stories one Tweet at a time in exchange for nothing more than social media followers.

Do you feel the need to see your book in a physical print form, to hold it in your hand like a real novel? Self-publishing is easier and cheaper now than any other time in history[12] and that book feels really, really good in your hand.

Do you want to see your name emblazoned across a book that's sitting upon a bookstore shelf, right next to your favorite Big Name author? That, like getting into the NFL or the NBA, requires a lot of time, effort, dedication, and luck, but it is not impossible. And when you do, the crowd goes wild, and confetti falls...

No, not really. It is a hell of a moment though. But like those professional athletes, you have to put work and time into getting there. It doesn't just happen.

Do you want to make a living at your writing? That's not easy either. Many famous authors don't earn enough to make a living, but options are limited only by your imagination and determination. And a lot of luck. The authors, in general, who are doing best at earning that income right now seem to be self-publishers putting out several (like 8 to 12) books a year, often in a continuous or same-world series, and marketing the heck out of them. These authors have two or three full time jobs: writing, publishing, and marketing, and they run a business. A huge portion of their income is put back into advertising. But it works for them.

Over the last decade, even traditionally published authors have been getting in on self-publishing. It's called a hybrid approach. Being both traditionally and self-published gives self-published books a chance to earn more by capitalizing upon advertisement, exposure, and fans gained from traditional publications.

If you've been thinking that somewhere in here my sports analogy fell apart, consider someone like Tony Hawk who managed to become a household name as a skateboarder when skateboarding was considered a pastime for delinquents. (Yes, that is true. I grew up in that archaic time where many public places had signs banning skateboarding. And sometimes roller skates or rollerblades. But I digress.) Mr. Hawk was not the first pro skateboarder, but he had a lot to do with making it a respectable sport, a legitimate way to live life. He did that through a lot of work way beyond his skateboarding skills: obtaining deals with companies for sponsorships, brandings, appearances, movies, video games, and more.

---

[12] In the months before this going to publication, the COVID-19 pandemic has dramatically affected costs, production times, and distribution capabilities. Hopefully that will all be a "blip" and nothing more than a memory by the time you read this.

Eventually other sports that weren't popular with the general public, but very popular within specific subsets, began to open up in much the same way as skateboarding, eventually becoming known as extreme sports and spawning their own Olympic-style competitions. This was largely in part from Mr. Hawk and his contemporary peers creating a pathway by remaking the world into what they wanted it to be; a place that accepted the sport of skateboarding.

Writing in today's quickly changing media ecosystem is similar. The internet opened up a myriad of ways to publish (see **What is "Published?"**), and people are still finding new ways to put their stories and art out into the world. Some even find new ways to make money at it, and others quickly follow the newly blazed paths, creating a burgeoning industry that is constantly in flux.

Because of this, there really is no right way or wrong way to be published anymore. There are only the ways that work for you and those that don't.

Some people may not like what works for you. It may be jealousy, as they may not like that it works for you but not for them. Or it may be bias: they may hate that you write fanfiction[13], or only in emojis, or they may think that if you crank out eighteen novels a year, you can't be a good writer. Or still think that only traditionally published counts. Or that if you don't…or if you…or…or…

What those people think doesn't matter. What matters is you get to do what you love, and that you find a way to accomplish your goals, big or small, doing it.

If your goal is to publish fanfiction, there are websites that would love to have you post with them[14]. Research what they offer (fan forums, blogs, etc.) and find the one you want. Watch for **Your Second, and Maybe Biggest, Mistake.**

If your goal is to self-publish, there are a lot of ways to accomplish it. For a breakdown of some of the better-known services, check out **An Intro to Self-Publishing.** Be aware success, or income, doesn't come quick or easy. Sometimes it doesn't come at all. Look into online forums, social media groups, and local people who are doing the same thing you are. The industry changes so quickly you need to stay on top of it. This is a situation where "a rising tide lifts all boats." Authors helping each other makes a difference. You can't just write a book and walk away and hope to make money; you'll need marketing and promotion[15]. Take your time, don't get overwhelmed. Resist the temptation

---

[13] Unlicensed fanfiction, as of this writing, is still illegal and a theft of intellectual property. Be careful what you put online. It could come back to haunt you.

[14] I cannot condone unsanctioned fanfiction. Some authors/publishers allow it with some of their Intellectual properties, and that is fine, because permission was granted. This is my disclaimer: I do not advocate the publication of unsanctioned fan fiction.

[15] 20Booksto50k, with a Facebook group and an annual conference (not cheap), is a good place to start learning. There will be a lot to learn, but they can help you avoid a lot of pitfalls. Remember, what works for one author may not work for another.

to just start trying things willy-nilly or you will make mistakes you regret. I promise.

If your goal is to get into bookstores with a huge bestseller, you've got a long, slow, tough haul ahead of you[16]. I suggest researching agents, acquisition editors, and publishers who have previously published books similar to what you have written. Don't bother trying to pitch or sell an idea to any of them unless you are already famous or have an established writing career; you need a completed manuscript to pitch to them. Seriously. Write the book first.

There are a ton of books devoted to getting agents. If the agent you are interested in wrote one of them, read it. They'll know if you didn't. If there are conferences you can attend, go there in person and meet the agents who are attending[17]. The best way to get published with a bigger publisher, I think, is to meet the agents in person, as humans, and allow them to see you as a real person, too. Especially if you are a nice person. A friendly person. A person who is not pushy or obnoxious or demanding or angry or resentful…you get the idea.

Talk with them, find out what they would want to see out of you beyond your writing. The truth of today's market is that even the big publishers expect you to have an online presence, and they expect you to work hard to promote your books. If you don't have a website, or a social media presence, I am sorry to say that lack may, for some, be a strike against publishing your work.

On a side note, you should never pay money out to an agent or a publisher. They should always pay you[18]. Agents or publishers who want you to pay them are not interested in getting you published, they are interested in getting your money. Do not pay office fees, submission fees, editing fees, or anything else to someone claiming to be an agent or publisher. They are likely very poor service providers scamming you by pretending they can get you published.

Real agents don't make any money unless you do; they get paid a percentage of what you earn. (If real agents have real expenses you are responsible for, those will be named in your contract with them and won't be due until after they help you earn money.) Real publishers pay you in advance

---

[16] I've been told this can be done by self-publishers, but I don't personally know any of those who claim to have accomplished it. I know a lot who have tried and, as of yet, not succeeded. Most small publishers I know of have yet to succeed at this.

[17] I live in Colorado and find Superstars Writing Seminars and Pikes Peak Writers Conference to be great for this, but there are many others here and around the county. Some are free, some expensive, some great, and some not so great. Ask other authors what they thought of them. Check for conferences near you; you may make some new friends and that is always worth it!

[18] Kind of. Agents earn a percentage of your earnings (around 15%). Traditionally, the publisher pays the agent, who takes their percentage and then pass the rest on to the author. Agents are going to have their fingers in your contracts and in your money so make sure you have one you trust. There have been bad contracts with agents, just as with publishers, where the agents did a rights grab

for the right to try to make money with your story. This is what selling rights to your story is all about[19].

With all of that in mind, the easiest way to put that first notch in your publishing belt, I think, is to sell a short story. I realize short stories aren't for everyone, but there are websites, magazines, and anthologies always looking to purchase short stories. Some don't pay at all, some pay "token rates," which are generally less than 1¢ per word but can range from $1 to copies of the publication to maybe $50, and some pay semi-pro rates and pro-rates. As of this writing, SFWA (Science Fiction & Fantasy Writers of America) defines pro rates as 8¢ and up. The key part there is *and up*. Don't think that's the most you should get paid. While I don't usually like to talk numbers or drop names, the best I was ever personally involved with was around seven times that.

Don't be ashamed to not get paid pro-rates. It's not easy to sell a story to a pro-rate market, even for (most) Big Name professional writers. But we all start somewhere. Once you get going, don't sell yourself short and not move up the ladder. It feels really good to have someone think your story is good enough to publish. It feels even better when someone thinks your story is good enough to pay you $200 or $2,000 for that story. You can take my word on that.

My advice is to always aim high. If your story doesn't sell at pro-rates, then try dropping your search to semi-pro paying markets, then, if you have to, drop down to token or free. Or hold onto it until you become famous! But, if you start a story out published for free, you (most likely) will never be able to sell it at pro-rates in the future. (See **What is "Published?"** for more on this.)

If you decide to go the short story route, there are places you can search for open submissions. There are websites, forums, and social media groups where authors and publishers routinely post new and upcoming submissions. Follow your favorite publications on their social media; they often announce upcoming projects you can submit to. Some of these are national or international, and some are local. Local publications (especially if you know the local community and it knows you) are often easier to get into, though they often don't pay well. There are also websites, like Duotrope, Ralan, and The Submission Grinder, which keep up with new listings for anthologies and keep track of which magazines, websites, and publishers pay, how much they pay (sometimes), and which are accepting submissions. They can also warn you of places that charge a "submission fee" before they will consider your story. I highly recommend never paying anyone a submission fee, reading fee, or whatever new name they call their money-grab.

An internet search can help you find specialized listings for specific genres. An example is the SFWA's Market Report, but there are many places with lists.

Make sure you research places you've never heard of before you submit!

---

[19] For an interesting take on selling rights, I recommend Dean Wesley Smith's book *The Magic Bakery.*

If you think a publisher/editor/agent/business seems sketchy, try to find out more about them. You can check places like Writer Beware and Predators and Editors, or ask around of other authors.

A great way to keep up with goings-on is to become an active member of your local writing community and attend conventions and events in your area. Fellow authors are a great resource for many things, especially friendships.

NOTES ON SELF-PUBLISHING

Self-publishing is neither for the faint of heart, nor the work adverse. If you decide to self-publish, you will need to learn how to format your writing properly for conversion into e-books and print, which kinds of files you need, and what to do with them. Or you can pay someone to do that for you.

The problem with paying someone is that you just never really know how good of a job they are going to do, or if they are going to do what you wanted. Not to mention prices and services vary wildly.

This is where it is helpful to know your local writing community. Other authors who have already gone through, or are going through what you are, can help you. Some of them have learned to do it themselves and may be willing to teach you. Others may decide to make a job out of it and be available for hire. Some can tell you which services you need and which you don't, and some can tell you whose services you definitely don't want.

This is such a huge topic, and it is ever-changing, that I am only going to go over basics here. If this is something you decide to do, remember: this is either a job or a hobby, and you need to pick which it is and treat it appropriately. As a hobby, it can get too expensive really quickly, and as a job, it can break you. And I don't mean just take your money, which it can, I mean it can leave your soul beaten, bloodied, and in a metaphysical coma in a back alley while you wander the world, a dead-inside zombie, searching for it.

Prepare yourself. You need to be thick-skinned and willing to bend like the proverbial reed while still standing strong like the oak.

In this section, I will go over some terms and some ideas to get you started down this path. Keep in mind, things change constantly. Anything I put in here was subject to change yesterday and may not be useful or helpful tomorrow.

What is "Published?"

A general definition of published is to have made something available to the public. See the similarities in the words? PUBLic and PUBLish. That should help you understand when something was published. It doesn't have to have been "for sale" or advertised or really much of anything; it merely needs to have been made publicly available, even if that was in a pretty limited way.

This is different than sharing your story with your writers group, which is there to help you make it better, or reading your story at a convention, which is not "making it available" (unless it is recorded and released), and people can get kind of iffy about this idea. They want to say things like "it was only available to members of the club," and then hope that means it will be considered "never before published." But if anyone can join the club and get a copy, it was available to the public. Even if none of the club members picked up a copy, and the author took all fourteen copies back home with them, head hung, tail tucked between their legs, it was still, technically, made available, and therefore published.

A more modern comparison would be authors making stories available on Patreon, Wattpad, Medium, or the like. Arguing that it was only to a small group, or behind a paywall, or that no one bought/read it, does not invalidate the argument that it *was* made available.

Why does this matter?

Once a story has been made available to the public, even if no one buys it, the first publication rights, or the ability to be the first to publish it, is gone. It is used up. This is why many publishers don't want stories authors have already had posted on their blog, website, social media, or whatever. People, especially those who already knew of the author (being the people most likely to purchase something from that author) have already had a chance at the story, so if they didn't buy it then, why would they buy it from a different publisher now? And if they already got it, why would they want to pay to get it again?

While some publishers may be understanding of some situations, publishers are in the business to make money. Any potentially lost revenue makes it that much harder for them to make money and therefore much less likely to want to pay you for your story.

(Yes, there are always exceptions, but the odds of you being one of them are very small.)

What is a "Publisher?"

A general definition of a publisher is a person or a business that prepares works (like books, videos, music, etc.) to be made available to the public. Easy. Someone who publishes, right?

Not really. Not in the modern publishing industry.

This idea is a bit complicated, and honestly, it sticks in my craw, so this is going to be bit of a rant. I'll temper myself as best as I can, as the war is already over, and my side lost.

First, let's look at what being a publisher entails. If you prepare your own works for dissemination, you are your own publisher. A self-publisher.

When you self-publish a book, you may need to utilize an array of services to accomplish this. You may need to hire an editor, a formatter, a cover artist, a cover designer, someone who can manage all that into one package, someone to turn it into the appropriate kind of computer files, a printing company that can use those files to make an end product for you, possibly a place to store that product once it is made, a distributor to disseminate the product to points of sale, and finally, those points of sale (a retail outlet to sell the product).

Some of these things you can do on your own, others you will likely have to outsource. (It can be really hard to print up 5,000 copies of your book and then deliver 5 copies to each bookstore around the country, and that's assuming the bookstores want them.)

So, self-publishers outsource; they pay others to help.

Once upon a time, a self-publisher may have had hundreds or thousands of copies of books printed up at once, because of costs, and then they had to store them in their garage, or basement, or somewhere more expensive, and then they called or drove around and tried to sell them at discount to retail stores to resell to their customers. (Well, some self-publishers did it that way. Others sold their books at seminars, or to their students, or to their church, or…)

Today, self-publishing is easier than ever, because of Print On Demand (POD). Now books can be printed one at a time, affordably, instead of hundreds at a time to be affordable. This eliminates a lot of storage problems, because you don't make it until someone orders it, and it reduces distribution down to almost nothing more than mailing it to whoever ordered it. But that's still really hard to do on your own.

So, self-publishers make use of services to do it for them. Places like Kindle Direct Publishing (KDP), Barnes & Noble Press (B&N), IngramSpark, Lulu, BookBaby, and such. And that is what those places are: services. They are *not* publishers.

While some of these places may actually be publishers for some authors (some, like Amazon eventually opened up publishing houses on the side), I don't consider them publishers because they do not pay for the permissions or rights to publish the books. In fact, a lot of them charge a lot of money to publish books.

But some will call themselves publishers even when you are the one paying them to use their services. Some will list themselves as your publisher on your book and on their website. But they are not your publisher. They are a service you utilize when you self-publish. Even the "free" ones, in exchange for those services, take a percentage of your earnings before they pass it on to you. That is the exact opposite of what a traditional publisher does. What they are actually doing is taking a commission, not paying a royalty. Like a consignment store.

A traditional publisher pays in advance for permission to publish your story and then they try to make money selling it. (An advance is "against royalties." That means two things. First, you don't get paid more until after they sell enough to have earned back the advance you were paid. Second, if they don't earn enough, you (usually[20]) don't have to pay back the advance—because they were the ones taking a chance on your story. They paid you for the right to publish it.) Traditional publishers spend the time and money to make a book salable, and then they spend more to market it, to try to earn that money, and more, back.

Meanwhile, most of the service providers that call themselves publishers never risk anything at all. They put no effort into the editing, formatting, layout, or marketing of your product unless you pay them to. With POD, they don't even have to store the book before they ship it out. When they print a book, the cost of manufacturing the book is included in the price, in advance, because they don't print it until someone orders it and pays for it. They never lose money on what they do. They never even risk any money on what they do.

While I admit it is a smart way to do business, it is not what publishers do. At least it didn't used to be.

Now these places habitually call themselves publishers, and so does (nearly) everyone else, so…that's what a publisher is now.

At least one kind of publisher.

Why does this bother me? Because I am hiring them to print, distribute, and then place a product on consignment. They are doing nothing in advance, and little to nothing beyond providing the printing and distribution services, and sometimes sales. And they are being paid for those as they do it. How does that make them a publisher? Why does that give them the right to take my publisher name of off my publication and put their own, or "independently published," on it instead?

In the end, no matter what they say, you are the real publisher. You are the one who put in all the work, you are the one who took all the risk. Not them.

And that leads me into why some people get irritated at ISBNs nowadays. (Or at least why I do.)

ISBNs

This is full of information that comes at you fast. Don't sweat it. Skip to **Do I Need an ISBN**. If you decide you do, then come back here. If not, don't

---

[20] There are a few exceptions to this. Imagine an author making headline news for something illegal and terrible just as the book came out and everyone refused to buy the book. The publisher may demand their money back because the author ruined their ability to make money on it. (Think books by actors and politicians who get million-dollar advances and then…do what actors and politicians tend to do.)

worry about this too much. It's not worth it.

An ISBN (International Standard Book Number), is a number used to identify a specific edition of a book or related type media, such as an audiobook, e-book, CDs, PDF, etc. (They do not apply to periodicals. ISSNs are used for serial publications.) Once upon a time, ISBNs were ten digits, now they are thirteen, referred to as ISBN-10 or ISBN-13. There is no difference between the two, other than the ISBN-13 is the newer system, implemented in 2007, and it is replacing the older system. That is why older books have only an ISBN-10 and some books have both an ISBN-10 and an ISBN-13. Eventually, all new books will have only an ISBN-13.

Each ISBN can only be used once. If a book goes out of print, the ISBN cannot be recycled to a new (different) book. Each edition or format of a title needs its own ISBN. An e-book edition of a novel will have a different ISBN than the paperback, which will be different than the hardback, which will be different than a trade paperback, which is different than the audiobook.

New editions, or re-issues, of a title need new ISBNs, but only if they have "added value" (which also means value removed). According to guidelines, making corrections and even changing the image on the cover is not enough to require a new ISBN. However, changing the spelling (or abbreviations) of the author's name is, as is adding (or removing) forewords, appendices, content, or changing the trim size or media format of the book. A re-issue by a new publisher, even with no other changes, also warrants a new ISBN[21].

Some places and people argue that e-books don't need ISBNs, while others claim that each file format (MOBI, PDF, EPUB, etc.), and each distributor needs its own unique ISBN. ISBN guidelines generally agree with the latter, but with a caveat for the former. For more on this idea, read **Do I Need an ISBN.**

There is only one agency in each country officially licensed to issue ISBNs. In the U.S. it is Bowker. Any other place or person in the U.S., selling or giving away ISBNs, either purchased them through Bowker, or they are not real ISBNs. When an ISBN is purchased, it is automatically registered to the purchaser, who is automatically listed as the publisher. Anyone other than Bowker (or the official issuer in your country) offering ISBNs and claiming you will be listed as the publisher is lying. The closest to publisher you can be listed as on one of those ISBNs is an imprint of the company that originally purchased the ISBN. This makes it look like your company is a subsidiary of their publishing house. Also, if you purchase ISBNs from anyone else you are at their mercy to update and register the metadata information of the ISBN, because ISBNs, and access to them, are linked to the original purchaser's account.

ISBNs were originally intended to identify specific works for purposes of tracking sales, inventory, shelving in libraries, etc. That is part of the reason the publisher, as well as the author, is named in the ISBN. In fact, ISBNs are registered to the publisher, not the author, as they identify versions of the book

---

[21] You can find more from the source here:
https://www.isbn-international.org/content/isbn-assignment

put out by a specific publisher. Think how many different publishers have issued editions of classic novels or religious texts. ISBNs make it a lot easier to find that exact version of the Holy Bible that your religious studies class is requiring.

But, like everything else in the publishing world, things are changing.

Print on Demand (POD) service providers, like IngramSpark, Kindle Direct Publishing (KDP), Barnes & Noble Press (B&N), and others, use ISBNs for more than what they were intended for. They use them as file identifiers for the services they provide (most specifically printing). This means that if a publisher wishes to use the services of more than one place, a single edition of a book, which should have had to have only one ISBN no matter how many different printers were used to create the physical copies, will require a separate ISBN for each place utilized.

This is because these places tend to use the same printing company, which means if I publish a book using IngramSpark as my printer and distributor, and then I try to also publish it with KDP or B&N, it causes problems. When KDP and B&N try to utilize Ingram's services (the printing and distribution company most publishers use in the U.S.) using the same ISBN number I already have registered to my account, they cannot, as it is already in use under my account.

So now these places pretty much all require separate, unique ISBNs for any editions you publish with them. This causes new problems because, while free in some countries, in the U.S. ISBNs are $125 for one, or cheapest individually when purchased in bulk at $1,500 for 1,000. This could be why so many of these places offer "free" ISBNs if you use their services—to entice you to self-publish with them by lowering the costs. Note: According to IngramSpark: "Once you have an IngramSpark account, you can purchase single ISBNs directly from Bowker through your IngramSpark dashboard for just $85."[22]

Sidenote: Barcodes (the scan lines on the back of the book) are often offered for sale alongside ISBN numbers. My opinion is you should not purchase them. Not only can they be obtained for free from some places, but many of these services providers will slap their own barcode over the top of yours anyway.

Second sidenote: ISBNs have nothing to do with copyright and offer no legal protection. You do not need to have one to submit your book to a publisher. If you are not going to self-publish, forget everything you just read. You don't really need to know it.

---

[22] https://www.ingramspark.com/blog/isbn-facts-for-self-publishers

Do I Need an ISBN?

If you are not self-publishing, the answer is a resounding No. ISBNs have to do with publishing, so if you are not going to publish, you do not need one. ISBNs have nothing to do with copyright and offer no legal protection. You do not need to have one to submit your book or story or poem to a publisher for consideration to be published.

Please note, any publisher asking you for an ISBN, when you submitted a book to them for consideration for them to publish, is likely not a company or person you want to be doing business with.

Publishers use ISBNs, writers do not.

If you intend to self-publish, you may or may not need, or feel you need, an ISBN. Some of this was covered in **ISBNs**, so make sure you read that if you need to know more.

Most places you can self-publish with today will provide a free ISBN for your book, if you want. They do this (in my opinion) for three reasons.

First, because most of them tend to use the same printing and distribution company, Ingram, which uses ISBNs as file identification numbers for the books they print and distribute. (See **ISBNs** for more on this.)

Second, because ISBNs can be expensive. By offering them for free, they attract authors who don't want to, or can't, invest money up front when they self-publish. In order to keep up with the competition, even Ingram, which was originally set up for publishing houses, eventually created IngramSpark, a self-publishing platform, and now offers free ISBNs.

And third, because if you use their ISBN, it lists them as the publisher of the book. Are there advantages to this? Eh… Kind of. It makes these companies look like a Big Publisher, because they have thousands and thousands of titles registered to ISBNs which are registered in their names. But really, it is more of a disadvantage to you, because it doesn't list you as the publisher.

Why would you care about that?

Registering an ISBN yourself allows you full control of the name of the publisher, the name of the imprint, and all associated metadata (author, genre, keywords, etc.,) along with the title. Part of this control is making sure that information gets input at all, let alone the way you want it to be. This can be important to sales as registering an ISBN lists the book in *Books In Print*, a database used by retailers and libraries to order books. Having the bane of small bookstores everywhere (aka one of the large online companies that compete with them) listed as your publisher can deter many of those bookstores from ordering your book, as they know buying it supports the competition. This may be part of the reason some of those service providers now list the publisher as things like "Independently published." Which can also deter small bookstores. Not only because small bookstore owners are not stupid and realize what that means, but because it reeks of a lack of professionalism and indicates the quality of the writing, editing, and formatting (or all of the above), may be subpar, which may lead to dissatisfied customers and returned books.

Now these are largely subjective observations. I cannot prove any of them beyond anecdotally, and I'm not going to cite people I have had conversations with, so your mileage may vary, especially if you are asking a small bookstore owner or a large online company's representative about this issue. Which either may or may not answer honestly, for sake of appearances.

Moving on to why you might not want to provide your own ISBN, beyond the cost: it might not matter or make any difference to you.

If you choose to publish your books through only one of the service providers, chances are you won't be concerned about the metadata listing of the ISBN or a listing in *Books In Print*. Many people who publish with Barnes & Noble Press are perfectly happy to publish only with Barnes & Noble Press. Many more are very happy to be exclusive to Kindle Direct Publishing. (Though there are disadvantages to going exclusive. See **Popular Self-Publishing Platforms** for more on this.) Choosing one service as your printer and distributor can pretty much eliminate a need for a personalized ISBN. B&N only distributes to B&N, so why bother? KDP can distribute worldwide by using only Amazon, but that is often the only place a self-publisher cares about, so why bother?

On top of that, self-publishers often have good control over keywords and genre listings within these services. Better control than over the ISBN's metadata.

Then there is the issue of ISBNs for e-books. As before, if you are using one distributor, why bother? But on top of that, some authors only do e-books, and bookstores don't order e-books, so why care about *Books In Print*?

Some people argue e-books do not even need an ISBN. There is validity to this point. While the International ISBN Agency states "...each different product form (e.g. paperback, EPUB, .PDF) should be identified separately,"[23] which implies every different file format of an e-book needs its own ISBN, it also states: "Some retailers are the sole providers of e-books in a proprietary format that can only be bought through their website. An example is Kindle format e-books which are only available from Amazon. In this particular case as there is one source of supply, the retailer does not require ISBNs and so it is not strictly necessary for the publisher to assign an ISBN to this particular version."[24] This basically means Amazon doesn't have to use one because they distribute their e-books as MOBI files that can only be read by Kindle products.

This is why Amazon doesn't automatically assign ISBNs to e-books and instead only uses an ASIN (Amazon Standard Identification Number), which is nothing more than an internal tracking number for the items they sell.

You may see where this can lead to confusion with people thinking that e-books don't need ISBN numbers. It also seems to be a huge, money saving thing for Amazon, not needing to purchase an ISBN for each e-book, especially

---

[23] https://www.isbn-international.org/content/what-isbn

[24] https://www.isbn-international.org/content/guidelines-assignment-e-books/26

when compared to a place like Smashwords, which will convert your file into eight different formats, which, according to the International ISBN Agency should mean eight different ISBNs. But then again, Smashwords states you do not need to have an ISBN with them, but not having one will affect your distribution, as some retailers require it, and it will not be distributed to them without it[25].

So, do you need an ISBN for an e-book? Probably not. Do you care if the ISBN for your e-book lists someone else as a publisher? Probably not.

So, then why would you want to pay for your own ISBNs for self-published e-books? To maintain a professional appearance and to track sales. Beyond that, I got nothing. I'm sure there are other reasons, but I don't know them.

What Do I Need to Know About Copyright?

Copyright is confusing to many people, not just authors, hence all the problems with fanfiction. But before I go any further, let me reiterate, I am not a lawyer, I have no legal background. I am neither attempting to provide, nor intending to imply, legal, or any other professional advice or service. If such advice or services are needed, professional council should be sought. Before you decide to do something based upon anything I say here, assume I got it wrong and don't do it without researching it yourself. For the latest official information on copyright, start at https://www.copyright.gov/

Okay. Just so that we're clear. These are my thoughts and opinions on copyright. Others will disagree with me. This is a huge topic and law schools teach multiple classes on it. It is a specialized subject. Obviously, I can't (and don't) know everything about it. I know professional writers, who have been living off the earnings of their writings for fifty years, who don't understand it. I know lawyers who have problems with it. I also know a law professor who specializes in intellectual property law, and he's set me straight a time or two. You can get a good, free, crash course on the basics of copyright from him here:

https://writerinlaw.com/2014/01/17/copyright-class-1-originality/

Again. That stuff is not legal advice. If you need that, you need to hire yourself a lawyer. One who knows this stuff; not the car accident guy or the real estate lady you see on TV all the time. They don't know it.

While you consider whether to tackle that learning adventure, I am going to cover what I think are important introductory ideas to help you get your footing.

---

[25] https://www.smashwords.com/about/supportfaq#isbn

Because plagiarism and copyright infringement and misinformation seem to run rampant online nowadays, let's start with some common misconceptions:

Regarding the idea of the "**poor man's copyright**," wherein people think they can mail their manuscript to themselves or others and keep it sealed with a postmark to prove they wrote it; that is worthless. Don't do it.

Titles, names, and phrases are not copyrightable. You can, however, trademark them, but that is more expensive and requires upkeep. Trademark is also the way Disney will hold on to Mickey even after the original cartoons fall out of copyright in 2024. (See **Don't Use Names of Real Businesses** and **Don't Use Names of Real Products** for more on trademarks.) On the flip side of that, song lyrics are copyrighted, and even small snippets of them can be copyright infringement. See **Don't Use Song Lyrics** for more on this idea.

Ideas are not copyrightable. While the movie *E.T.* is copyrighted (and probably trademarked), the idea of a kid meeting a friendly lost alien in the woods and bringing him home and then helping him get home, is not. But the way you write that story is. If someone writes a book with an idea that is a lot like yours, they have not infringed upon your copyright. Unless it is too much like yours. In every way. Like scene for scene. With the same characters. And then things get murky real fast. Ugly in fact.

Just because something is on the internet does not mean it is in the public domain. Things on the internet are still copyrighted, just like everything else. Think twice about using that image or text you found online. Find out if it is public domain before you use it. If you can't verify it is, then don't use it.

Fair Use is actually very limited. You can't just quote everything you want for no reason in whatever type of writing you want. There is no percentage or word limit involved. It is how it is used that matters, and that can be murky too.

Fanfiction is not "fair use." For some reason people think that writing fanfiction is okay. It is not. Not without express permission from the copyright owner. But that doesn't stop people from doing it anyway. And then things can get really ugly again. Combine this idea with the previous one, and you end up with lawsuits and debates like the 2018 one over stories written in the "Omegaverse." You can research that yourself. It's quite a read. (Warning: the stories themselves are a form of erotica, so you may not want to look too far into them. Or maybe you do.)
Moving on.

You do not have to use the copyright symbol (©) to protect the copyright of your work. Once upon a time it was required to show the work was still under copyright, but it no longer is. That doesn't mean you shouldn't use it, only that you don't have to.

Something you write is copyrighted as soon as you put it in a fixed form, meaning as soon as you write it down. Or record yourself saying it. Or anything that is a "tangible medium of expression." This means you don't have to worry about whether or not your story is copyrighted. It was, as soon as you wrote it. Even if that was on a napkin, in the back booth of a diner, with coffee as ink and a toothpick as a quill.

Are you still thinking about writing it but haven't yet? It is not copyrighted. So, write it down. Or dictate it. And then it is copyrighted. But that does not mean it is registered.

Registering a copyright is a different thing. You do not have to register your copyright, but if you do want it registered, you have to actually contact the Copyright Office to do that. It is easiest to do it online here:

https://www.copyright.gov/registration/

And it is easiest to do with digital editions, which, you can upload, but only if it does not yet exist in print form yet. If you are self-publishing, and choose to do this, it should be done before you actually publish the book.

Now comes the big question: **Should you register a copyright?**

If you are submitting your novel to publishers, the standard answer is no. Most larger publishers will register a copyright for you. If you register it first, and substantial changes are made in the editing process, another may need to be registered. That can create confusion. And it costs money.

A lot of self-publishers, if not most, don't bother to register copyrights.

So, what's the point then? First, if you are going to sue for copyright infringement, you will have to register the copyright before you can sue anyway. Second, it registers the date of the copyright in official records, just in case there ever is a lawsuit. And third, "When registration is made prior to infringement or within three months after publication of a work, a copyright owner is eligible for statutory damages, attorneys' fees, and costs.[26]"

If you choose to register your copyright, have heart, it has gotten simpler since I first registered one, probably because the influx of self-publishers created logjams in the process, and it only costs $65. (It was $35 the first time I registered one.) It is simple enough that I do not recommend using any of the various companies that will happily charge you hundreds of dollars to do it for you.

Do I need to submit my book to the Library of Congress? No. In fact, it probably won't do you any good to try. Books published by Print on Demand are not eligible, and there are few other ways to self-publish[27].

[26] https://www.copyright.gov/circs/circ01.PDF
[27] https://www.loc.gov/publish/cip/about/ineligible.html

What Software Do I Need to do My Own Layout and Formatting?

Like everything to do with writing, there is no one answer to the question of software needed for formatting and conversion of files for publishing, and what works for one person may not work for another. On top of that, in this situation, there are many possible answers, and they are changing all the time. What I list here is based upon my experience. I am sure there are many more out there I don't know about, and I'm sure some of them are probably fantastic.

As the industry grows, more free resources have become available online. When I first started self-publishing, the only (free) online resource for converting files into different e-book formats that I knew of was Smashwords' "meat grinder," the name they gave their program that converted .doc files into the files Smashwords would then distribute. It was a difficult program to use, but only in that they had very specific formatting requirements you had to follow within your .doc file before uploading your file to them. Many authors got very frustrated with it but used it because it would make all the files necessary for e-books (EPUB, MOBI, PDF, and more), and then Smashwords would distribute those files to all of the retailers. This meant the authors didn't need to figure out MOBI vs EPUB vs PDF, or anything other than formatting the .doc file for use by Smashwords.

If you are considering Smashwords, it is easier to use now than it was then. And it is no longer the only place that will do that. Nearly every place you can self-publish will allow you to upload a .doc file, and they will convert it for you into an e-book file to use on their platform. But again, you need to have your formatting done correctly in your .doc file or you will not have good final results, and each place has varying finished results anyway, so make sure to check the results you get, and make sure you're happy with them, before you publish.

The publisher I was working with at the time was not happy with the results of automated conversions, so we made our own files. More on that in a few paragraphs from here.

My current favorite online file converter is Draft2Digital. They will make EPUB, MOBI, and PDF files for you, in moments, online, for free, that you can download and use as you like, where you like. In other words, for free, you could use D2D to format your .doc file into a MOBI file to upload to Amazon yourself, if you choose to do so. Very nice of D2D, I think. And, I think, the files their converter creates are some of the better ones from automated converters.

If you are on a budget and don't want to learn programs for formatting and converting, I suggest you check out what D2D has to offer. Unless you feel you need to do something fancy with your books (like interior images or fancy dingbats), you will likely be happy with what they will do for you for free. (Again, only if you format your .doc file correctly. Make sure to read their guides.)

When it comes to doing the layout and file conversions yourself, there are a myriad of choices. Personally, though I have heard many people say it can't be done, I use MS Word to format my PDFs for print books. Because it can be done, and I already have MS Word, so I don't have to pay for another monthly fee-based software.

Like Adobe InDesign.

Which is basically the industry standard. I have used it. There are advantages to using it, but there is the hefty price. As of this writing, it is $19.99 a month if you pre-pay annually, or $31.49 for one month. Few people other than publishers will use this program even once a month, and that makes it hard to justify paying that price. (And saving up several projects to do all in one month is an aneurysm waiting to happen. Trust me on that one.)

The upside of Adobe InDesign, once you get past the steep learning curve, is that it can create EPUBs for e-books, PDFs for print, and PDFs for your book covers, and it is the industry standard. This means you can exchange InDesign files with others easily, and it means the output files it creates are compatible with what you need.

Once upon a time, about ten years ago, I tried six or seven free "Adobe alternatives" that were "100% compatible," to try to create print-ready PDF files for upload to CreateSpace and Ingram. They all were continually auto-rejected, especially at Ingram. I heard other self-publishers complain about this issue as well, and the conspiracy theory was there must be an Adobe watermark of some sort on their PDFs that allowed the other files to be rejected. I don't know if there was any truth to this or not, but, long story short, I made use of Adobe InDesign while working with publishers.

The point of this story is to make you aware that sometimes the free stuff just doesn't do what it says it does. If you go the route of free software, be prepared for setbacks and frustrations.

At the time I used Adobe InDesign, the publisher I was working with was not happy with the results of the e-books InDesign created, so I used a program called Jutoh to create e-books, both for EPUB and MOBI files, and for the final .doc file that would be uploaded to Smashwords for conversion into other formats.

I still use Jutoh, as I am happy with the control and options it gives me, but many people I know have been using Vellum for a few years now and are happy with it. Not only do they use it for e-books, but for PDF files for print books as well. But there are a couple of drawbacks to Vellum.

The first is a big one; it is Mac only, meaning you have to have a Mac computer to run it. The cost of the program, $200 for e-books only or $250 for e-books and print books, and the cost of a Mac computer, put this out of the range of many people who don't already have a Mac computer. (And, as I have mentioned before, the industry standard for manuscripts is the Microsoft .doc file, which, despite claims of 100% compatibility by many programs, does not do well when passed back and forth between Macs and PCs, which is why so many writers have PCs.)

I have been told there are a lack of formatting options in Vellum, such as when it comes to putting in graphics and charts, but I have also been told this is continually improving.

I recently heard of an alternative to Vellum called Atticus. I call it an alternative because everyone keeps comparing it to Vellum. I have no experience with it, but I have heard favorable things, starting with *"you don't have to have a Mac."*

Some authors swear by Scrivener for writing, and I have found it to be an interesting tool for helping write your book, or at least gather notes and research, but many of the authors I've spoken with have been disappointed in Scrivener's ability to make e-books and print-ready PDFs. Others say it works great. I haven't used it for that, so I can't attest either way.

In the end, as I already said, I use MS Word to make the PDFs for my print books. You should use whatever program you feel does the best job for you, that you feel is the easiest for you to work with.

On a side note. The most common error with PDFs for print books, no matter the program that made them, seems to be a problem with embedded fonts. There are several solutions, depending upon the program you used. If you are having problems, I would start by researching that on the internet. The next most common problems tend to be color profiles and PDF standards. More on those in the next section, **Book Covers.**

Book Covers

Book covers are arguably the most important thing about your book. Anyone who says they don't judge a book by its cover is wrong. We all judge books by their covers. We may not think we do, but we do.

Try this: imagine a bookshelf full of books.

There, just off center, on the second from the top shelf, is the one that catches your eye.

Now, at this point, I would expect you to expect me to ask what it was about that cover that caught your eye. But I'm not going to. Instead, I want to know how you pictured all of the other covers, the ones that didn't catch your eye because they were just part of the whole of the bookshelf.

Those books all got judged by you, even in your imagination. Yes, one caught your eye, one was special. But it was because all of the others weren't as special. Which is judging.

We all do it. We can't help it.

Book covers are important.

Before you decide to download a stock photo for a cover, realize there is an artform to book covers. Each genre has "rules" they follow, that slowly change and grow over time. The rules not only apply to the images, but to the fonts, the layouts, and sometimes the titles, the authors' names, or more.

I'm not saying you have to hire a professional cover designer, but I will say that doesn't hurt. (Except maybe in the bank account.) And sometimes (okay, a lot of times) an amateur looking cover can really hurt your sales. The cover I made for the first edition of this book is a good example.

Some self-publishing platforms have tools to help you build a cover yourself. Be wary, you may end up with a generic cover that looks pretty much exactly like everyone else's who used that cover generator.

On top of that pitfall, when you use or create your own images to make your cover, it is easy to get caught in a feedback loop that prevents you from seeing how terrible something you are doing really is, especially if any outside advice you are getting is from someone more interested in getting paid than doing a good job, or if they have no experience in art or book covers. Reference again the aforementioned cover to the first edition of this book. Everyone I asked thought it looked fine. I thought it looked fine. And then it was published. And then people looked away instead of meeting my eyes. (Literally. That happened.) And whispered things to other author friends of mine. Things like, *"Why did you let him do that?"* (Again. Literally. That happened.) So, learn from my mistakes. Don't get caught in a feedback loop with yourself or people who say what they think you want to hear.

A good thing to do is browse through the current titles in the genres you are publishing in and look at the similarities between the covers. Especially look at the bestsellers. Little things, like which way a character is facing, or if the background is red or blue, can make a huge difference, but those subtleties won't matter if you've used funky looking CGI characters or anime-style drawings in a genre they shouldn't be in.

Another thing to keep in mind is what the cover will look like as a thumbnail image, which, unless your book is in a bookstore, is the way most customers will see your cover. If it is nothing more than a little blob, then…it's just a little blob. It does you no good. It won't sell the book.

If you hire someone to do the work for you, make sure you agree to get more than the final product. Most artists work in programs that allow them to layer text and images on top of one another and easily move them around as needed. If you can, you want to end up with a copy of the file that has these layers. Some artists won't give them up. These may be artists you don't want to work with. If you ever need to make changes down the road and only have a finalized, flattened image (meaning no layers), you may have problems that will be difficult to overcome, especially if you can no longer contact the artist for corrections, which they will likely want to charge for. Or they no longer have the files, which happens way, way too often. I have helped out a few times when all that was available was a .jpeg or a .pdf, and I have to say, it basically takes an artist to fix that problem.

For e-books you generally need something like a .jpeg file sized at 2,560 pixels x 1,600 pixels, which is what Kindle Direct Publishing recommends. That size will work most anywhere, but some places want special sizes. You may run into compatibility problems with other image file types, like .bmp or .png, or even if your .jpeg is formatted for CMYK color profile, as most places deal with RGB. (Which is the opposite of printing.)

A word of caution: do not create your cover the small size of an e-book cover to begin with. If you ever choose to make a print book and want to use the same cover, you will be disappointed to find upscaling an image for a print book will make it blurry or jaggy. I recommend always assuming an image will eventually be used on a print book (or a bookmark, or a poster, etc.) and start out with a size at least large enough to make a print book, if not a full poster, then scale the end result down as needed.

Some places will help you make a cover for your print book, but again, be careful of the quality of your final cover. Generally, you need print covers to be 300 dpi no matter what size they are, and most places require a PDF, correctly sized to the book trim, which must take into account the bleed.

Print books come in different sizes, called trim size. When the books are printed, they are printed larger than the final product and then the pages (and cover) are trimmed, or cut, down to final size. In order to not have white edges, which may not be symmetrical, around the cover image, the cover art must "bleed" out farther than to where the final product will be trimmed.

Unless you are doing something that is not a novel, you will probably use a 6x9 or 5.5x8 trim. (Those are in inches, and, at least in the U.S., usually referred to in that way). The typical "pocket book" paperback size you find in bookstores, and the cheaper paper making up the pages, are not usually options for Print on Demand.

Trim size is something you'll want to consider for a few different reasons. First, the genre you are writing in. An 8x11 trim size works great for an illustrated children's book, but no so great for a romance novel. (Unless you have pictures, I guess…) Second, the distribution service you are using. Some self-publishing platforms have non-standard sizes they print books in, which can be cool, but many distributors won't carry non-standard sizes, so you won't be able to get sales outlets to carry your book. The third consideration is cost.

POD books usually don't cost by the trim size of the book but rather by the number of pages in the book. (This is not always true. Pay attention to how the service you use charges.) So, a 250 page book at 5.5x8 will cost the same as a 250 page book at 6x9. But you can fit more text on the larger pages of a 6x9, so it becomes cheaper to go with the larger size, as you will need fewer pages[28].

Finally, when you create a PDF file for the cover (very few places will let you use a .jpeg, and then you probably won't have a back cover image, just text they put there for you), you have to take into account the trim size and the bleed. You also probably need to use a certain standard of PDF file (usually an older

---

[28] This book in your hands, for example. The first edition was sized 5.5x8. A size I actually prefer. But as this edition was being prepared to go to press, the cost of POD has gone up enough during the COVID pandemic, that we changed to 6x9 and saved around 35 pages, or almost 50¢ on the production cost of each unit.

one) such as PDF/X-1a:2001. Also, unlike the .jpeg for an e-book cover, which usually has to be uploaded in the RGB color profile, the PDF likely needs to be in the CMYK color profile (but not always). If you are playing with color images inside your book, it can become confusing switching back and forth. Some programs won't work with CMYK color profile .jpegs for interior images, but then convert the RGB images to CMYK when exporting a .pdf file. I tell you this because I spent a week troubleshooting that problem once.

A lot of this may sound like gibberish, but I wanted to point it all out, to give you a place to start looking, to try to save you hours of figuring out why something doesn't work. Most places have information on their file requirements, but some are hard to find. Try to know them in advance so you get it right the first time and save yourself a lot of frustration, especially if you are paying someone to do it for you. They may charge you to make changes if you don't specifically state what you need up front, and sometimes, when they think they know what you need—and they're wrong—it can be really hard to make them get it right.

Popular Self-Publishing Platforms

This is a section of the book that will go out of date very quickly. Make sure you don't take any information here as set in stone, but rather use it as a stepping-off point for your own research.

The self-publishing services available are in constant flux, not only in what services they offer but even in what companies exist. New ones pop up all the time, especially predatory sites that want to take advantage of authors. They also disappear quickly. (Usually. There are a couple out there that have been around for many years.)

I'm not going to list companies I definitely don't like, partially because they may be gone already by the time you read this, partially because I don't want to open myself up to the attacks I may receive from doing such a thing. I will talk about a couple I wouldn't choose to use, because I know some people do like them, and I feel you should have a basis for comparison.

Before we get to that, I want to start with an opinion, a word of advice based upon what I think, what I believe. Take it as such and then make up your own mind.

There are two kinds of self-publishing platforms, and neither of them care if you make money. They are only interested in making money for themselves. The one kind costs you very little, if any, money to use. They will make money off of you as you make money. (I rant about this in **What is a "Publisher?"**) The other kind makes nearly all of its money from you directly, when you pay for their services, and doesn't care if you make any money at all.

I personally don't use the second kind. I refer to the legitimate ones as Turnkey Publishers, because they are like renting a furnished apartment. All you need to do is pay enough money and they hand you a key and you are good to go. Of course the problem with that is you won't *really* know the quality of the furniture you're paying for until it's too late.

These places generally make their money from editing services, formatting services, printing services, distribution services, cover design, marketing and more, that you pay them for, in advance. This can cost you thousands of dollars. I have met people who have done this and were thrilled with the end results. I have also met people who were terribly upset by the results, or, more accurately, the lack thereof.

And those are the legitimate services. There are others I consider predatory, out to steal money from desperate authors who just want to get published. This kind will lie, mislead, and misrepresent in order to get your money. If they do anything at all after they have your money.

Again, I am not going to call places out by name, but before you use any place asking you to pay for any of their services, you owe it to yourself to do detailed research on them and read contracts or terms of service carefully (See **Your Second, and Maybe Biggest Mistake.** There are complaints about how copyrights, or at least the right to publish, have been stolen.), and don't trust random review sites for honest reviews. Often the worst places use sock-puppet reviews, meaning they plant fake reviews, or they review themselves. Do your research by looking up blogs and posts by other authors willing to share their experiences. Check places like *Writer Beware* and *Predators and Editors*.

I have seen books published this way that authors, whom I met, paid hundreds of dollars for editing, and the books still had "hte" errors. That is a mistyping of the word "the" that I have a hard time keeping in that sentence because autocorrect keeps fixing it. That also means that after getting paid hundreds of dollars for editing, that company didn't even bother to run a spellcheck.

I have seen authors stuck with piles of books they were contractually obligated to order as part of the service provided. I have found out authors paid hundreds of dollars to have their books distributed to Amazon, and only Amazon, when that can be done easily, for free. I have listened to authors complain that no one buys their books, then found out the books are only available at the webpage storefront of the company that was paid hundreds of dollars to publish them, and then only at a very high, if not completely unreasonable price.

The list goes on, and I'm ranting. My point is, before you decide to pay a company to edit, format, market, or publish your book, you need to learn enough about those things, and the company, to make sure they aren't ripping you off.

Again, let me reiterate, this is a bias of mine, and I know it. The flip side, not using these services, is that you have to find a way to get your book edited and formatted, and find cover art, and design, and more, all by yourself. Which usually still costs you money. There are people out there who really like some of these full-service companies, feel they did a great job, and will use them forever. My bias leans toward not paying a company several hundred dollars for something I can do myself for free in a matter of minutes. But then, I took the time to learn how to do that stuff. Some people don't want to do that, and for them, companies that do it (those that aren't a scam, but actual service providers) are a good thing.

But back to the first kind of self-publishing platforms I mentioned, the ones that cost you very little to no money. These are becoming easier and easier to use. They keep updating their user interfaces and offering more services all the time. The information I provide on them should be considered out of date, and I may have made mistakes (sorry if I did), and you should research them thoroughly before choosing one. Also, assume there are others I did not list that may be better. Though I believe these are the most popular and widest distributing, go searching and find out for yourself. There may be Newer, Bigger, Better by now.

When I started out self-publishing, CreateSpace was probably the most popular platform for self-published print books. It has since been replaced by Kindle Direct Publishing, which now does both print and e-books. KDP is now probably the most popular platform all around. Many people have no desire to publish anywhere except Amazon, and KDP is the best way to do that. It can also get you to other booksellers if you choose to use their expanded distribution. (With print books. They distribute e-books only through Amazon sites.)

So why would anyone want to go with any company other than KDP and Amazon? Well, some don't like the idea of Amazon being the only bookstore, so they publish with others just to try to keep competition alive. Others go with the idea that casting the widest net catches the most fish, meaning the more places your book is available, the more people there are to purchase your book.

Personally, I use several of the service providers for most of my print and e-book distribution. Here's why: once I have gone through the effort of creating the files needed to self-publish books, it takes very little more effort to change two or three tiny details (like the ISBN number) and then upload them to other retailers. The advantage to that is each retailer offers a higher royalty rate on purchases of books made through their storefront, that they published for you. So, it takes me an extra fifteen minutes (I'm pretty quick because I've done a lot of them while working for publishers) to upload my book to all the places I want to use, and for that effort I can get an extra 5% to 20% or more on each sale from individual retailers. And that adds up.

Here is a quick example: For print books, KDP states "If you enroll your paperback in Expanded Distribution, the royalty rate is 40% of the book's list price effective in the distribution channel at the time of purchase, minus printing costs, applicable taxes, and withholding."[29]

But for sales of print books at Amazon through KDP: "KDP offers a fixed 60% royalty rate on paperbacks sold on Amazon marketplaces where KDP supports paperback distribution. Your royalty is 60% of your list price. We then subtract printing costs, which depend on page count, ink type, and the Amazon marketplace your paperback was ordered from."[30]

Basically, if you use KDP's expanded distribution to get your books on Barnes & Noble's website, you are earning 20% less for each book sold at Barnes & Noble than at Amazon. So, I go to B&N Press, re-upload my files with a new ISBN (a lot of people use the free ISBN from B&N Press, because B&N Press only distributes to B&N, so they don't care who the ISBN says the publisher is), and now my print copies sold on B&N earn "…a 55% author royalty rate of the List Price, minus the per book printing cost."[31]

I could be wrong, but I think it used to be a better rate than that, but still, that's 15% more per sale[32]. That adds up over time, and that's why I do it. A

[29] https://kdp.amazon.com/en_US/help/topic/GQTT4W3T5AYK7L45#royalties
[30] https://kdp.amazon.com/en_US/help/topic/G201834330
[31] https://press.barnesandnoble.com/legal/royalty-payment-terms
[32] Printing costs are in flux as of this writing, because of COVID-19. That is affecting book costs, which affects earnings.

similar thing happens with e-book distribution.

My personal preference, which has changed over time and will likely change again, is to use IngramSpark to publish paperbacks and/or hardbacks with wide distribution, then use KDP to publish paperbacks and e-books to Amazon, then use B&N Press for paperbacks and e-books to B&N, then use Rakuten Kobo (formerly Kobo) to distribute e-books to their storefront and global partners, then use Smashwords to distribute e-books to their storefront as well as other places I haven't yet covered, then I use Draft2Digital to round off the last few places they distribute e-books to I still have not yet covered[33].

Now, that sounds like a lot of work, and initially, setting up the accounts and learning what to do can be. But like I said, at this point, I can upload files to them all in 15 minutes, more or less, so that extra 15% is worth it to me. A lot of people feel it is not. They like to stick with one place that does it all, an aggregator, because it is easier to keep track of sales, to keep track of payments, or they don't care about wider distribution, or they just don't want to learn more than one user interface. Also, more than one version of the book can split up reviews, which can affect visibility (or a spot on the bestseller list).

And that is fine. Each to their own. We all need to figure out what works for us. Which is what your next step is, if you are going to self-publish.

Remember, my list of places and the services they provide are subject to constant change, so don't expect it to be accurate or complete, and make sure you do your own research before you make decisions. This is here to help get you started, not to tell you what to do.

In the following summaries, I include quick stats that will hopefully help you to see at a glance if the company does what you want. As time goes on, these companies have become more alike as each races to come up with something that makes them stand out, and then the rest race to apply that feature, too. But there are differences.

There are two things you should look out for. First, do you have to already have a finalized, finished file, or will they make an e-book or print book file for you? Not all of them will create a book for you; some require that you upload a finished e-book or print-ready PDF file. And not all of them that will turn a .doc file into a book for you will make something you will be happy with. A quick way to tell if they make the books for you is the files they accept. If the only thing they accept (file in) is an EPUB (which is already a formatted e-book) or a PDF (which is already a fixed layout), then you've already made the e-book and formatted the print book, and they're not going to. But if they are accepting a .doc, .docx, or .rtf type file, then they are likely converting the files into e-books or print books for you. (See **What Software Do I Need to do My Own Formatting?** for more on this.)

The other thing to watch for is, where will they sell your books? You'll be

---

[33] Draft2Digital now also distributes print books. This, along with their payment splitting program, is the reason I am currently using them as sole distributor for my publishing house, Knight Writing Press. (I am not affiliated with D2D.)

disappointed if your books don't show up someplace you thought they would. Don't expect Apple Books to list your book on Amazon, or vice versa.

But this kind of stuff is always in flux. Where I could, when I knew, I listed the distribution partners and if they could be restricted. Some services will, some won't, and some restrict only some. Pay attention to this. It causes problems if you put up an e-book on Amazon with KDP, then do it again with IngramSpark, then do it again with Smashwords, then again with Draft2Digital.

Or rather, it used to cause a lot of problems, so now Amazon has made it a lot harder for those other places to do that, which means there can be some hoops to jump through to get your e-book on Amazon through those other aggregators. But that doesn't mean it can't be done or that you shouldn't do it. Just make sure you pay attention and find out. (Print books are a bit easier to deal with, kind of, because of the ISBN thing. See **ISBNs** for more on this.)

I also listed whether or not you can restrict the regions in which a book is sold. This won't apply to 98% of people who read this, but I had the information for myself, from working with publishing companies[34], so I went ahead and put it in here.

Again, don't trust any of this to be accurate. Things change.

One last thing to keep in mind. When you set up an account with any of these places, you will have to provide Tax ID information (usually a Social Security Number or, if you have a business, an EIN) and set up a way to receive payment. Some places will pay via PayPal, some with a check, some with direct deposit into your bank account. Some let you choose (this is becoming more common). Make sure you figure out if what they do works for you before you have your heart set on using one of them, especially if you live outside the U.S.

---

[34] Sometimes when an author sells rights to a publisher, they only sell rights to publish in a certain region. If I sell first publication rights in North America, I still have the right to publish (or sell the rights to publish) my book in the rest of the world. In that case, I can self-publish a book that another publisher is also publishing, and I can restrict the regions in which my book is made available so I don't also sell the book in North America and violate the rights I sold to a different publisher.
Restricting regions can be tricky, as they are not always clear cut, but you likely won't have to deal with it. As a self-publisher, unless you've sold or given away some of your rights, you can publish anywhere you want.

Kindle Direct Publishing

Kindle Direct Publishing started out as the way to self-publish e-books to Amazon. Eventually print books were added to it, and it replaced CreateSpace as a way to self-publish print books to Amazon and other places. As of this writing KDP has added the ability to print hardcover books, but they are "case laminate," meaning the cover images are printed directly upon the laminate case of the book instead of on a dust jacket. Note that these hardcover books are not eligible for Expanded Distribution, so they will not be sold anywhere except on Amazon websites. Hardcover and paperback royalty rates are the same, but the cost of printing the books is different.

Kindle Select and Kindle Unlimited are programs only available through KDP. Use of those programs requires exclusivity with KDP, so make sure you research them and understand what they are, how to use them, and if they are right for you. Some authors prefer them and only use Amazon and KDP.

Amazon is the largest book and e-book distributor by far, although numbers are hard to come by because Amazon rarely releases sales information. It is estimated that Amazon has nearly 70% of the e-book market and around 50% of the print book market. For this reason alone, many self-publishers feel no need to try to publish anywhere else.

Also, KDP makes use of Ingram for publishing and distribution of print books, so if you plan to use IngramSpark as well, be prepared to deal with multiple ISBNs and "multiple editions" of your paperback. (See **ISBNs** for more.)

Recently, KDP has changed something about the way they do print books. You can only order author copies after a print book has been set "live," or published to Amazon. In the past, KDP (or rather CreateSpace) could be used to print up a couple dozen copies of a book you only wanted to share with family. This is no longer true.

**As this guide was being put together, KDP announced, "Starting August 1, 2021, we will no longer support MOBI files for reflowable eBooks. Use EPUB, DOCX or KPF to publish new or update reflowable eBooks." I have not used KDP since that announcement and cannot confirm the effects this has on publishing with them. (See what I mean about everything changing all the time?)

Stats at a glance:

- Cost: No set-up fees. Variable "distribution fee" based upon file size for e-books.
- ISBNs not needed for e-books, can be provided for free for print books. Amazon provides ASIN numbers for e-books. (Amazon Standard Identification Number, which is nothing more than an internal tracking number.) **As this edition went to press, KDP announced the ability to make hardbacks.***
- Can setup pre-orders.
- Cannot offer e-book for free unless in Kindle Select, and then it is limited.
- 60% royalty rate on books sold through Amazon marketplaces, 40% for Expanded Distribution to other booksellers. "...royalty is 40% of the book's list price effective in the distribution channel at the time of purchase minus printing costs." **Note: Hardcover not eligible for Expanded Distribution.**
- 35% or 70% royalty rates for e-books, depending. E-books must be priced between $2.99 to $9.99 for 70%. The 70% rate option has an added "delivery fee" based upon the size of the file.
- Distribution: Amazon only (but all over the world). Can restrict regions and set individual region prices.
- Titles must be enrolled in KDP Select to be eligible for 70% royalty in Brazil, Japan, Mexico, and India.
- Files accepted for conversion into e-books: .doc, .docx, .html, .mobi, .epub, .rtf, .txt, and .kpf (Kindle Package Format from Kindle Create.)
- E-book format produced: MOBI ?**As this guide was being put together, KDP announced they would not be using MOBI.
- Digital Rights Management (DRM) at author discretion.

Barnes & Noble Press

Barnes & Noble Press distributes only to Barnes & Noble and, despite tantalizing glimmers of hope sprinkled around their websites, it is still practically impossible to get your self-published paperback book carried in their physical bookstores. If you self-publish with B&N Press, it is MUCH easier to get a local B&N bookstore to order copies to have at their store for an event, but don't get your hopes up about having your books on the shelves all around the country.

B&N Press can print hardbacks (with dust jackets or with printed case) as well as paperbacks, but again, they only distribute to B&N. They do, however, also allow you to print books for "personal use," which means, unlike KDP, you do not have to make your book available to the public before you can order more than a couple of proof copies. (Useful for printing up a bunch of advance copies for promotional purposes.)

Also, they make use of Ingram for publishing, so if you plan to use IngramSpark as well, be prepared to deal with multiple ISBNs and "multiple editions" of your paperback. (See **ISBNs** for more.)

Stats at a glance:

- Cost: No set-up fees.
- e-books and print books, also hardback books.
- ISBNs free from B&N or use your own. Cannot use same ISBN you used elsewhere.
- Can setup pre-orders.
- Can offer book for free.
- E-book royalty rates: 40% if priced $0.99 – $2.98, 65% if $2.99 – $199.99.
- Print book royalty rate: 55% of list price, less the printing cost of the book.
- Distribution: Barnes & Noble only.
- Files accepted for conversion into e-books: .doc, .docx, .txt, .html and .epub.
- E-book format produced: EPUB.
- Files accepted for print book: .doc, .docx, .pdf.
- Digital Rights Management (DRM) at author discretion.

Google Play Books

I have never used Google Play. In 2015, they declared themselves "Temporarily Closed" and stayed that way until sometime in 2020. During that time, only select publishers were permitted to publish.

Prior to the closure, I had been warned off from publishing with them, as they would randomly drop the price of e-books, sometimes to free, without warning to, or permission from, the author. Now this may not sound like a bad thing, as they paid the author full royalties on every sale, even when the book was free. Great, right? No.

Amazon would price match the sale price, but wouldn't pay the difference, as they weren't the ones who initiated the sale price. And sales on Amazon were many, compared to few on Google Play, so authors lost money on Amazon when books were priced at free on Google Play, and the authors had no control over it. That led to some authors asking people to purchase the free book on Google Play, at the discounted price, in exchange for the author personally reimbursing the purchasers what the author earned, in an attempt to try to make the free version so expensive to Google Play that Google Play would raise the price, then the author could make money on Amazon again.

Supposedly, now that Google Play Books is open to the general public of self-publishers again, this doesn't happen anymore. I have heard, secondhand, good things about them recently, but after over 30 minutes of searching, I was not able to access the Google Play Books Terms of Service. I found a lot of information, but not the TOS. The closest I found was the Google Play TOS, which did not cover Google Play Books, and this mention in how to use Google Play:

> **Quick steps**
> 1. **If you don't already have one, create a new account.**
> 2. **Agree to the Terms and Conditions.**[35]

Because creating an account is often considered acceptance of a TOS, I don't work with companies that put their TOS behind the login. Disappointing, as I generally use Google as a whole.

---

[35] https://support.google.com/books/partner/answer/4492574

Stats at a glance[36]:

- Cost: No set-up fees.
- e-books only.
- ISBNs not needed. Like Amazon's ASIN numbers, Google assigns GGKEYs which are only used with Google
- Can setup pre-orders.
- Can offer book for free.
- 70% royalty rate on e-books sold through Google Play
- 52% royalty rates "for partners who have not accepted our updated TOS and for e-book sales in certain countries."[37]
- Distribution: Google Play only (but nearly all over the world). Can restrict regions and set individual region prices.
- Files accepted for conversion into e-books: .epub, .pdf (basically you need to give them a finalized e-book, they don't really turn your files into e-books).
- E-book format produced: EPUB.
- Digital Rights Management (DRM) at author discretion.

---

[36] Remember, I couldn't verify *all* of this myself, as some of it is behind the sign-in wall of creating an account first, so take this as "rumored" and not factual.

[37] https://support.google.com/books/partner/answer/9331459

Apple Books

Apple's self-publishing platform has been, in my opinion, a bit of a mess over the years. They keep changing the name, they move where and how to purchase e-books from one app to another, sometimes you have to have Apple products to purchase or even see items, other times, that doesn't seem to be true. All in all, in my experience, it is a difficult platform to work with whether you want to purchase or publish.

While I have never self-published directly to Apple Books, I have published other authors' works directly to iBooks (the older version) when I was working for other publishers. I chose not to self-publish directly to iBooks as it required Mac hardware and software until July, 2020, and I chose not to personally invest in Apple products to do so. Now publishing to Apple Books can be done from iCloud.com, which means any computer browser will work. I have not done this, so I have no suggestions to offer. According to Apple Support, you can "Publish your book directly to Apple Books from Pages on your iPad, iPhone, iPod touch, Mac, or online at iCloud.com."[38] iCloud is done through the online Pages app, and iTunes Connect, which is different from iTunes. Basically, you can let Pages make an EPUB for you from your text or you can upload an already finalized EPUB. Either way, in my experience, you need to log in more than once and bounce between programs. I don't enjoy it, which is why I use a different distribution platform to get my books on Apple Books. This is the only digital storefront I could directly upload my books to that I choose not to, but that doesn't mean you shouldn't. Look into it for yourself. If you're an Apple person, it may all make perfect sense to you.

Apple Books is the second largest seller of e-books. Even so, it still has only an estimated 10% of the market. This is a big reason why so many self-publishers are perfectly happy to stay with Amazon only. But that 10% market is also why I do like to have my e-books available there.

---

[38] https://support.apple.com/en-us/HT208716

Stats at a glance:

- Cost: No set-up fees.
- e-books only.
- ISBNs not needed, can provide your own.
- Can setup pre-orders.
- Can offer book for free.
- 70% royalty rate on e-books.
- Distribution: Apple Books only (but all over the world). Can restrict regions and set individual region prices.
- Files accepted for conversion into e-books: .epub, or directly from the Pages app (a .pages file).
- E-book format produced: EPUB.
- Digital Rights Management (DRM) automatic. Restricts use on non-Apple readers.

Rakuten Kobo

Rakuten Kobo, once just Kobo, has been a sort of dumping ground for readers' libraries as other e-book companies have gone out of business, including Borders and Sony Reader, and transferred customer accounts over to Kobo. This gives Kobo a group of customers that stay with them for their virtual library. In addition, Kobo manufactures a popular e-reader that is strongly preferred by some readers.

Kobo is more popular outside of the U.S. than you might think. It is the most popular e-book company in Canada (where it is based) and has worldwide sales partners. It has been reported to have better e-book sales than Amazon in Japan and Australia.

If those were not good enough reasons not to pass Kobo over, in 2018, Kobo made a deal with Walmart to carry Kobo e-readers and sell Kobo e-books. (Some of that has fallen through, but some of it still exists.)

To access Kobo as a self-publisher, look for the Kobo Writing Life (KWL) website (kobowritinglife.com).

Stats at a glance:

- Cost: No set-up fees.
- e-books only.
- ISBNs not needed, but Kobo warns not all distribution partners will sell your book without one.
- Can setup pre-orders.
- Can offer book for free.
- 70% royalty rate when e-books are priced at $2.99 or more. 45% for under $2.99 on the Kobo Store. Public Domain Works are only eligible to receive a royalty rate of 20% of list price.
- Distribution: Kobo website and 22 distribution partners across 14 countries, including Walmart and OverDrive (a catalogue libraries order from).
- Can restrict regions and set individual region prices.
- Files accepted for conversion into e-books: .epub, .doc, .docx, .mobi, .odt.
- E-book format produced: EPUB.
- Digital Rights Management (DRM) at author discretion.
- Kobo Plus—Kobo's subscription reading program (Similar to Kindle Unlimited) currently available in Belgium, Portugal, Netherlands, and Canada, but still growing into new territories.

Smashwords

Smashwords has alternately been both adored and despised by some self-publishers. One of the early e-book aggregators and distributors on the scene to help self-publishers get their books out to multiple storefronts from one dashboard, it was loved by people who wanted to have to deal with only one account. But dealing with the "meat grinder," Smashwords' name for their automated, online software that turns files into e-books, which was one of the first ways non-techie authors could affordably make e-books, was (and still can be) a fiddly process. So much so, literal books were written on how to use it, including a 28,000 word style guide by Mark Coker, the founder of Smashwords. (See **What Software Do I Need to do My Own Formatting?** for more.)

Personally, I haven't had a problem with the meat grinder or the AutoVetter (an automated checker) in years, but then, I've been formatting my own e-books for years...

A more recent, and disappointing for some, development is the terms for distribution to Amazon. According to the Smashwords' website:

> If your book has earned over $2,000 at Smashwords retailers and you would prefer to consolidate your distribution via Smashwords to Amazon as opposed to uploading direct with them, please click the "support" link at the bottom of this page and let us know you're in the $2,000 club and would like to be considered for our distribution to Amazon.

Smashwords also has a coupon code generator. It is only good at the Smashwords storefront, but still...coupons! And it has a way to set up multi-author box sets (for e-books, of course) if you are working at cross promotion with other authors.

Stats at a glance:

- Cost: No set-up fees. 33¢ transaction fee for purchases at Smashwords storefront.
- e-books only.
- ISBNs: free from Smashwords or provide your own.
- Can set pre-orders but not at Amazon, only at Smashwords, Apple Books, Barnes & Noble and Kobo.
- Can offer book for free and let reader pay what they want (Smashwords storefront only).
- Approx. 60% of retail price for 99¢ and up. Varies due to wide range of partners. 45% for libraries. Up to 85% of "net proceeds" at Smashwords storefront (this means it could still be similar to the 35% royalty rate).
- Distribution: Kobo, Inktera, Baker & Taylor, Gardners, Tolino, Apple Books, Barnes & Noble, Library Direct, OverDrive, Scribd, cloudLibrary, Odilo, Smashwords. Limited on Amazon (If your book has earned over $2,000 at Smashwords retailers…).
- Cannot restrict regions, only distributors. You have to manually restrict distribution partners if you don't want to use them.
- Files accepted for conversion into e-books: .doc and .epub, (won't convert to other formats from .epub).
- E-book format produced: MOBI, EPUB, PDF, .rtf, .lrf, .pdb, .txt, online reader
- Digital Rights Management (DRM): none.
- Coupon codes!
- Maximum file size: 15MB for Word documents, 20MB for professionally designed e-book format files.

Draft2Digital

Draft2Digital is currently a popular choice for people wanting to use a single distributor, especially because they keep implementing new features, such as print book distribution (still in beta as of this writing), automated end matter (automatically updated information, such as "Also by," at the end of e-books), and royalty sharing between co-authors, which allows multiple authors to share the royalties of a single title. This requires a D2D account for each person receiving payment, as payment is issued directly from D2D to each person receiving payment.

They also offer free conversion of your files, online, into e-books and print-ready PDFs that you can use anywhere, not just on Draft2Digital. (See **What Software Do I Need to do My Own Formatting?** for more.) This converter is simple to use and does a good job, as long as you are not trying to do anything fancy.

But there are a few drawbacks. The number of distribution channels they use are smaller than some other distributors, and distribution to Amazon can be slow and requires a few additional steps. **If you don't pay attention, you could miss those steps, and your book won't go to Amazon.**

Royalty rates are a bit ambiguous, as individual rates with partners are not (as far as I can find) disclosed. On top of that, Draft2Digital takes out their 15% fee. This, by my reckoning, puts royalties at somewhere around 55%. When I look at "projected royalties," which are nothing more than estimates, on my D2D author dashboard, they are closer to 60%.

Print book distribution cannot be region restricted and is world-wide. If you already use Ingram for your print books, using D2D for print books will be of no benefit, as it does not have its own storefront, like Amazon, B&N, and some others do, and the book will appear on Amazon, B&N, and everywhere else. The reverse is also true. If you choose to use D2D's print book program, Ingram will likely be of no benefit to you as an additional service.

Stats at a glance:

- Cost: No set-up fees.
- e-books and print books (still in beta).
- ISBNs: Free from Draft2Digital or provide your own.
- Can set up pre-orders, but only for e-books and not at Amazon.
- Can offer book for free, but not at Amazon.
- Maybe 60% royalty on e-books. For print books it is 45% of the list price minus the printing cost.
- Distribution: Kobo (including Kobo Plus), Baker & Taylor, Tolino, Apple Books, Barnes & Noble, Hoopla, OverDrive, Scribd, Bibliotheca, Biblio, BorrowBox, Amazon (has extra submission requirements). *There is no D2D storefront.
- Cannot restrict regions, only distributors. Can manage territorial pricing.
- Files accepted for conversion into e-books: .doc, .docx, .rtf, .odt, .pdf, and .epub (won't convert to other formats from PDF or EPUB).
- E-book format produced: MOBI, EPUB, PDF.
- Print book format produced: PDF (4.5x6 and 5x8 sizes.)
- Digital Rights Management (DRM): none.
- Royalty sharing program.
- Automated end matter.

IngramSpark

IngramSpark, often referred to as Ingram, is the self-publishing side of Lightning Source (sometimes referred to as LSI), which is a printing and distribution branch of the Ingram Content Group, which prints and distributes books world-wide. Nearly all of the other self-publishing services that make print books, as well as traditional publishers, make use of Ingram's services in some form, including printing and distribution. Ingram began re-directing self-publishing authors to IngramSpark from Lightning Source around 2013, so some authors and small publishers may still have LSI accounts, but some, like me, were not given the option to stay with LSI and were moved to IngramSpark for various reasons. Mine, I was told, was that LSI was for publishers and I had less than 20 titles. Others, some publishers with more than 20 titles, were told that those movement of accounts were voluntary, and it was training issues that caused many of the changes (which were not always changed back). Either way, that kerfuffle was long ago, and most services and options most self-publishers need are the same, and IngramSpark is more user friendly than LSI. Which is important, as there is a learning curve with Ingram. Overall, it is not as easy to use as the other services, though it has improved.

My understanding is that LSI considers itself to be for "mid to large-sized publishers" of over 30 titles, and that you have to apply for membership, and that you will most likely be given an IngramSpark account anyway.

Many self-publishers, like myself, use IngramSpark to distribute print books widely, then also use KDP or B&N Press for print books to Amazon and B&N. There are multiple reasons for this.

One is that many small bookstores won't carry books made or sold through Amazon, as they consider that helping the competition, so in order to make sure bookstores are willing to order their books, many self-publishers use Ingram.

Another is the differences in royalty rates. In order to get bookstores to want to carry your books, you need to give them a percentage of the cover price, which means selling them the book at a discount. This is generally 40%, but Ingram takes an additional 15% as a fee, so in order to give bookstores 40%, an author needs to set the discount to 55% off the cover price. If you're good at math, which I am not, that puts the author's earnings at around 45%. But none of this takes into account the price of printing the books yet, which Ingram also takes out. (I feel a headache coming on, so let's ignore that and keep it simple.) In comparison, books printed through KDP and sold at Amazon earn the author 60% of list price, less the cost of the book. (That rate drops to 40% if you use KDP's Expanded Distribution, so there is little benefit over IngramSpark there.) Books printed and sold through B&N earn 55%.

In way of practical example, my book *Blazing Uncanny Trails 2*, in paperback for $14.99, earns approximately $3.24 per copy when sold through IngramSpark, but $6.00 when sold on Amazon through KDP and $5.07 when sold through Barnes & Noble Press on B&N. You can easily see the monetary advantage of using KDP and B&N Press to publish directly to those businesses.

In contrast to that, if I use KDP's expanded distribution, to the U.K. for example, I earn £2.71, but through IngramSpark I earn £2.98, making IngramSpark the better way to get out to the rest of the world. (Part of the reason for this, again, is other publishers use Ingram as a printer/distributor, so Ingram gets a cut of their profits as well.)

You may see why some authors find this overwhelming and not worth dealing with, choosing instead to use one publishing service.

Important note: if you choose to use IngramSpark (or LSI) to distribute print books, be wary of "Returns." Many bookstores will not order books they cannot return, so it becomes "recommended" and tempting to allow returns on your book. I strongly recommend against it unless you have deep pockets. I have met people who were stung by this when a bookstore, often mistakenly, orders a bunch of books, sometimes hundreds, and returns them. This causes problems in multiple ways. First, the author is responsible for paying for the printing costs of each book. Going back to *Blazing Uncanny Trails 2,* that would be $3.51 for each copy. So, if a bookstore ordered 100 copies and returned them, I would owe Ingram $351, an amount which I would have had to have sold 109 books to earn. Worse, I still wouldn't have any books.

The cheapest return option is to have the books destroyed. Which means you pay $351, and you get nothing for it. Or, you can have the books returned to you for an extra $2 per book ($20 each outside the U.S.). If you do that, now you have to pay $551 to have the 100 books shipped to you, and then you'll have to figure out what to do with them from there.

How many times could you afford to have that happen to you? What if a bookstore screwed up and ordered a thousand, or more? Be careful and pay attention to your options.

E-book distribution through IngramSpark has a couple of major caveats for people who use multiple platforms to self-publish. From the IngramSpark website:

*If you have provided any ebooks to Amazon for the Kindle in the past 12 months we will not be able to provide service to Kindle through the IngramSpark program.

**If you currently have ebook content available on Apple, you will need to remove those ebooks from the iBook store prior to uploading those same titles into IngramSpark. Also note that any reviews or ratings of that content will not transfer when your titles reappear in the iBook store.

IngramSpark also has an e-book royalty rate of 40%, which is comparable to some other distributors, in certain pricing situations, but nowhere near the 70% of some of the others when you publish to them directly through their platforms.

There are a couple of reasons why people use IngramSpark for e-book distribution anyway. Consolidation: not only one account to deal with, but one version of the book. This keeps all reviews together instead of splitting them up. Widest distribution. Conversion of print books into e-books. Sometimes the 40% royalty rate is higher (like when compared to Amazon's 35%, or when Amazon's "delivery fees" are high because of large file size). IngramSpark allows larger EPUB file sizes than some other places (important if you are using images). IngramSpark can set up preorders nearly everywhere, including on Amazon, which others cannot. And there are a few other things that vary in usefulness from person to person.

Once upon a time, Ingram required ISBNs to be provided by you. They now will provide them for free, if you want to use theirs, or, alternatively, if you have an account with them, you can purchase one from Bowker at a discount. (I have never done this, so I don't know if there are any gotchas involved.)

Something to be wary of; each time you revise a book that you've already published (to fix typos or whatever), there is an additional fee.

Overall, there is an initial cost, and a steeper learning curve, to using IngramSpark, but many people feel that the benefits and additional options outweigh those issues.

Stats at a glance:

- Cost: $25 setup for each e-book, $49 setup for each print or print and e-book.
- $25 fee for each revision to live book.
- E-book conversion from print book available at 60¢ per page.
- Sometimes coupons/codes are available to set up titles for free.
- E-books and print books. Can do hardcovers.
- Can print books without distributing for sale.
- Can do preorders, even on Amazon.
- ISBNs: Free from Ingram or provide your own. *"Once you have an IngramSpark account, you can purchase single ISBNs directly from Bowker through your IngramSpark dashboard for just $85."
- Royalties: For print books, set vendor discount yourself (33% to 55%). 40% for e-books.
- Distribution: "…to 40,000+ Retailers…" and library services, etc., including Amazon*, Apple*, B&N, Kobo (including Kobo Plus) *note: special problems involved with distribution of e-books here. See summary text for more.
- There is no IngramSpark storefront.
- Can restrict regions, but it is fiddly. Cannot restrict distributors. Can manage territorial pricing.
- Files accepted: .pdf for print (which can be converted to an EPUB for a fee) and .epub.
- E-book format produced: multiple. Depends upon distributor.
- Digital Rights Management (DRM): none.

Example Turnkey

I don't promote turnkey publishing services much, and I wasn't going to include any, but I felt it would be disingenuous not to offer any comparable information on them, so, with the knowledge you (hopefully) gained from the previous sections, here are some quick stats to compare with, to make your own decisions. Remember, some people swear by these services and love them. I am neither saying these services (the legitimate ones) are good nor bad, merely to me, as I am able to accomplish what they offer for much less money (or free), they are not worth paying for. Also remember, this information may be out of date before this book is published.

By using BookBaby as an example, I am neither endorsing nor condemning BookBaby. While I have met authors who used them (some loved them, some did not), I have not used them and have no personal experience. I chose BookBaby to use as an example because their information is easily available online, without need to create an account or request a quote. A good start, in my opinion. Most places I considered for this section wanted me to create an account before I could see what I thought to be worthwhile information regarding services and costs.

Each turnkey publisher is different, not only in prices, but in services offered, what those services actually entail, and the quality of those services, so make sure you do a deep-dive when learning about them, and read reviews from other authors (not sock-puppet reviews), before you choose one, if a turnkey publisher is the path you choose. You might also want to spend some time reading the articles on the SFWA site for Writer Beware:

https://www.sfwa.org/other-resources/for-authors/writer-beware/

BookBaby

- "Our on demand printing and book distribution service means that we only print a book when a retailer or wholesaler orders it. This enables you to sell your book in thousands of stores with minimum upfront costs and no warehousing. Just add $399 to any printed book order of 25+ books."[39] ($99 for distribution only to Bookshop, BookBaby's storefront.) (These prices are per title.)
- According to BookBaby's online quoter[40], at the time of this writing, one (1) 250 page, 6x9, softcover POD book is $49 plus $42.03 shipping. Prices don't drop until you order 25 books, then books are $11.94 each, totaling $364.29 for 25, with shipping.
- Black Text Formatting add $649.00.
- Professional Book Cover Design add $599 (only available with orders of 25 copies or more).
- BookBaby ISBN (listing BookBaby as the publisher) add $39 or supply your own. (Required).
- "...titles will generate between 10% -30% royalties."[41]
- Print distribution: Amazon, Powell's Books, Books-A-Million, Barnes & Noble, Ingram, Baker & Taylor, NACSCORP, Bookazine, Diamond Comic, BPDI, Christian Book Distributors, and 50+ others.
- $99 to convert file to EPUB, MOBI, $2 charge per image (even when you supply an already fully publishable EPUB files).
- "Keep 100% of your Amazon eBook royalties when you publish with BookBaby!"[42] (Requires purchase of $299 e-book conversion and distribution package.)
- 85% e-book royalty is with sales at Bookshop only.
- "There is a $50 base charge + $2.00 per editorial change/typo, per round of proofs. For example: if you have 10 typos to correct, the editorial/typo change fee will be $70."[43]
- "If you need to submit a new file for eBook, there is $100 file reconversion fee for dynamic layout eBooks and a $100 flat fee + $3 per page fee for fixed layout. If you need to submit a new file for formatting, you will be subject to the full formatting fee again."[44]

---

[39] https://www.bookbaby.com/book-distribution
[40] https://www.bookbaby.com/Quoter/
[41] https://www.bookbaby.com/book-distribution
[42] https://www.bookbaby.com/amazon-book-publishing/
[43] https://support.bookbaby.com/hc/en-us/articles/213152108-Can-I-make-changes-or-fix-typos-to-my-ePub-or-formatting-proof-
[44] https://support.bookbaby.com/hc/en-us/articles/213152108-Can-I-make-changes-or-fix-typos-to-my-ePub-or-formatting-proof-

FORMATTING FOR SUBMISSIONS

There are a lot of places online where you can find lengthy explanations about what format a submission should be in. Some are good, some not so much. This section is comprised of things I think you should try to keep in mind as you move forward with writing and submitting for publication.

More importantly than anything I say here, remember not to make the **First Big Mistake**. Follow any and all of a publisher's guidelines before submitting your story.

My apologies to users of platforms other than MS Word on the PC. That is where my experience is, and the examples I give will be based upon that.

Most Editors Do Like Times New Roman

Despite what the internet says, most editors, especially those under 40 years of age or so, do like the Times New Roman font and actively dislike the way Courier looks like it came directly from a typewriter. Although there are still editors out there who prefer Courier, I would recommend going with Times New Roman unless the submission guidelines specifically say otherwise. (Note: this does not apply to screenplays, which are not covered in this guide. Standard font for screenplays is still Courier.)

Here's the deal: Courier (or Courier New) was the font of choice for a long time. Editors and publishers liked it because it is a monospaced font. That means each and every letter takes up the same amount of space, which meant a word count could quickly and easily be done, telling them how many pages a book would be. The number of pages directly relates to the printing costs.

Fonts can easily be changed, in MS Word, under the **Home** tab, so there is no excuse not to submit in a requested font.

Below is an example of Courier New font. I have aligned that text to the left, rather than setting it to justified, as the rest of this book is formatted, so that you can see how the spacing works.

```
Monospacing means each and every letter takes up
the same amount of space.
```

Here is the same sentence in Times New Roman (again aligned to the left), so that you can compare them:

Monospacing means each and every letter takes up the same amount of space.

Times New Roman is a proportional font. That means skinny letters, like *i* and *l* take up less room than wide letters, like *w* or *H*.

After that, it becomes more a matter of preference for a font's appearance. Some people hate Times New Roman, others hate Courier. I think it kind of comes down to an old guard vs. new guard type of thing. (You know, the way things were vs. the way they are becoming.)

Either way, I would caution you to remember this: **Everyone hates Comic Sans.** I don't know why, but they do.

This is what Comic Sans looks like.

Don't use Comic Sans. Ever.
(One of my editors added in the "Ever." So, there is her opinion!)

If you are going to self-publish, take the time to think about fonts. If you are thinking of using a strange font, think about it a long time, and then don't do it. Look at books published by some of the more well-known publishers to get an idea of what to use. (None of these font examples I used here translated over to the e-book versions. I had to use an image of the fonts to demonstrate. See **Don't Use a Bunch of Strange Fonts** for more on this.)

The thing about fonts is they need to be invisible. It's important that the reader never think about them. Whether it is because the reader can't decipher the font, or because it looks silly, weird, or whatever, if it comes to the reader's attention, it is a problem. A font, like everything else in your writing, is a tool, and the best tools are the ones you can work with invisibly. (For more about fonts with e-books see **Notes on Self-Publishing This Mess!**)

Below are some popular fonts for printed books. They are all in the same front size (11), and style, and aligned for comparison.

Calibri-	Here is an example.
Cambria-	Here is an example.
Garamond-	Here is an example.
Georgia-	Here is an example.
Helvetica-	Here is an example.

This book is printed in Garamond.

Don't Use A Bunch Of Strange Fonts

This is a headache all the way around. For starters, you might be the only person in the world who likes a particular font. Some people may not even be able to read it, finding **hieroglyphics** more decipherable. But there can even be a **LEGAL** reason why you should not use a font:

Fonts are copyrighted.

Really!

Just like artwork.

You can't print your book in a particular font unless you have permission. This can be obtained by purchasing a license to use it. It is possible the font is in the public domain, and free to use, but you need to make sure. You may own a computer program that provides the font *and* grants a license to use it, but be warned: **Some computer programs come with fonts that are not licensed for commercial use!** This can lead to a lot of headaches for publishing companies, so they don't like to mess with strange fonts.

A final thought on fonts:

E-books don't play well with fonts or formatting. If you try to use your favorite non-standard font in a self-published e-book, you will most likely spend a long time regretting the headaches it causes you. (See **Notes on Self-Publishing This Mess!**)

Normally I would chuckle here, because I got away with using all of those different fonts while telling you not to, but guess who is going to be doing the formatting for this book.

O.o

Here is what that page looked like when transferred to e-book format:

Don't Use A Bunch Of Strange Fonts

This is a headache all the way around. For starters, you might be the only person in the world who likes a particular font. Some people may not even be able to read it, finding hieroglyphics more decipherable. But there can even be a legal reason why you should not use a font:

Fonts are copyrighted

Really!

Just like artwork.

You can't print your book in a particular font unless you have permission. This can be obtained by purchasing a license to use it. It is possible the font is in the public domain, and free to use, but you need to make sure. You may own a computer program that provides the font *and* grants a license to use it, but be warned: **Some computer programs come with fonts that are not licensed for commercial use!** This can lead to a lot of headaches for publishing companies, so they don't like to mess with strange fonts.

A final thought on fonts:

E-books don't play well with fonts or formatting. If you try to use your favorite non-standard font in a self-published e-book, you will most likely spend a long time regretting the headaches it causes you. (See **Notes on *Self-Publishing This Mess!*)

Normally I would chuckle here, because I got away with using all of those different fonts while telling you not to, but guess who is going to be doing the formatting for this book.

O.o

Most Editors Want Double-Spaced Lines

Double-spaced lines are easier to read and, if the editors print out your submission, it gives them room to take notes. That's a good thing. When editors want to take notes on your story, you are winning! Hooray!

This is also for formatting purposes. If the formatter starts with a clean manuscript, they will have less trouble setting everything up the way the publisher wants it. While they do usually change double-spaced lines to single-spaced during the formatting process, it can be a mess to clean up if the story has varying line spacing, fonts, page breaks, and goodness knows what else. Especially if the author has created double-spaced lines with hard returns to force the text to appear that way on a computer screen, as would be done with an actual typewriter.

Imagine you want to format a story, but it is so full of junk formatting that you must first copy and paste the entire text into a new file to clear all of the formatting out. Then you have to go through and find every new paragraph and indent it again, one at a time. And anything that needs to be italicized. Or marked in bold. Or superscripted. (Superscript is what the *st* does in 1st.)

Formatters hate that.

See **Don't Use the Tab Key or the Spacebar to Indent Paragraphs** for information on how to set line spacing to Double.

Most Editors Want Font Size 12

Not too big, not too small. Just right, I guess.

Part of it may be a holdover from being able to judge page count based upon the word count. The smaller the font, the more words will fit upon a page. But mostly this is a preference due to readability.

Most guidelines and style guides say to use a font size 12, so as a standard, nearly everyone is used to it.

As mentioned in the last section, doing strange things with fonts, font sizes, line spacing, or whatever (especially in a short story, where it will be different from all of the other stories) causes problems down the production line for editors and formatters, so I don't recommend it.

Font sizes can easily be changed in MS Word under the **Home** tab, so if you want to write in 14-Point Font or a 9-Point Font, go ahead. Just make sure you change it to a 12-Point Font (or according to the submission guidelines) before you send it off for consideration.

You also will want to stick with the font the guidelines tell you to. (See **Most Editors Do Like Times New Roman** for more.) A 12-Point Font size for Times New Roman does not look the same as the 12-Point Font size for all other fonts. Sometimes, though the same font size, text can be very different sizes. (See **Don't Use A Bunch Of Strange Fonts** for more on this.)

This has to do with the way font sizes are determined for manual typesetting. Just as the em-dash and en-dash were sized based upon typographical size (see **Em-Dashes, En-Dashes, Hyphens, and Ellipses** for more on this), so was the idea of the font size. It is based upon the "point," or the smallest typographic mark, as well as the size of the tiny, rectangular piece of lead the printed letter was on. (Think of something like the metal heads of typewriter keys, where they smash the ink ribbon against the paper.)

The problems is, with the advent of computer printing, we don't (usually) use physical typesetting anymore, and the idea of the "point" becomes malleable, which means fonts sizes are now like clothing sizes. They don't mean much from one manufacturer to the next.

Most Editors Don't Want Underlines For Italics

It used to be standard practice, in manuscript format, to indicate italics by underlining words the author wanted to have italicized in the final version.

Now, just as most editors no longer wish to see the manuscript in Courier font, they don't want this either. With the advent of desktop publishing, it is easier for writers to do some of this stuff on their own and save the formatter a little bit of work. In fact, changing the underlining into italics is extra work now.

Personally, I think editors just finally started realizing that if something was underlined no one, except the author, really knew if it was supposed to be underlined, italicized, or both. (Not that fiction authors generally underline things, but it does happen.)

Most Editors Want An Electronic File

There are few publishers or editors left still who want authors to send in a physical copy of their manuscript. If they do, their guidelines will clearly say so. Most editors today actually dread receiving real, live, physical mail. Because it might be live…or something.

Whatever it is, they don't want to be responsible for it, or have to send it back, or have to explain it to their boss, or their spouse…

So, they prefer you send things to them electronically.

When you send an electronic file, make sure to use the formats they request. If you are not sure which to use, try to use a **.doc** file (a standard MS Word file format that nearly all word processors can recognize and use) or an **.rtf** file (rich text format). Avoid **.docx** files (a newer MS Word file format). Many places, not just editors and publishers, won't accept a file in the DOCX format because of a fear of computer viruses or because they run older versions of software that can't open it. (Though this is changing.)

To save a file in the format you prefer, use the **Save As** option under the **File** tab in MS Word. When the **Save As** pop-up window opens, choose the **Save As Type:** pulldown menu to select the file format you wish to save your document in.

Marking Scene Breaks

If you are not familiar with the idea of **Scene Breaks**, please check out that section for more information on what they are and how to use them.

In the formatting of a manuscript for submission, it is important to clearly mark your scene breaks for the editor and the formatter so they can do their jobs properly and adjust your story to match the formatting and style of any other stories they are publishing.

When self-publishing, many writers make the mistake of merely leaving a space between paragraphs to indicate a scene break. This can cause difficulty for the reader in recognizing changes in location, time, or point of view. Sometimes writers don't even leave an extra space. That can be really rough on a reader. (See **Changing Focus** for more on this.) It can also be hard on an editor, who will be trying to figure out what just happened in your story and how to fix it, and it can be rough on a formatter; as text flows, shifts, and changes as we write, meaning blank spaces could end up at the top or bottom of a page and no longer be an obvious break in text.

There is a long history of the ways breaks have been used and how they have been demarcated. I've heard them called hedera, fleuron, asterism, dinkus, dingus (I suggest not using that one), glyph, dingbats, wingdings, and other, not as specific terms (like scene break markers, or printer's ornaments). Most writers I know just call it a scene break and tell you to mark it.

Generally, when formatting a manuscript to be submitted to an editor, I use the pound symbol (#) between the paragraphs where a scene break occurs. This is a pretty common way of representing it. I learned it early on when I was directed by submission guidelines to refer to the Shunn Manuscript Format. Most publishers and authors consider the Shunn Format to be the business standard: **www.shunn.net/format/**

The pound symbol is quickly recognizable by the editor, it doesn't often show up in the text of fiction writing, and it can be easily searched for and replaced by the formatter. It also doesn't impinge upon a publisher's idea of what kind of pretty graphics (if any) they want to use in their stories.

Some editors hate seeing homemade scene breaks like:

{------------------}

or

These raise questions like: *"What font is that? I don't want to mess with fonts!"* or *"Is that a graphic? Who owns the copyright to that graphic? I don't want to mess with graphics!"* or *"Does this writer think that is part of the story? Are they going to be hard to work with when I try to tell them I can't use that?"*

This is also, to an editor, a pretty good indication that they are not dealing with a professional writer, and it may become something they use as an excuse (at least in their own mind) to reject your story. (Not often, but it could be.)

If you are self-publishing, be aware that you can cause yourself a lot of headaches dealing with trying to format fancy images as scene breaks.

Also beware of infringing upon copyrights to images you don't have the rights to use.

Don't Use The Tab Key Or The Spacebar To Indent Paragraphs

Formatters *hate* that! Unfortunately, many of us writers do one of those when we are first starting out in our careers. I suspect it's because we are trying to make the page match what we think it should look like, but we aren't paying attention to the underlying formatting in the word processing programs. (And why would we? That's the formatter's job, right? Right?)

To set paragraph indentations in MS Word, select (highlight) the text you wish to format and then go into the **Paragraph settings**, which are under the **Home** tab. Under **Indentation**, set the **Special option** to **First Line**.

This is also where you can **Set Line Spacing** to Double, with the before and after line spacing set to zero. (Apologies to those who don't write in MS Word, I am not familiar with other platforms.)

Be careful, these settings can be set globally or to just one line, so double check what you have selected when you apply the setting. Select the entire body of the text to format the whole story, or just place the cursor at the start of a sentence to select that one sentence. Don't select your title or your heading, as it will mess those up.

If you've already used Tab to indent your paragraphs, you can get rid of them by using the Find and Replace function in MS Word.

Just as with words and letters, the hidden formatting marks, like Tabs and Paragraphs, can be found and replaced. You can do this by clicking on the **More>>** button in the **Find and Replace** pop-up window. Then click on the **Special** button to open a pulldown menu to select Tab. Leave the **Replace with** field empty, and the Find and Replace will remove all of the Tabs. Or use Find Next to check out each one individually. If you are going to self-publish, be aware that tabs generally have to be taken out for properly formatted e-books.

If you used spaces to indent your paragraphs, see the next section, **Don't Use Two Spaces Between Sentences**, for help fixing it. The same idea applies.

Any time you use a search and replace function, run it multiple times to make sure it catches all instances of the thing you are searching for. Especially on longer documents. Many programs seem to have problems finding everything on the first try. Or maybe that's user error on my part, but it works for me.

Don't Use Two Spaces Between Sentences

This can be a tough one for old folk (like me!) who learned to type on typewriters. (For you youngsters out there who didn't know what I was talking about when I mentioned typewriters and the Courier font earlier, a typewriter is similar to the typical Steampunk Analog Single Page Printing Machine.)

Putting two spaces between sentences was supposedly done to make it easier to read print when a monospaced font was used. (I have seen articles that dispute this theory, but if you are geeky enough to care then you've probably already seen them!) In the digital age of easily adjustable, proportional fonts, the use of two spaces is not only unnecessary, it can look odd at times.

If you can't break the habit, it is easy to clean them up by using the **Find and Replace** function in MS Word. Just enter two spaces in the **Find** field and one space in the **Replace** field. Easy-Peasy!

Again, anytime you use a search and replace feature, run it multiple times to make sure it catches all instances of the thing you are searching for. **When eliminating more than two spaces (such as three or four), replacing two spaces with one will still leave you with more than one**, so you should continue to repeat the search and replace until it doesn't find any more instances of two spaces together.

Don't Separate Paragraphs With An Extra Hard Return

A hard return is when you press the Enter key. This signifies to the word processor that you have reached the end of your paragraph and are going to start a new one. Once upon a time, in a decade long gone, those of us older than sliced bread found it necessary to use a hard return at the end of each line to keep from running our text off the side of the paper. Like using two spaces after a period, the hard return became ingrained into us. When we wanted an extra space between paragraphs, we hit the carriage return a second time. (A carriage return is the old steampunk-style lever mechanism on the typewriter that resets the page back to the start of the next line.) Now, with text automatically wrapping around to the next line on the screen, that is not necessary at all. Hitting Enter is only used at the end of a paragraph. But doing so more than once messes up the formatting.

A formatter must go through and take out all of the extra hard returns us old timers accidentally put into our documents. This can be especially hard if the writer, as I have in this guide, intentionally set some things apart (like the examples). Now the formatter has to look at each one individually and try to decide how the author intended the page to look.

It never turns out well when the formatter has to second-guess the author. Never.

If you feel your paragraphs need to have some extra space between them (something I've seen many times but don't personally understand), you can use the **Spacing Before/After** options in the **Paragraph** settings. This is something a formatter can easily change to whatever the publishing company wants the final text to look like.

See **Don't Use The Tab Key Or The Spacebar To Indent Paragraphs** for instructions on how to set up the indentation for a new paragraph.

Sample Cover Letter

On the next page is a sample of how a cover letter generally should be set up, just to get you started. Remember, everyone has their own submission guidelines, so read and follow those. If they ask for a certain font, use it. If they specify not to use a certain font, then don't.

Sometimes they will ask for things like your two most recent publications. This is usually not a big deal if you don't have any. Sometimes they ask for you to let them know if you've never been published before. This is usually because they have a soft spot and want to help new authors, so tell them. Either way, it is usually okay (unless it is a submission requirement) to leave out that kind of information.

If you have other qualifications or memberships that are applicable (such as you are a member of the Science Fiction & Fantasy Writers of America and SFWA is sponsoring the anthology, or you are a veterinarian and this story is about a veterinarian hospital) then feel free to include that information.

Where things are not specified, something like my example will get you by pretty well. If you know who the editor is, you may want to address them by name instead of the generic *Dear Editor,* but make darned sure you spell their name correctly if you do!

Notice the *Jane Doe (writing as Sam Knight)* part. **If you choose to use a pen name, you need to let your publisher know.** See the section on **Pen Names** for more information on why. Also note that you really need to provide your contact information. They cannot accept your story if they can't contact you with a contract.

In the end, generally, you are better off if you resist the temptation to provide a full curriculum vitae, unless it is applicable. Also, resist the temptation to use pink stationary, crayons, and fun fonts.

Definitely don't use perfume or glitter.

Ever.

Jane Doe (writing as Sam Knight)
1234 South NorthWestern East
Happyville, OZ 11111
(888) 555-5555
sam@samknight.com

October 1, 2122
Ya Ya Publications
http://www.yayapublications.yaya
publisher@yayapublications.yaya

Dear Editors,

Thank you for considering my submission to *Ya Ya Presents: Yahoos and Yoyos*.

My story, *Walking the Dog in a Basket Full of Nuts*, approximate word count 5,385, is a YA Fantasy that follows a young juggler/dog walker as he encounters a mime-turned-assassin, and her rabid, radioactive squirrel sidekick, in his neighborhood park.

I am the author of six children's books, five short story collections, three novels, and over 75 stories, including three co-authored with Kevin J. Anderson, two of which were media-tie-ins: "Wayward Pines: Aberration" (Kindle Worlds, 2014) and "Of Monsters and Men" Planet of the Apes: Tales from the Forbidden Zone (Titan, 2016).

Examples of my writing, a full bibliography, and a bio can be found at samknight.com.

Thank you for your consideration,

Jane Doe
Writing as Sam Knight
Member HWA, IAMTW

Formatting A Submission

At the end of this section is a sample submission manuscript, showing how the formatting should generally be set up. Remember, everyone has their own submission guidelines, so read and follow those, but where guidelines are not specified or say something like "standard," this should get you by.

Most publishers and authors consider the Shunn Format to be the industry standard: **www.shunn.net/format/**

I recommend the Modified Shunn Format, as it is becoming the more common to use. It is also worth the read for more than just the formatting, and there are a lot of other great resources at that website.

Take particular note that contact information is provided in the header for the story. Treat this like a return address in a business letter, because it is. If you don't provide your information, the editor or publisher cannot contact you to purchase your story.

Really.

This has happened before, and it will happen again. It is a silly enough thing, and it happens often enough, especially in this day and age of quick electronic message exchanges, that it bears repeating:

If you don't provide your information, the editor or publisher cannot contact you to purchase your story.

That said, some publishers do not want personal information on the submission itself, only in your cover letter. They may do this to facilitate what are sometimes called blind submissions, which means they don't want their decision-making process to be influenced by who wrote the story, only the story itself.

Also, note the placement of the author's name and the story title at the top of every page (except the first, which should already have the business heading and title), along with the page number:

Doe/Grabbing the Stallion by the Horn/2

This part is important for editors who like to print copies off. When they drop your manuscript, and they will (along with a pile of 14 other stories), they like to be able to put it back together again. The only time you don't want to do this is when the guidelines say not to. Also (and this is important!), do not place the page numbers on the page manually! Use the page numbering function of your word processor to do it, otherwise a formatter will have to strip them individually from your file, and they will not be happy about it.

This applies to things like using spaces for tabs or indentations or using hard returns to make paragraphs. For more on these kinds of issues, please see **Don't Use The Tab Key Or The Spacebar To Indent Paragraphs** and **Don't Separate Paragraphs With An Extra Hard Return.**

Make sure you know how to use your word processor's functions. I know small publishers, who often do the editing and formatting themselves, who will reject stories over these kinds of issues because it takes too much time and effort to correct them into proper formatting[45].

Always mark your scene breaks. I use a hashtag symbol (#) to mark mine, some people use an asterisk (*). Don't use images. They can cause problems in a couple of different ways. If strange icons or fancy artwork are to be used between scene breaks, they are added in during formatting. Please see **Marking Scene Breaks** and **Scene Breaks** for more information.

Remember to make sure you put END, The End, or something similar at the end of your story. That way, if the editor does drop your pages, they know they managed to pick them all up!

Like anything in life, a failure to provide a "proper" submission will quickly show your ignorance, your lack of desire or concern to learn the standard conventions, or that you will be difficult to work with. None of these are impressions you want to give.

---

[45] I am now one of those small publishers. I may be more forgiving than some, but it will definitely make me curse.

Jane Doe (writing as Sam Knight)
1234 South NorthWestern East
Happyville, NY 11111
(888) 555-555
sam@samknight.com

Approx. 471 words

Grabbing the Stallion by the Horn
By
Sam Knight

"I am here, Margie. Do you remember me?"

The gentle voice roused the old woman enough to flutter her eyelids. Rheumy, faded blue eyes searched the hospice room, but saw only the blur of subdued colors.

"Over here." The voice spoke with a rich, yet subtle accent.

The woman, white hair thin and wispy against her pillow, struggled to turn her head. A large, dark maroon blur contrasted against her normally bright room, blocking the light from the windows.

"Margie? Do you remember me?" the blur asked.

At the sound of her name, Margie felt the world come into focus in a way it hadn't in years. Her vision still failed her, but she knew where she was and why she was here. Hot tears formed and trickled down her withered cheeks. Life was so cruel, but the cruelest thing of all was the way it stole the memories of who she'd been and what she had done.

Her mouth was dry, and licking her lips didn't help, but she tried to speak anyway. Little more than a rasping croak, her words were unintelligible even to her own ears, but her visitor seemed to understand.

"It's all right, Margie. I will help you remember. Here. Take hold."

A warm, smooth cylinder, with ridges like finger grips, pressed into Margie's hand. Stiffly, arthritic knuckles complaining, she closed her fist around it.

A lightness of being, like the first kiss of the warm morning sun, enveloped her old body and her pain began to fade. Her unquenchable thirst vanished, followed by the lifting of joint pains and the heaviness of gravity pulling down upon her tired body, and then, mercifully, the weariness that had been in her soul for as long as her feeble mind could recall.

She took a deep breath, feeling her old ribs painlessly expand to their limits, and sighed contentedly.

The object in her hand tugged at her to stand. Margie, relishing the absence of pain, held tight and used it to rise. Unable to remember the last time she had been on her feet, it took her another moment to realize the room around her was sharp and clear, and that the object in her hand was the pearlescent horn of a claret-colored unicorn.

Letting go of the unicorn's smooth spiraled horn, she stared into the equine's blue eyes, enjoying the disparity between the vibrant blue and the softer wine color of the creature's coat. "I think I should be disquieted by the fact I am standing here talking with a unicorn, but…you seem so familiar. I feel I know you."

#

That was a strange dream, Margie thought. She sat up, grabbed her stuffed unicorn, and squeezed him tight. "I'll never forget you, you know that, right?"

The red fuzzy toy didn't deny that it knew.

END

OFT OVERLOOKED UNTIL TOO LATE
(Way, way, waaayyy too late…)

There are some things people just don't think about until it is too late. Hindsight is 20/20, they say. Foresight is 2 to 1 odds in your favor, I say. Actually, that's the first time I ever said that, but I wanted to try to sound cool.

If you need more of a resource, or a second opinion, for some of the things I mention in this section, make sure you research properly. Don't just trust the crap you will find on the internet.

Many lawyers will not be familiar with what you need to know unless it is one of their areas of specialty, so be cautious. You won't save money by going to an unspecialized lawyer who charges you for their time as they research what you want to know, and you won't have the benefit of past experiences a specialized lawyer may have had either.

Always Run A Spell Check On Your Writing

This is a very simple and quick thing you should always do. I have seen published books with "hte" errors, and there is no excuse for that. (An "hte" typo is when you type "the" too fast and get it out of order.)

Some people complain that spell checkers do not work very well, and I have to agree, sometimes they don't. But that's not a good reason to not use them. They still help. On larger documents, you should run a spell check three or four times in a row to make sure that it catches everything. This will at least give you a chance to get rid of most of the obvious typos.

Remember, once you have run a spellcheck, and told it to ignore certain words, it will continue to ignore them in that document. Just because it says the spellcheck is complete and no errors were found, does not mean there aren't any errors. To reset spellcheck for your document in MS Word, go to **Options**, under the **File** tab. Go to **Proofing** and select **Recheck Document**. This should give a pop-up menu warning about resetting the spellcheck to recheck words you have previously told it to ignore.

I always try to make sure I run spellcheck on everything one last time before I send it out. It is really, super, I-hate-myself embarrassing to notice an ugly typo mere seconds after you've sent something out professionally.

Don't Trust A Grammar Checker

Those damned blue underlines just keep taunting you and taunting you, don't they? Like something out of an Edgar Allen Poe story, they torment you and niggle at your brain until you finally break down and accept the changes they keep suggesting. And then you send your story out, and it comes back from the editor marked to change it. And you see they want it changed to exactly the way you had it before. Grrrr…

While grammar checkers can help you spot things you missed, they often make mistakes like suggesting plural when something is singular, or commas where no commas are needed, or telling you something is wordy, or offensive, or the wrong tense, or should/shouldn't be capitalized when it has no idea what you are writing and if what you did was relevant to the text.

Don't ignore a grammar checker. Treat it like an editor you don't like much. Read their suggestions, consider what they are suggesting, as it may have merit, and then make your own decision as to what to do. But don't blindly trust. (See **Software Assisted Writing** for more on this.)

Read What You've Written Before You Send It Anywhere Else

I have seen stories where it is painfully obvious the author did not even read it themselves before submitting it to someone else. It doesn't matter who you send something to—your friend, your writers group, your editor, or *anyone*—you need to read it yourself first.

I've seen huge chunks of sentences missing, strange typos, broken plot lines, and generally weird things that nearly anyone would notice had they read the story. These are all big clues to an editor that you didn't read your own story.

And if you didn't care enough about your story to read it, why should they?

On a side note, this idea applies to artists as well. Be very careful of what kind of work in progress you show/give to a client. You may find out they used it when it was still a concept sketch. That's fine if it saves you time and effort and earns you money, but it sucks if you felt it wasn't up to snuff yet or if you didn't have a formalized contract in place yet.

I have had this happen to me with both my art and my words. Learn from my mistakes: Don't do it. It will leave a bad taste in your mouth that never really goes away.

The Title Of Your Story Should Make Sense

The title of your story doesn't have to be perfect. It can be silly. It can be misleading. Intentionally, for dramatic or ironic purposes, for example. But it needs to make some kind of sense.

The title of a story is a milestone for the reader. It is something that tells them what they (think) they are getting into. If you betray this, you will betray the reader, and you may lose a fan forever, or worse, create an internet troll who will actively chase down everything you do so that they can berate it for the next twenty years.

For example, don't title your book *Candy Corns and Pumpkin Spice* if it is about a space-fighter pilot whose brain is being eaten by multidimensional ear-worms. If you think you have found a way that connects that title to that story, two things need to happen. First, the reader had better be able to understand why you named it that by the time they finish the story. Second, they need to know from some other source, like the cover image on the book, that this is some kind of horrific space story, not a holiday-food magazine article.

Consider the title to be a part of your story. Use it to set up the reader's expectations. Take advantage of the fact that they are reading it, and try to make them feel as though they have already started your story and want to keep reading.

That's a tall order, I know, but just keeping that in mind will help prevent you from naming a heartwarming, romantic love story *Oil on the Garage Floor*, no matter how sure you were that was a good title.

Unless it is about robots...

Hmm...

Pen Names

If you are using a pen name (nom de plume, pseudonym... Whatever you want to call it), editors don't need to know. Other authors around you don't need to know. Your fans don't need to know. **Your publisher, however, needs to know. Even if no money is involved**.

When a publisher publishes one of your stories, you will have to sign a contract. (Goodness gracious let me tell you now, if you are doing business with someone who doesn't want to mess with contracts, RUN!!!) Contracts are legally binding. That is what a contract is: a legal agreement. You will be signing away some or all of the rights to your story in exchange for...something, I hope. (For more on contracts, please see **Contracts Are Your Safety Nets**.)

In order to legally sign a contract, you need to use your legal name. **To sign a contract under a false name is FRAUD!**

Some people don't realize that, but it is. If you have any questions about that, contact a lawyer and get some good legal advice. **I am not a lawyer, this is not legal advice, nor is it intended to be, and you should not listen to anything I say, let alone act upon it without first consulting a lawyer.** (*Whew* Does that cover my butt?)

If you are using a pen name, make sure the publisher knows. If you feel the need to hide your real name, there are some options available, but even then, you can't completely hide from everyone behind a pen name.

You can use an agent, who can sign contracts on your behalf with your pen name, but your agent will still have to know your real name. If you use a lawyer as an agent or representative, they also have to know your real name. If you create a business and fill out the necessary form in order to be legally allowed to use a DBA (Doing Business As), this will become public record and anyone who researches it will find your real name. If you self-publish, you will have to create an account of some sort with the company you choose to use, which may require tax ID numbers and bank accounts. (Especially if you want to make any money.) As a last resort you could change your real name legally, but that also becomes public record and people could look up what your name used to be.

Seriously, if you feel the need to hide your identity, check with a lawyer. For the rest of us who just want to write under a cool name, make sure anyone you do business with knows your real name so that you aren't committing fraud. This applies to anyone who pays you, anyone you pay, anyone who grants you rights, and anyone you grant rights to. You should have some form of contract between you and anyone you are exchanging or sharing money or rights with.

Who would you pay? You would pay a developmental editor, a copy editor, a proofreader, a cover designer, the person in charge of renting out spaces for tables in the dealer's room at a convention so that you can sell your books in person…lots of people, theoretically. While you can get around revealing you name to many of these people, being deceitful will eventually cause you problems if for no other reason than people felt like you were being deceitful.

As for the publisher, if they know you want to use a pen name, they will usually add a place in the contract that says what name they will publish your story under.

If you are self-publishing, you need to create accounts with your real name, your real tax ID (social security or EIN if you have a business), and some form of account money can be deposited into by the companies you are doing business with. Trying to do this stuff with pen names is terrible. Doing it with business names is much easier. Either way, there will be opportunities to use a pen name later, after the accounts are created. None of the self-publishing places care what pen name you use, or even how many of them you use, but they need to know who you really are in order to do business with you.

A few final thoughts on pen names: First, it's not all it's cracked up to be. It sounds sexy. It seems like the thing to do. But it can be a pain in the tuckus, and it is something you continually have to deal with. Don't be surprised when it confuses your family and friends. Don't get upset when someone calls you the wrong name in the wrong social situation. Don't be a jerk when you find out someone else is using (or really has) the same name.

Second: **Don't be stupid about it.** You can get into a lot of trouble if you try to write horror under the name Stephen King or romance under the name Nora Roberts. Depending upon how you present yourself, you could be accused of fraud or identity theft for doing so.

Don't try to use a trademarked name. Calling yourself Batman will not serve you well in the long run.

Don't pick a name you can't stand to be called. If you become famous for a story written as Boogerty Twosnoots, people will call you Boogerty the rest of your life, and you may get a little tired of it. And the jokes. Which will not be original or funny.

A pen name offers you no legal protection against things like defamation or slander. If you do those things, you did those things. Using a pen name does not give you permission to do things you shouldn't do just because you are in a strange town and no one knows your real name. Don't be stupid.

Writing something new under a new pen name will not (usually) get around any contractual obligations that you have.

You can't cash or deposit a check made out to your pen name unless you have set up a business banking account that recognizes that name as part of the business. You can get in a lot of trouble for trying to cash a check made out to someone else!

Checking into a hotel room reserved under your pen name can be very difficult. Make sure promoters/convention staff/venue owners know your real name so that accommodations they provide are accessible to you. Contracts with some of these places can get confusing when it comes to pen names. They are not always as used to it as publishers are, so keep that in mind and try to make it easy for yourself in the long run even if that means more problems trying to explain the situation in the short term (you know, when setting things up six months in advance of an appearance.)

Contracts Are Your Safety Nets

As long as we are on the subject of contracts, I feel the need to try to save you a lot of misery in the future.

Never do business without contracts. There's not much else I can say about that. I can't be any clearer. Not having a contract will lead to terrible, terrible things. Loss of money, loss of friends, loss of rights to things you created, liability for things you had little or nothing to do with, family feuds over money long after you are dead... The list could go on for pages. This is important.

Always read and understand any contract before signing it. Yes, the rumors are true. There are authors who have even lost the right to use their own names, or to prevent their name from being used, on future publications. I cannot emphasize this enough.

Always use contracts. Always make sure that you fully understand a contract before you sign it.

If you take only one thing away from this book, let it be those last two sentences. If you have any doubts about a contract, take it to a lawyer. Not just any lawyer, either, but a specialized one. Seriously. Some of the nasty things in contracts are so slick that the average Josephina Lawyer won't know about it. You need a Specially Trained and Experienced Josephina Lawyer to recognize potential pitfalls and potholes. If you are getting a movie contract, get a lawyer who deals with those. Maybe you'll need an Intellectual Property Lawyer. It will be worth the avoidance of future problems, I assure you.

Also, and this is important, a lawyer who works for the publisher is **not** a disinterested third party. You need your own lawyer. Don't trust someone else's legal representation to explain it to you. This goes for your agent, too, if you have one. They are not disinterested parties either. They make their money from you, but that doesn't mean the best way for them to make money is the same as the best way for you to make money. Don't trust them to tell you what a contract means, especially contracts they want you to sign about your business relationship with them.

If you have any doubts about a contract, get your own lawyer. If someone can't wait for you to get a lawyer, if they say the deal *has to* happen right now or it's gone forever, then I suggest you walk away. There's a 98% chance they are trying to take something from you they don't want the lawyer to tell you about. (Percentages were calculated in my head based on made up facts and imaginary figures that were, in the long run, ignored before the final result was posted. ± 98% margin of error.)

Even when collaborating on a story with your brother, you should set up a contract between the two of you, describing in detail who does what jobs, who owns what rights, who has final say-so, and more. If you are headed down the route of collaboration, I suggest you look into *Writing As a Team Sport: The Complete Writer's Guide to Collaboration,* by Kevin J. Anderson and Rebecca Moesta. (Full disclosure, I personally know both of the authors.)

Don't Use Song Lyrics

Song lyrics are copyrighted. Just like the story you are writing. If you want to use the lyrics from a song in a story, you will need to get the permission of the copyright owner first. Even if you are just putting your story or blog up on the internet for free.

Yes, really. Fair use is not what most people think it is. (Please see **What Do I Need to Know About Copyright?** for more on this.)

There are some cases, like for a critical review of a song or an album, where you are allowed to reprint a small portion of the lyrics, but that is not what this book is about. Trying to go around the rules by perhaps having a character, who is a reviewer, using the song lyrics on his fictitious blog, won't work. You still need permission.

If you have your heart set on using copyrighted lyrics, I suggest that you start the process to obtain permission months in advance. Sometimes, it can take a very long time to figure out who owns the copyright to something. Also, **do not** accept verbal permission. Contracts should always be used to protect yourself from misunderstandings and problems in the future. The copyright is not always owned by the person or business that says, or thinks, it does. Sometimes, even if everyone involved wants you to have permission, there can already be a legal embroilment, and the courts may say you can't use them just to prevent muddying the waters further.

How will you feel if you base your story on the lyrics of a specific song, but then find out you can't use them? You may have to scrap the whole story. Forever. Even if you are under contract for it and have been paid an advance. In addition to all of that, some editors will flat out turn down a story with song lyrics because they don't want to deal with…all of that. If you are trying to sell a story with song lyrics in it, it might all be a wasted effort on your part even if you have obtained permission. Example why, point of interest, and word to the wise: I have a writer friend who used song lyrics in his novel. Prominently. After some effort, he managed to secure the rights to use the lyrics and his book was published. Fast forward a few years, the book went out of print and my friend reacquired the published rights from the publisher. He wanted to re-publish the book with a new publishing house. Guess what? He was forced to re-secure the rights to publish the lyrics, because it was a new edition of the book.

And the lemon juice on that papercut? The owners of the copyright to the song had changed. There was a whole new process, with a whole new set of people, and a whole new licensing fee, he had to go through in order to get permission to use those lyrics again—in a book that was already published. With those lyrics in it.

If you're going to pursue using song lyrics in your novel, it's probably time to buy stock in analgesics too, because it'll give you a headache.

Don't Use Names Of Real Businesses

This isn't quite as difficult as the whole song lyric-thing, but you need to be cautious here as well. You either use the name of a real business or you don't. You don't have to get permission, but the problem is, if you use the name of a business, and they find out, and they don't like how you've used it, they may sue you for damages, claiming you have cost them business. If they feel you have portrayed their company in a disparaging way, they might try to sue for defamation. They may not be right, and they may not win, but when all is said and done, you will probably be a much poorer, unhappier camper.

If you are thinking about using a real business in your story, you should probably ask yourself, how important to the story is it, really, that you call the store your character shops in *Wal-Mart* instead of making up a name like *S-Mart*? How important is it that your characters eat dinner in a *Denny's* instead of a *Paul's Eggs and Beans*?

Now in those two examples, the companies probably wouldn't care. But what if your setting is in a real bank, and most of the characters in the story, from the bank manager to the tellers to maybe even the head-honcho in New York, are crooks. What if you portray them as seedy, money-grubbing criminals who steal old ladies' pension money?

I don't think that would go over so well. I think their lawyers will call you, and you'll be wishing you would have had a lawyer of your own tell you not to use a real bank's name in the story before you published it.

This same rule applies to characters' background information as well. You might not want to say someone used to work for (insert real business name here) but quit because the manager kept doing disgusting things to the food. This puts (insert real business name here) in a bad light. It could make them lose customers who might think some part of your story is based in truth. It could make the business upset enough to try suing you for defamation.

And, I know this is repetitive, but in addition to all of that, some editors will reject a story with real business names because they don't want to deal with any possible future problems. Like maybe a movie deal. Where you would have to obtain permission to show the business's trademarked logos and such in the film. Wouldn't you hate to miss out on a movie deal because you set your story in Disneyland, but Disney refused permission to use anything referencing them in a movie? (Hey, it could happen.)

Don't Use Names Of Real Products

This is pretty much the same idea as not using the names of real business, but here, I would worry even less about it, unless, again, you are saying something disparaging.

Generally, it is fine to say someone made copies at the Xerox machine, or that someone is choosy and chooses Jiff Peanut Butter[46], or that you like to drink milk and Pepsi before bed at night. (Laverne and Shirley? Anyone? No? *Sigh*) It might even be kind of funny to have two characters always arguing about which is better, Candy Bar A or Candy Bar B, but things get fuzzy when one of them starts to say Candy Bar A sucks.

What if the character who likes Candy Bar B eventually turns out to be an unforgivably bad guy? Suddenly you are associating a product with a bad person or maybe saying that a good person doesn't like a certain product.

What if, in your story, someone claims to have found cockroaches in a brand-new unopened box of Brand X Foodstuffs? Some people will have that image in their head forever and NEVER buy a box of Brand X Foodstuffs again. (My grandmother was like that. Come to think of it, so is my wife…)

Generally, businesses don't mind if you shine their products with a positive light. In fact, sometimes (not very often) sponsorships can happen that way. But woe betide the poor soul who actively slams a big brand-named product belonging to a company with deep pockets and lots of lawyers.

And, to repeat myself once again, some editors will reject a story with real product names because they don't want to deal with possible problems. This doesn't happen as much as with business names or song lyrics, but still, it's something to consider.

Another thing to consider is the use of trademarked product names as a common term. In real life, people tend to substitute a brand name item for the whole idea of the item.

Examples of this are Thermos®, Kleenex®, Xerox®, and Vaseline®.

---

[46] Hey! Look at that! The Mandela effect in action! I am sure I would have looked that up before publishing the first edition of this guide. Surely one of my two editors or umpteen proofreaders would have caught that, right? Right? Really? Are you sure it was Jif and not Jiff or Jiffy all along?

People have used the brand names as generalized names for these products to the point where the brand name recognition is lost. Companies don't like losing their trademarked names that way.

If you become a bestselling author and every time you write a story, you have a scene wherein someone makes xeroxes, or blows their nose with kleenex, without showing that these are actually specific products, you may find yourself on the receiving end of a lawyer's cease and desist letter[47].

The way to write those would be: someone makes photocopies with a Xerox machine or blows their nose with Kleenex tissues. Or just leave out the brand name.

No, you don't have to use the ® symbol like I did the first time I used the names, but the companies that own the trademark do. They have to use it to protect their trademark, much as copyright was once required to be indicated with the copyright symbol (©).

Don't Be a Dick

I can't take full credit for this section. The day I met Kevin J. Anderson and Rebecca Moesta, I was lucky enough to be in a class they were instructing, and they gave a talk on this. They've since renamed their talk something a bit more family friendly, but I'm going to stick with this name for shock value. To make you think about it. Because it is important.

In their class, Kevin and Rebecca talk about being nice to everyone, all the time, because you never know who someone is, or who is seeing you act like a dick to someone else and judging you for it. They could be your biggest fan, or an editor with a big publisher, or your favorite writer you hadn't met in person and didn't recognize. On top of that, we all deserve to be treated kindly anyway. If you get the chance to hear Kevin and Rebecca talk about it, I recommend it. They have some great stories that go along with their talk.

But on to what I wanted to say. When you get a rejection (yes, I said when, not if), you probably should not reply to it. You definitely should not send them your opinion of their opinion. You should never, ever tell them they will rue the day, or threaten their mother, or mail them dead fish[48].

At most, if you got a really nice rejection letter with a lot of feedback, you might consider thanking them. But that's it. Stop there unless their rejection letter actually requested to initiate dialog with you. Really.

If you meet an overzealous fan, keep your calm. Be nice to them. Remember they are a fan. They are there because of you. If you are mean to

---

[47] Actually, the odds on that are very low, but it could happen, so why risk it?

[48] The reverse is also true. Not too long ago a small publisher began rating and listing (by title and author name) the stories they received and rejected. Word got out and there are now a lot of authors who will never submit to that publisher or the persons involved in that action.

them, they will take that personally. Maybe as personally as if you were a lover jilting them. Because books can be that personal to people, and it hurts them that much to be rejected by their favorite author who they deeply felt "gets them." And if you are not nice, if you are mean, you may not like how they respond in kind.

When you meet another writer who wrote something similar to what you did, and that will happen, too, you should not tell them you had the idea first, or that you did it better, or that they stole it, or any of the other things the internet has lied to you about and said you should do. Because you shouldn't, and you know you shouldn't. So, don't.

You should be polite and express interest if you can. You may make a new best friend. Or, if you can't bring yourself to do that, you should politely excuse yourself and find a quiet corner to choke down those nasty feeling before you vomit them all over the place and permanently embarrass yourself in front of your peers, friends, and colleagues.

The ONLY exception to this is if they actually plagiarized from you. Even then, you need to approach it civilly and legally, not scream in their face and make a scene. No matter how badly you want to.

Now, I realize I may sound a bit harsh here. Usually, I try to be very supportive, but this is important.

If you're a dick, people won't like you. If people don't like you, you won't be able to sell any books to them, they won't help you sell your books to other people, you won't sell stories to them, you won't be sought out for opportunities, you won't make friends, and worse, people will remember that you were a dick and they will avoid you.

They will also tell other people you were a dick. And then those people will avoid you too. And then those people won't buy your stories or contact you with opportunities.

Being a dick can and will ruin your writing career. And, if you have acquaintances in the writing community everyone associates with you, it can ruin their writing careers too. I've seen it happen. This is important.

Don't be a dick.

Don't be a dick.

Don't be a dick.

Don't be a dick.

Don't be a dick.

Yes, it really is important enough to repeat that many times.

Don't be a dick.

COMMON ISSUES WITH PUNCTUATION

So, just in case my high school English teacher is reading this, I want it to be perfectly clear that any and all faults were with my learning and not her teaching. Any mistakes in this book stem from issues she was unable to correct because I had already left her sphere of control. Also, thank you, Mrs. V. (Yes, I am still in contact with her! Social media can be a wonderful thing.) for teaching me the five sentence paragraph and the five paragraph essay. They are, after learning to read and write, probably the most useful academic tools I ever received.

So, all brownnosing aside, the biggest problem with punctuation for authors is this whole poetic license thing. New authors tend to break nearly all the rules, nearly all the time, whether they know and understand them or not. That leads to a loss of any positive effect that can be generated by knowingly breaking the rules, and then the story can become messy and unreadable.

Know the rules and understand why they exist before you break 'em!

This is important. I am constantly surprised by the number of writers who start out believing that if they just write a good story, it's the editor's job to clean up all the mistakes. Here's the deal: as cool as that would be, it's not someone else's job to fix your story after you write it.

Well, it is, but it isn't. The thing is, no one wants to touch a story that is a mess unless you pay them to do it. A publisher wants to put as little work into fixing a story as possible, as spending time and money on a story cuts into their profits.

If you use punctuation correctly the first time, it doesn't need to be fixed later, and an editor can focus on making your story better, not just readable. In order to get the most out of an editor, it behooves you to give them the best, cleanest story you can. So learn the rules, and then pay attention to the editors when they point out places where you should have followed them.

Punctuation In Dialog

This really is the elephant in the room, and many people angrily point it out and get upset that it won't leave. Many novice writers have problems in this area because there really are so many ways to be expressive and so many ways to write dialog around action. (A related issue is discussed in **Impossible Dialog Tags**.)

I often see simple mistakes such as:

"Hello." He said. (This is Wrong.)

"He said." is not a standalone sentence. It needs to be connected to the dialog with a comma and the capital removed.

"Hello," he said.

Mistake examples:

"Hello," he said "how are you?" (This is Wrong.)
or
"Hello" he said "how are you?" (This is Wrong.)

"How are you?" is a clause capable of standing alone. It needs to be separated out from the rest as a sentence, or correctly joined with the rest as a clause. This can be done with either a comma or a period.

"Hello," he said. "How are you?"
or
"Hello," he said, "how are you?"

Another mistake is:

He said, "My name is John," and walked over to her, "How are you?" (This is Wrong.)

This is an example of a comma splice. (See the section on **Comma Splices** for more on that.) It needs to be broken up into separate sentences. Unlike correcting a comma splice in narrative text, you cannot correct them in dialog merely by adding conjunctions.

Multiple dialog tags confuse the issue further:

He said, "My name is John," and walked over to her, and said, "How are you?" (This is Wrong.)

Correct examples:

He said, "My name is John," and walked over to her. "How are you?"
or
"My name is John," he said and walked over to her. "How are you?"
or
"Hi," he said.
She replied, "Hello."
"It's a hot day." He wiped the sweat from his forehead.
She nodded. "Yes, it is."

The proper use of question marks, exclamation points, ellipses, and em-dashes tend to confuse people a bit. Treat them as commas when using dialog tags.

"Hello?" she asked into the darkness. "Is anyone there?"

"Hot dog!" he cried, jumping into the air and pumping his fist.

"I love—" he cried out and suddenly stopped, realizing it wasn't her after all.

"You're so…" she whispered breathlessly.

Multiple sentences of dialog occasionally confuse writers as well. Here is an example:

He turned to her and said, "I love you. I have always loved you. I will always love you. I don't know how else to say it. I love you."

There are several sentences there, but they are all part of the words being spoken right now, by this one character. This makes them all one action, and as such, they are all included with what appears to be the same sentence, within the same quotation marks.

This does not always hold true. Sometimes a character rambles on so long they need a new paragraph to continue speaking. When that happens, you leave off the quotation marks at the end of the first paragraph to indicate the speaker has not stopped speaking, but you do include them at the beginning of the next paragraph to show it is still dialog.

He turned to her and said, "I love you." His expression became vacant, and as though he had rehearsed a speech, he began walking around the room, adjusting flowers, candles, and photographs as he

spoke. "I have always loved you. I will always love you. I don't know how else to say it. I love you.

"You are my dearest love. No one will ever come before you. You have usurped my heart for now and for always."

Caution!

Avoid describing other characters' actions during dialog, unless the speaking character is observing or involved, as it can get really confusing.

Confusing example:

He turned to her and said, "I love you. I have always loved you." Susan turned away from him. "I will always love you. I don't know how else to say it. I love you."

When Susan turns away from him, it starts to read as though she speaks the rest of the dialog. If you need to say she is turning away, break up the sentences into separate paragraphs, or change the action to a stand-alone sentence to show how he is observing her actions.

He turned to her and said, "I love you. I have always loved you." Susan turned away from him.

"I will always love you," he continued. "I don't know how else to say it. I love you."

or

He turned to her and said, "I love you. I have always loved you." He winced as Susan turned away from him. "I will always love you. I don't know how else to say it. I love you."

Use Of ALL CAPITAL Letters And Multiple Punctuation Marks!!!!?

This is an easy one. Should you or shouldn't you? The easy answer is: Don't. Ever. And that is what most editors will tell you.

Obviously, I can't complain too much if you do. As you might have noticed I have used them both in this book (to the great dismay of many sticklers, I am sure).

My point is, if you are going to do this, make sure you know your audience. Not only who you are writing for, but what style they like to read. Using all capitals and/or multiple punctuation marks can emphasize something in your writing, but it can also be very distracting. And distracting is bad. Distracting breaks the reader "out of the zone" and makes them aware they are reading and not just watching a movie come to life out of the black and white squiggly things on the page in front of them.

If you are intentionally writing a story that is very much like a comic book, and you are going to be consistent, then by all means, use comic book techniques. This has been done to great effect and success in the past. But if you are writing a romantic scene, in a serious mystery, and you suddenly change up your style for emphasis, it looks shoddy, unprofessional, and makes the reader remember they are reading.

Not only that, betraying their genre like that makes the reader forget about the story as they begin to wonder about the author, even if you are consistently using the technique. It's just not what the typical reader of that particular type of story (or most types) is used to or wants.

Instead of:

"What?!" he asked angrily.

Try to use other words to convey the meaning.

"What?" His voice thundered throughout the small room as he turned and glared at me.

I also strongly recommend against the use of the interabang (sometimes called the interrobang). It is a combination of the question mark (?) and the exclamation point (!), and it is intended to replace using them together (!? or ?!). It looks like one of these:

‽ ‽ ‽ ‽ ‽

Yeesh! I had a hard time even finding fonts that had the interabang symbol! I wanted to give a couple of examples to show what it looked like, as they are a bit different. It turns out the Garamond font, which this text is written in, doesn't even have one. That should start to give you a clue as to why an editor, formatter, or publisher wouldn't want to have that symbol in your story.

While we are on the subject of what not to do, I should mention general overuse of punctuation marks. Some people will tell you to never use an exclamation point. Some will tell you to use no more than one in your story. These rules fall under the same category as "your first million words are crap." They are right, but they are wrong, too. The whole reason people have made up these rules is to stop other people from doing things like ending every third sentence with an exclamation point. It can be horribly distracting for a reader.

For more things you shouldn't overuse, see **Pro Tips**.

Comma Use When Joining Two Sentences

This gets tricky for some of us. Probably because there are both so many ways to do it and too many misconceptions about when to use a comma. (See also the sections on **Comma Splices** and **Other Times You Shouldn't Use A Comma** for more on the comma, and **Because "As" is Also…** for more on comma use with the word *as*.)

When joining two sentences, you need to use both a comma and a conjunction.

Example:

Julie was amused, and she said so.

These are two stand-alone sentences jammed together.

Julie was amused. She said so.

There are other ways to combine them, but if you are using a comma, the above way is the correct one. Leaving out the conjunction (and) creates a comma splice. When merely adding a clause to a sentence, you do not generally need the comma.

Example:

Julie was amused and said so.

As *said so* is not a complete sentence, you have not combined two sentences and do not need a conjunction. Putting the word *she* in there makes the second clause into a separate sentence instead of a fragment and changes the way it should be connected.

Sometimes these sentences need to be broken apart for clarity.

Examples:

Julie thought Jack was funny and said so.

Julie thought Jack was funny, and she said so.

The first sentence makes it a bit confusing as to whether it was Jack or Julie who "said so," but the second clarifies that nicely.

Of course, you could always break them up entirely.

Julie thought Jack was funny. She said so.

Comma Use When Using Prepositional Phrases

Most of us learned to set prepositional phrases apart with commas, but this can be very confusing. Really, sometimes we should and sometimes we shouldn't. It is an issue of both clarity and necessity. Generally, you do not need a comma to set apart the prepositional phrase unless it is an introductory prepositional phrase (at the beginning of a sentence), or it is a nonessential phrase.

Examples:

As though he were going to faint from the shock of his offended sensibilities, Ronald put the back of his hand to his forehead and swooned.

Ronald put the back of his hand to his forehead and swooned as though he were going to faint from the shock of his offended sensibilities.

Notice the part of the sentence *as though he were going to faint from the shock of his offended sensibilities* is not essential to the sentence at all. You can take it out and the rest of the sentence still works just fine.

Ronald put the back of his hand to his forehead and swooned.

An easier way to see this is to determine whether or not the prepositional phrase is essential. If it is essential, you don't need to set it apart.

Example:

I took the dog with the floppy ears to the vet.

Here, *the floppy ears* identifies which dog. Without that phrase, you might not know which dog I took to the vet. It is essential to the sentence.

Example:

I took the dog, despite his growling at me, to the vet.

While *despite his growling at me* is informative and adds meaning to the sentence, it is not an essential phrase. It didn't add any identifying information that could have prevented some sort of misunderstanding. We still don't know for sure which dog it was.

I took the dog that growled at me to the vet.

Now we know which dog. We turned that bit of information into an essential identifier, so no commas are needed.

Just to confuse the issue, some style guides say that if an introductory prepositional phrase is short (less than three words or so), generally the comma is left off.

Example:

On my birthday we went to the baseball game.

This introductory prepositional phrase is short and clear enough that there is little chance of it being confusing, so it is acceptable to leave the comma off. It is also acceptable to use the comma.

On my birthday, we went to the baseball game.

Where you don't want to leave a comma off is when the introductory prepositional phrase could be misconstrued as a verb affecting the subject.

Example:

After painting my mother went back to working in the garden.

Here the introductory prepositional phrase is short, but it is not clear. This sentence sounds like someone painted my mother, and then it gets confusing. The comma is definitely needed there.

Another example could be:

Posters had been stapled to the walls wrapping around the whole room.

Without a comma after *walls*, this sounds like an oddly redundant sentence telling us that walls wrap around the room.

For more on this type of problem, see the section on **Misplaced Modifiers**. See the section **Because "As" is Also...** for more on comma use with the word *as*.

Comma Splices

A comma splice is when you splice two sentences together using only a comma, no conjunction. While some people find it acceptable to occasionally use a comma splice for effect, overuse is distracting, confusing, and the biggest culprit leading to run-on sentences. (See **Semicolons, Comma Use When Joining Two Sentences, Run-on Sentences**, and **Because "As" is Also...**for more information.)

Part of the problem is the way we speak aloud. While it may sound like we are talking with two sentences joined by a comma, it's still not written that way.

Example of a comma splice:

My mom went to the store, I went to the movies.

A correctly punctuated single sentence would be:

My mom went to the store, but I went to the movies.
or
My mom went to the store, so I went to the movies.
or
My mom went to the store; I went to the movies.

Some editors don't allow comma splices at all. I personally feel they can be excellently used stylistically, but you need to use them sparingly and only when you want to make the sentence stand out.
Example:

The monster roared, it screamed, it wailed, it died.

This clearly has more of a dramatic effect than if it were correctly punctuated.

The monster roared. It screamed. It wailed. It died.

To me, that seems too drawn out for such closely related ideas.

The monster roared; it screamed; it wailed; it died.

This seems too stilted and formal for the climax of a story. But, technically, both of those last two are correct, while comma splices are not. If you are going to use the comma splice, realize that you are making a stylistic choice and do so wisely, not in a haphazard shoddy way.

Other Times You Shouldn't Use A Comma

First, let me reiterate what I said before: part of the problem is the way we speak aloud. It is not the same as the way we write.
Now let me pooh-pooh a rule you may have heard as a kid.

"Put a comma wherever you pause while speaking."

No.

No. No. No. Bad.

Example:

I wanted to go home but, I couldn't. (This is wrong.)

or

In a letter, to tell your mother, that you weren't coming home for Christmas, I saw you mention you had, a new girlfriend. (This is wrong.)

People pause all the time when speaking, but the written language follows a different set of rules. The comma is not really for pauses, it is for clarification. Don't separate a clause with a comma as you would a compound sentence.

Example:

I went to school, with my brother. (This is wrong.)

Don't use a comma just because you think you see a conjunction.

Example:

I went to the mall, and the gas station. (This is wrong.)

The Oxford Comma

The Oxford comma, also sometimes called the Harvard comma, is a serial comma. It is a serial comma used to separate out things in a list. Specifically, the Oxford comma separates out the final thing (person, or whatever) on the list. It is called the Oxford comma because the style guidelines for the Oxford University Press famously required its usage. How or why this recently became an issue I don't know, other than to speculate that ignorance of the use of a comma is at the root of it all.

Some people have begun arguing against the use of the Oxford comma, and some have vehemently argued back for its necessity. Some claim that the context of the sentence removes the need for the Oxford comma, others say that if you need the Oxford comma the sentence has been poorly written and should be re-arranged properly.

The truth, I feel, lies in the middle. Sometimes you should use it, other times you shouldn't, but mostly, you need to pay attention to whether or not the idea you are trying to get across has been clearly expressed.

As I said before, **the purpose of a comma is clarification**. The improper use of a comma can be very confusing and misleading.

Here is an example of serial commas with the Oxford comma in use:

I went shopping with Mary, Bob, Tom, and Sue.

Here is the same example without the Oxford comma:

I went shopping with Mary, Bob, Tom and Sue.

Not much difference, right? Maybe. Maybe not. To me this now looks like Tom and Sue are somehow related. Like they are always together. A brother and sister team, or a married couple. As in I wouldn't go shopping with Tom without Sue being there also. But whether or not they are a thing together is not a big deal. Until it is.

If I wanted to make sure you knew Tom and Sue were a couple, I would write it like this:

I went shopping with Mary, Tom and Sue, and Bob.

Notice the Oxford comma shows that Bob is not with whatever form of sub-group Tom and Sue form within our group of people who went shopping.

Let's say that Tom and Sue are a couple I always want to group together. In that case, I wouldn't put a comma between them at all. Then, if I take out the Oxford Comma, strange things start to happen:

I went shopping with Mary, Tom and Sue and Bob.

Now it looks like Bob is part of Tom and Sue's subgroup after all. That could be all right, but if I wanted to make sure that you knew Bob was with Tom and Sue, it would be much better to rewrite the sentence as:

I went shopping with Tom and Sue and Bob, and Mary.

This is where things start to get sticky. Because now some people think that looks wrong because you only have one serial comma, and it is the Oxford comma. We are starting to run into a problem I talk about later: We don't speak the same way we write. (See **Don't Write The Way You Speak** for more on this.)

Things get worse when you use pronouns that may be ambiguous.

I went shopping with my cousins, Mary, Tom and Sue, and Bob.

Are my cousins Mary, Tom and Sue, and Bob? Or are my cousins even more people, beyond Mary, Tom, and Sue, who are involved in this expedition into the world of consumerism?

Maybe it's time for a stretch break.

Hopefully you are beginning to see that how you use a comma is dependent upon what you are trying to say, and following a steadfast rule is a sure way to get yourself into trouble. When you use them, try to make sure you do so in a way that gets your idea across as best as you can. Remember that while poetic license can be a matter of preference, you don't want to sacrifice clarity. Or your sanity.

Semicolon

The semicolon is an often misunderstood tool. Many people are afraid of it. I am. It's scary.

Some people seem to think it is good for all kinds of things and use it to replace all sorts of other punctuation marks. This is usually a side-effect of learning that you have been using it incorrectly all along and then overcompensating.

I wouldn't worry about it too much. Modern usage of the semicolon is falling by the wayside. But that doesn't mean you shouldn't know when to use it, even if you choose not to.

A comma splice (please see the section on **Comma Splices**) is really a comma doing the semicolon's job. A comma splice can be fixed simply by replacing the comma with a semicolon.

Whereas commas are supposed to be used with conjunctions (and, but, for, nor, so, therefore, etc.), semicolons are meant to be used without conjunctions.

When you use a semicolon to put two sentences together, it should mean that these two ideas are closely related, and you want to keep them close together.

Example:

I can't drive tonight; my car has a flat tire.

These sentences don't have to be connected with a semicolon but doing so shows how they are important to each other. Using a comma instead of the semicolon makes it a comma splice.

Here is another example of a correctly used semicolon, and why authors don't like to use it:

I can't drive tonight; my car has a flat tire; I am low on gasoline; my battery is dead.

Dialog written like that tends to make you feel as though you aren't reading a character's spoken words. They feel like printed words on a page. Which they are. Which breaks the illusion of the storytelling and kind of ruins the whole thing. Personally, I suggest that you try to avoid the whole issue by breaking the sentences up into bite-sized chunks the reader can enjoy.

Like this:

"I can't drive tonight." Zach shifted nervously from one foot to the other. "My car has a flat tire." He glanced sideways at Nancy and then down to his own feet. "I am low on gasoline. My battery is dead."

But don't be afraid to use the semicolon in your narrative. It can help vary your sentence structure and ease a repetitive cadence. (See the section on **Repetitiveness** for more information on that.)

Note: some people feel that you cannot connect more than two independent clauses with semicolons, as I did in the second example above. They consider it a run-on sentence. I won't argue with that, as I can't see myself ever writing that kind of sentence again, but I wanted to point out that others say it is fine. Mostly, you should aim for clarity.

Colon

The use of the colon is often confused with that of a semicolon, probably because not only do they look similar, but in some situations they are interchangeable. The colon can also sometimes be used in place of a comma. This usage can be confusing, and when used in fiction writing, they tend to feel too formal.

I would recommend, unless you are comfortable with this punctuation mark, that you stick to using it for listing things.

Example:

(See where I used the colon up there, next to the word *Example*?)

Example:

He bought all kinds of candy: lollipops, chocolate bars, taffy, and even popcorn balls.

You can use the colon even when listing only one thing.
Example:

He knew who had stolen the cake: Sadie Cakestealer.

The colon can even be used for dialog.

Example:

Mac put his cheek next to mine and spoke: "I'll kill you."

And finally: A big pat on the back to myself; for resisting all of the colon and semicolon jokes in the last two sections.

Run-On Sentences

Sometimes people complain a sentence is a run-on merely because it is too long. While this may be true, **a run-on sentence is actually two or more sentences jammed together without correct punctuation.** There are many ways writers make this mistake.

Typical example of a run-on sentence:

My mom went to the store I went to the movies.

Example of a run-on sentence because of comma splices:

My mom went to the store, I went to the movies.
or
It's getting late, go eat dinner.

While the last example looks pretty good, and it is pretty typical of the type of writing we see nowadays, it is still a run-on sentence.

Also, just because you know, or think you know, how to grammatically construct a three-page sentence so that it is not technically a run-on doesn't mean you should.

Example:

My mom went to the store with my Aunt Sue, who is really younger than I am, which is really weird, and I went to the movies with my nephew, Mark, who is really older than I am, which is even weirder, and my sister rode horses all afternoon with my Uncle, who should never be trusted with any animal, while my dad watched the football game with the world's greatest armchair quarterback, my grandfather, who once owned a football stadium that was used for the playoff game that had the half-time show where the cow rode the horse down the waterslide made out of popsicle sticks collected by all of the Boy Scouts and Girl Scouts who had been lucky enough to attend by winning family vacations from the cereal company that makes the little golden O's based on the movie by Stephen Spielberg, which was adapted from that book by Sam Knight about his own personal experiences with run-on sentences that made him say, "Oh."

Is that sentence technically correct? Crap. Who knows? Who cares? No one wants to read something like that. If you can write a sentence that long while being grammatically correct, you are just playing word games, doing a puzzle if you will. That kind of exercise may be fun and entertaining for you and a few of your friends, but readers just want a good story.

A longer sentence structure is a valid approach to writing, and one some people prefer. I don't want to discourage you from using it. (I know. Based upon what I said above it seems like I am.) My recommendation is, if you choose to continue using longer sentence structures, you should try to avoid wordiness. Just taking out a few extraneous words can help a lot.

When sentences are too long, they are difficult for the average reader to follow. Unless you want to make sure this is how your narrative voice sounds, I would advise against it. Super-extra-long sentences tend to become awkward, and that's when clarity falls apart and you lose your reader. Possibly to lack of oxygen from not being able to take a breath.

See the section **Because "As" is Also...** for more on comma use with the word *as* in relation to run-on sentences.

Periods And Commas Inside Or Outside of Quotes

This is another debated issue that causes red ink to go flying at computer screens everywhere. Do I put the period inside or outside of quotation marks?

There is a difference. First, the Americans and the British do it differently. Second, there are different times to do it, or not. And third, or maybe this should be first, clarity.

This is not an English 200 class, so I won't go into all the ways you should or shouldn't apply these rules to your final essay with a minimum of twenty citations. If you are dealing with that, find out which style guide your professor uses and follow that strictly.

But when it comes to dialog, the punctuation is easy. It generally goes inside the quotes. (See **Dialog Tags** for more information.)

"Hi," he said.
She replied with a sultry, "Hello."

But when you are referring to something you want to imply is something else, it becomes a bit fuzzier. If you are not sure what I mean, think of when people use their fingers to put air quotes around something they are saying, implying the use of *irony* or a *euphemism*.

I looked at the scared man. He was standing in a puddle of yellow "water."
        or

I looked at the scared man. He was standing in a puddle of yellow "water".

Which is right?

Both. Neither. Depends upon your editor. Personally, I like to use the second example. Here is an example of why:

"George," he said with an overly casual voice. "Do you have the 'bananas', or do you have the 'apples'?"

If you put the punctuation inside the quotes, I think it begins to look messy and hard to read.

"George," he said with an overly casual voice. "Do you have the 'bananas,' or do you have the 'apples?' "

That one isn't so bad, but what if the quotes are like that on both end? What if your character shouldn't be using that many words and is speaking quickly?

**"George," he said with an overly casual voice.
" 'Bananas,' or 'apples?' "**

Now it looks strange and hard to read to me. That's why I prefer to write it this way:

**"George," he said with an overly casual voice.
" 'Bananas', or 'apples'?"**

The real difference between the American style (punctuation inside of quotes) and the English style (punctuation outside of quotes) is that the English style prevents adding punctuation that did not exist before to a quote. To me this is the key factor. I don't like to see direct quotes altered, even subtly.

Bonus

Problems with formatting! Notice the spaces I used between the double quotes and the single quotes above. Formatters tend to put those in for clarity. As a writer, it's up to you if you want to or not, but don't be surprised if your story ends up published that way.

"George," he said with an overly casual voice. "'Bananas', or 'apples?'"

See how it all kind of runs together? Now here's the nasty part if you are a formatter. Look what happens to that sentence when I put that space in between the quotes:

"George," he said with an overly casual voice. " 'Bananas', or 'apples?' "

See that final quote at the end of that last example, floating all by itself out there? The word processing program didn't keep it connected to the rest of the sentence where it was needed, nor did it point the smart quote in the correct direction, so it had to be played with manually to fix its positioning. Part of the problem with this kind of error is that it's challenging to find. That's why you need a proof copy of the final product and a proofreader to help find them. (With e-formatting, just as with em-dashes and ellipses, this is a terrible headache, and it just won't ever turn out right. More on that in **Notes on Self-Publishing This Mess!**)

Some people don't like to use single quotes and try to always use the double quotes, even when nesting the quotes within each other. Don't be surprised if this gets changed by an editor as well. It looks terrible. (I think.)

"George," he said with an overly casual voice. ""Bananas", or "apples?""

Also, note how it looks like *he* stops speaking at the end of "Bananas", possibly making the reader think his dialog has ended when it hasn't. The double quote is awkward, and distracting. One of the most important things about writing, in my opinion, is to never let the reader get distracted from the story by whatever is printed on the page.

Using An Apostrophe To Show Missing Letters

This only applies to dialog, or a narrative where the narrator is a character of some sort, and slang contractions are being used. You shouldn't use these kinds of contractions in a conventional narrative.

Some people think the correct usage of the apostrophe in these situations is a big deal, others don't. It is one of those little things that, I think, tend to show whether or not someone is paying attention. When using an apostrophe to show missing letters, it should point to where the letters were missing.

Go get 'em!
not
Go get 'em!

I'm fine 'cept when you're around!
not
I'm fine 'cept when you're around!

Here is how you can tell:

Can't
not
Canʻt

Can't is short for cannot. The apostrophe points to where the missing letters should have been.

This is a relatively new problem. It seems to have cropped up with the advent of digital word processing and the automatic implementation of smart quotes, which are the quotes that point in toward the text they are surrounding. (' ' or " ") rather than the straight quotes, also called prime marks (' ' or " ") Obviously, if you are not using smart quotes, it wouldn't matter.

See **Notes on Self-Publishing This Mess!** for more information.

Note: You really shoudn't combine more than one contraction. It becomes too difficult for the reader to decipher.

Examples:

Shouldn't've
Couldn't've
Wouldn't've

Or

We'd've

People may talk that way, but remember, the written word is not the same as the spoken word and clarity is key. (See **could have vs. could of**, for more information on these types of contractions.)

By the way, *'til* is a contraction of *until*, so it only gets one *l*, not two (meaning that *'till* is incorrect). This word is a point of contention for some. Some feel that *'til* is a contraction of *until* (which it is) and should be written as such. Other feel that *till* is a word that means the same as *until* (which it does) and should be used instead of *'til*. You'll have to make up your own mind on that one, and I suggest always deferring to any editor who is paying you for your story. Actually, that piece of advice applies to everything in this book.

Just don't use *'till*.

Em-Dashes, En-Dashes, Hyphens, and Ellipses

Some people think I am picky about this, and I am. That's why each one is getting its own time in the spotlight. But I do have reasons. One is that improper use hurts your story by distracting the reader. Another is that some writers severely overuse these, which can also detract from a story. (A term I have heard for one is ellipsis-itis.) And finally, it can be a formatting nightmare for the publishing company. If you use punctuation correctly the first time, it doesn't need to be fixed later.

I have seen them all used to replace the others, but they each have a specialized function, which is why we have them all.

First, here are the punctuation marks I am talking about:

em-dash   (—)
en-dash   (–)
hyphen   (-)
ellipsis (…)

In MS Word on PC, you can make an **em-dash** by pressing:
ctl + alt + (the minus symbol (-) on the number pad)

You can make an **en-dash** by pressing:
ctl + (the minus symbol (-) on the number pad)

The **hyphen** is next to the 0 (zero) key on the top row of the keyboard. (Yeah, I know you knew that, but since I explained how to make all the other punctuation marks, I felt silly not including this one.)

The **ellipsis** is made by putting three periods together in a row. Generally, MS Word's auto-formatting will replace those with the single punctuation mark that looks very similar but acts like one character for formatting purposes. (More on that in **Notes on Self-Publishing This Mess!**)

Some word processors will insert an em-dash or an en-dash automatically if you use two dashes in a row (--). If you choose to do this, pay attention; sometimes the autocorrect will change it, sometimes it won't. Some programs will replace it with an em-dash, some with an en-dash. If you use this technique, know what you are getting into. Also, some writers will use two dashes in a row (--) to signify an em-dash in their manuscript. Not a big deal, and pretty easy for the formatter to change, but be consistent.

Apologies to those who don't write in MS Word. I don't know shortcuts for other platforms. If all else fails, you can always copy and paste from an example of the character being used somewhere else, like looking it up on an internet webpage.

Bonus Note
Remember when we talked about monospaced fonts vs. justified fonts? The em-dash (—) is called *em-dash* because it takes up the same amount of space as the letter *M*. Or it did at one time, in that one font…

The en-dash (–), of course, was the same width as the letter *N*.

Em-Dash

While the em-dash is actually quite versatile, it should be used to represent interruptions or emphasis, not to replace semi-colons when combining sentences. As a fiction writer there are many times I would use it in dialog and in the narrative to represent an interruption.
Example:

"Hi, Bob! How are you? It's been a—"
"Duck!" Bob grabbed Tom by the arm and pulled him down just as a sticky popsicle whizzed over their heads.

There, Tom's words were interrupted by Bob's actions.
Example:

Tom stepped off the curb, wondering where Bob had gotten off—
Bob pulled Tom backward as a speeding taxi jumped lanes and swerved, nearly hitting them both.

Here I interrupted the narrative about what Tom was doing.
In both instances, the em-dash was used for dramatic effect and indicated an action interrupted. It can also be used in the narration in place of commas or parenthesis for emphasis and dramatic effect.
Example:

Joshua stared up at the gold starship—the same one that had killed his parents—and he readied his laser bazooka.

Again, this is used for dramatic effect, not merely to combine the sentences, and it is more impactful than commas as the em-dashes interrupt, instead of just setting aside, the other thought. In comparison, see how much tamer these versions are:

Joshua stared up at the gold starship, the same one that had killed his parents, and he readied his laser bazooka.
or

Joshua stared up at the gold starship (the same one that had killed his parents) and he readied his laser bazooka.

The commas feel more matter-of-fact, while the parentheses feel more like an aside whisper.

Another dramatic effect of the em-dash, for much of the same reasons given above, is to replace a colon in a sentence for emphasis.

Example:

He knew the truth now—she was dead.

Bonus example!
When someone is speaking, and they get interrupted, but they continue speaking anyway, do not capitalize the first word of continued dialog (unless they are resuming in some fashion).

"Hi, Bob! How are you? It's been a—"
"Duck!" Bob grabbed Tom by the arm and pulled him down just as a sticky popsicle whizzed over their heads.
"—long time," Tony said, as he slowly stood back up.
or
"Hi, Bob! How are you? It's been a—"
"Duck!" Bob grabbed Tom by the arm and pulled him down just as a sticky popsicle whizzed over their heads.
Tony slowly stood back up, nonplussed, and looked at Bob. "It's been a long time."

Bonus warning!
While it is generally acceptable to place emphatic punctuation after an em-dash, usually to show question or excitement, there should not be a period or comma after an em-dash. This is the same as the rules for the **Ellipsis**.

"Wow! You look—!" he said, shaking his head, suddenly at a loss for words.
or
"Wow! What did you—?" Tom asked, overwhelmed at the sight of Bob's new hairstyle.
or
"Bob? Bob is that—?" The figure vanished before Tom could finish his question.

but without the emphasis, no comma or period is used.

"Wow! You look—" he said, shaking his head, suddenly at a loss for words.

or

"Wow! What did you—" Tom asked, overwhelmed at the sight of Bob's new hairstyle.

or

"Bob? Bob is that—" The figure vanished before Tom could finish his question.

En-Dash

The **en-dash** is generally ignored in fiction writing, but as long as we are learning, we should learn as much as we can, right? The en-dash is used with a range of numbers such as "1–100" or "read pages 78–96." It can also be used when linking things, like the Bush–Cheney political ticket, or the Batman–Superman movie.

Use of the en-dash links things differently than the hyphen. The hyphen combines them into one. If you were to use the hyphen with the Bush-Cheney political ticket, I would assume that Bush-Cheney was the last name of one person. If you were to use the hyphen with the Batman-Superman movie, I would assume that, like the Fly, Batman and Superman had entered a teleporter together and exited as one being.

Hyphen

The **hyphen** is our standard linking punctuation. It is used to combine two things into one, making them a compound object or thought. (For more on compound words, see also **alloneword**.)

Example:

The cat-dog was brown-green in color.

This should have evoked an image of a creature that is half-cat, half-dog, and has a brownish green color. The use of the hyphen in this manner allows us to combine two things into something new.

Let's look at some of the examples from the em-dash and en-dash to see how the hyphen changes them.

He knew the truth now-she was dead.

Unlike when we used an em-dash here, this sentence gains the appearance that "now-she" is the name of person or a creature.

Hi, Bob! How are you? It's been a-"

"Duck!" Bob grabbed Tom by the arm and pulled him down just as a sticky popsicle whizzed over their heads.

This sentence, instead of appearing interrupted as it did with the em-dash, now looks like Tom may be from Wisconsin, with a local idiom in his speech implying that "been a-" is a slang contraction of *been a while* or *been a long time*.

The hyphen is also what many of us remember seeing in printed books, when we were kids, to break long words off at the margin and carry them onto the next line.

(For those of you who are younger, a book is that other version of this text. The one that you didn't buy because it's not compatible with your e-reader and you don't have room for it on your shelf full of... Hey... What do you kids use shelves for nowadays, anyway?)

Ellipsis

The **ellipsis** is a tool that confuses many writers because it means that something has been left out, but it can mean that in two different ways.

First, it is used in excerpted quotes.

For example:

"The president ... flew down to Mexico ... for the weekend."

This usage could be a shortening of this quote:

"The President and his family, along with the First Dog, boarded Air Force One last night and flew down to Mexico, where they plan to meet the President of Mexico and enjoy themselves for the weekend."

In this case the ellipses (plural for ellipsis) indicate things that have been left out of the original quote.

But in fiction writing, it is common for writers to use an ellipsis to indicate a trailing off, or incomplete thought. (This leads to the ellipses being referred to as suspension points in some style manuals.)

"I wonder where...?" The Professor's voice trailed off as he noticed the writing on the tomb wall for the first time.

Here, the professor had more to say, but he left it out. Unlike the em-dash, which would have indicated that he was interrupted.

An ellipsis can be used to dramatic effect, just as an em-dash, but it does have a different effect. Let's look at one of the previous examples again.

He knew the truth now—she was dead.
becomes
He knew the truth now...she was dead.

To me, the difference between the two is an emotion. The em-dash is harsh and violent, maybe angry, while the ellipsis is softer, sadder, and evokes sympathy from the reader (or at least sympathy from me).

Replacing the em-dashes here, though, just gets confusing.

Joshua stared up at the gold starship...the same one that had killed his parents...and he readied his laser bazooka.

Are the ellipses indicating a passage of time? A dreamy feeling? Is Joshua fading in and out of consciousness? All of those could be possibilities, but they would have to be taken in context with the rest of the story for them to work, and if the context doesn't fit, they won't work.

If you are going to do a stammer, I recommend not using ellipses, but rather something like:

"B-b-but...there has to be!"

Using ellipses just looks weird. It seems to convey too much time between sounds.

"B...b...but...there has to be!"

You may have noticed that in my very first example in this section, the one of excerpted text, I used a space before and after each ellipsis. That is a standard style for formal writing, which is where you would be most likely to encounter an abridged excerpt such as that. You may also have noticed that in my other examples I didn't use a space after the ellipses. This is a stylistic choice on my part.

Like many parts of punctuation, different publishing houses will have different house rules about how they want to format their text. Some like to stay with the formal style, and some like to do what I have done. Some like to have a space before and after the ellipses.

"B ... b ... but ... there has to be!"

To me, a space after the ellipsis means that thought trailed off and is not being picked up again. It is over, and the next thing is going to be a new idea.

"B-b-but... Okay. We'll do it your way."

Modern word processers may split ellipses away from the previous word and onto a separate line if there are spaces in front of them. In an e-publication, you may consider an alternate spacing, if the spacing affects the formatting too much. (More on that in **Notes on Self-Publishing This Mess!**)

Whatever you choose to use, be consistent within each manuscript.

There can still be normal punctuation marks at the end of the sentence when using an ellipses, with the exception of the period, which becomes redundant. The exception to that is complicated and lies within the purview of quoting things. It is outside the range of what I want to cover here, because I don't like to write non-fiction. **The use of a four dot ellipses in unexcerpted text is an unconventional stylistic choice**. I have seen it used to mean something that is being said trails off and is not going to be continued, but that is uncommon. Use it at your own peril.

"I wonder where…?" The Professor's voice trailed off as he noticed the writing on the tomb wall for the first time.

"I wonder where…!" The Professor's excitement trailed off as he noticed the writing on the tomb wall for the first time.

"I wonder where…," said the Professor, as he noticed the writing on the tomb wall for the first time.

Regarding that last example: some people say not to use a comma after an ellipsis. The Chicago Manual of Style says you should. Again, you will have to decide for yourself, but be consistent.

Notes On Self-Publishing This Mess!

Em-dashes, en-dashes, hyphens, and ellipses truly are a mess when it comes to formatting for self-publishing. If someone is paying you to publish your story, great! Let them deal with the mess. If you are going to do it yourself though, you might want to take note of the problems with spacing.

Generally, in printed text, there are no spaces around em-dashes, en-dashes, hyphens, or ellipses. But then, generally, a printed book always looks the same after you format and publish it.

An e-book, however, changes the formatting of the text as the reader uses a larger or smaller font, or switches to a device with a larger or smaller screen. This is called flowable, reflowable, or dynamic text, and it often creates situations where the text wraps around to the next line, sometimes leading to very ugly results. There is also (for some e-readers) the option to make what is called a fixed format layout. This is pretty much the same as making a PDF. The text and images do not "flow." It is like having an e-book made up of photographs of the pages of the print book. They are usually used for things like illustrated children's books or things with a lot of tables or images, like a cookbook. A big drawback is many e-readers can't use this format. Another big drawback is zooming in to read text, like you zoom in on a photograph on your smartphone (assuming your e-reader can zoom in). I highly recommend you don't use fixed format in your e-books unless you really need to make pages look just like they do in the print book.

Another issue with formatting e-books is that e-readers have a tendency to replace fonts. (See the example of what e-book formatting did to the font examples used in this book in **Don't Use A Bunch of Strange Fonts**.) When changing the fonts, the e-readers can change not only how the text appears to the eye, but where it is laid out in relation to other text.

For example, if you use three dots for an ellipsis (...) you might have one or two dots on one line and the remainder on the next, as the wrap around text adjusts to the screen. This is because the e-reader recognizes each dot as its own entity. By making sure you use the ellipsis character (…), which looks like three dots but is actually a single symbol, you ensure all three dots will stay together. But e-readers still mess with formatting and may drop the ellipsis off into a line all its own, completely separating it from any words it had been attached to.

This problem carries over to hyphens, em-dashes, and en-dashes as well.

Why e-books can't recognize these punctuation marks seems a mystery until you realize something like "Stratford-upon-Avon" becomes one word that would never be broken up, which can lead to strange formatting before and after the word on a device that uses adjustable font size and wrap-around text. On top of that, some e-readers will recognize something like that as one word and won't break it up, but other e-readers won't recognize it and will break it apart, putting the pieces on different lines.

If you let them break apart, they look strange. If you keep them together, they look strange. Many formatters have put a lot of time and effort into trying to get around this problem, with varying success and results. Even formatting each and every instance of the use of the punctuation mark may not work and sometimes they still come out weird.

Generally, for e-books, putting spaces around these punctuation marks (which usually don't have spaces around them in print) seems to be an acceptable way to go. Just be aware of what you are stepping into when you go down that path. There is no easy solution.

While non-breaking spaces can be a solution when setting up formatting to make a print book or a fixed format e-book, they don't work well in typical e-books, sometimes not transferring during conversion process and sometimes creating strange gaps in the text. (Ctrl + Shift + spacebar creates a non-breaking space in MS Word.)

Note: Sometimes transferring documents from one format to another messes things up as well. I have especially noticed this when transferring from an Apple machine to a Microsoft PC and/or the other way around. (Yes, yes, I know. It's all 100% compatible. All I can say is that if you don't believe me, you go right ahead and keep doing whatever it is you are doing. Don't mind me. It's not like I went out of my way to include it in a book to warn you or anything.)

If you are in a situation where you are transferring documents back and forth between programs, you need to pay special attention to the formatting after your final transfer of the documents. Sometimes there are obvious losses in formatting, like paragraph indentation, font changes, or margin sizes, but some are insidiously hidden. Specifically, I have run into problems with italicized text randomly being normalized in some places but not others, and normal text becoming italicized. That can be especially hard to spot on a quick once-over when checking the formatting of a proof copy.

Another problem, involving the smart quotes, was nearly unnoticeable at first, but later became painfully obvious. I have run into situations (even in my own stuff, *sigh*) where dialog in some sections, but not in others, have ended up opening with smart quotes and closing with straight quotes.

Like this:

"Hi! How are you today?" she asked.

Generally, I put the examples in bold text, to make them stand out. This time the bolding helps hide the issue, so here it is again without the bold text:

"Hi! How are you today?" she asked.

If you are transferring files back and forth between platforms or programs, I recommend removing all formatting and then re-formatting it all in the final program to be used, never to be transferred to another program to be worked on again. (See **Using an Apostrophe to Show Missing Letters** for more on smart quotes.)

COMMON PROBLEMS WITH WRITING

This guide is not meant to teach you how to write a good story, or even a bad one. It's meant to help you be aware of common issues that are rarely mentioned, and that is what this section will focus on.

If you need help finding a guide on how to craft stories, the number one recommendation I have, which came as a recommendation from Jim Butcher, is *The Fantasy Fiction Formula* by Deborah Chester, whom I have heard Jim credit for his writing success. Other writers are a great resource for finding guides. They are quick to tell you good ones they re-read and warn you off bad ones they are sorry they touched. (I bet you can't guess which category I hope this one falls into…)

If you're looking for books on how to make yourself sit down and write, I'll save you the money. Sit your butt in the chair and write. Don't play video games. Don't binge-watch Netflix. Don't watch TikTok videos of people all doing the same dance. Don't scroll Pinterest recipes. Just write. Mercedes Lackey once left me feeling vindicated and validated when she expressed the same sentiment I had been stating: when you were in school and had to write a report, you made yourself sit down and write it. This is no different. There really is no such thing as writer's block, there is only you not forcing yourself to write.

If you still have problems with writer's block, there are as many different solutions as there are writers. Personally, I juggle projects. I usually have at least three being actively worked on, with several ideas on the back burner. I have juggled many more. I have no idea what the most at once was. Maybe thirteen. Things like working on three different short stories, two novels, a children's book, artwork for said children's book, artwork for the cover of a novel, and an outline for an upcoming project. Currently, I am working on this, I just opened up my publishing company to accepting submissions for three anthologies (which means reading emails and going through submissions), considering ideas for an anthology someone wants me to curate for them, working on the covers for four different anthologies, writing a novel, trying to come up with an idea for a short story I promised someone I'd write, thinking about an idea for a short story that I probably don't have time to write but want to as it fits an open submission call that caught my eye, and clockwatching to pick my son up from school and get him to his allergy shot. With this many irons in the fire, I don't have time to have writer's block. Needless to say, things with deadlines take priority.

I have found that when I slow down or stall out on a project, I do well by picking up and continuing on with another. This is a big reason why I started doing a lot of my own artwork and cover design. The art/layout part of my brain seems to be in a completely different residence than the writing part, and when one is exhausted the other still seems to function fairly well.

I take advantage of this when I don't feel like writing. It also helps to have another job or big chore I *don't* want to do. Then writing feels like procrastination, and I can do that for a *very* long time.

Descriptions

New writers tend to have one of two problems with descriptions: too much, or not enough.

The seemingly unlimited choices of how to describe things, and the problems they can cause, manifest in so many ways that I considered making this a section all its own. Instead, I decided to include them all under the same heading of Common Problems With Writing. Many writers don't recognize a problem as being part of the use of description, and I worried that someone thumbing through would miss what they were looking for because it was under the Descriptions heading. As you read other examples of Common Problems with Writing, please keep in mind how many of them are actually a problem with description, and realize that, really, all a story is, is a bunch of descriptions.

Writing teachers like to tell us, "show don't tell," and there is some truth to what they are saying, but really, everything in a story boils down to *tell*. The trick is to make a reader think about what you are telling them, so that they infer things that you have not directly told them, so that they understand connections you did not explicitly point out to them. That is a big part of what *show* means.

Remember, a reader's imagination is better than anything you can write. What you want to do is give fertile soil with a great topiary frame for their imagination to grow in. After you give them the shape, let them fill in all the little details.

An occasional problem with descriptions is sounding literal when we mean them to be figurative. (See **literally** for more on this.) As writers, we love to be artistic and use our metaphors and similes, but sometimes, especially when writing science fiction or fantasy, it can be difficult to tell if something is actually that way in the story or if the writer is being poetic.

If a space traveler sets foot on a planet for the first time, and the author says the ground was ashen, I really don't know if I am being told it is gray or if it is really covered in ash. If a wizard opens a magical doorway to a gilded land, I really don't know if the land is literally covered in gold or just bathed in golden sunlight.

Remember to try to interpret what you write as someone else may. They might not see it the way you did. This is a good reason to have editors and beta readers. (A beta reader is someone, usually not a professional, who reads your early manuscript and helps you find problems and mistakes. You know. Like your mom. Or your writers group. Or, as you get going, a Facebook group of your dedicated fans who want to see the story when it still has warts.)

Location/Setting

Remember, the readers cannot read your mind. You need to let them know a few details about everything that is going on. Some writers completely forget to fill in the setting. This can be known as **white room syndrome**. Basically, your reader starts trying to imagine what is going on as soon as they start reading. If you don't give any information about the setting (or character descriptions), the reader ends up imagining two talking mannequin faces in a white room with no furnishings.

It doesn't take much to fill in a setting, but it needs to be done. It can be as simple as saying, "They met at the airport." And then the reader can imagine everything else that happens is taking place in an airport.

Or you can do what Hawthorne did in the *Scarlet Letter* and spend the entire first chapter describing the front of the jail and the rosebush next to it. Whatever works best for you.

But be careful.

Hawthorne was using the jail to describe the town and the people in it; their temperaments, attitudes, and history. He is also giving you a good idea of the time period the story takes place in. When you spend a couple of pages literally describing only a jail, you will lose your readership pretty quickly. (He pretty much lost me there anyway, though I love some of his other works.)

An important and often overlooked place to mention the location or setting is at the start of a new scene. When you have a scene break, the reader assumes time has passed or the setting has changed. But they have no idea how much or which until you tell them. At the start of a new scene, you need something, no matter how small, that will clue the reader in as to where, and when, the new scene is taking place.

Maybe an overhead announcement lets us know we are still in the airport. Maybe the moon outside the window lets us know night has fallen. Maybe a character is still chewing on the same bite of hamburger he was chewing at the end of the last scene, so the reader knows no time has passed at all. (More on this in **Scene Breaks**.)

The time period of the setting is also important. Most writers fit this into the story naturally, without thinking about it, but occasionally someone forgets. In a contemporary story, it is not usually a problem, but if the story is set in 1863 or 2172, and the reader doesn't find out until halfway through the story, it can cause a lot of confusion. Generally, this is more of a problem in short stories than novels, but it can still happen. The exception to this is if you are intentionally misleading the reader into thinking it is a contemporary story when it is not.

There are many simple ways to show the time period your story takes place in as well. Things like a calendar on the wall, or the date on a newspaper are a little too obvious and tend to upset editors, if not readers. Those are better used to show how long a place has been abandoned.

A reference to well-known historical events works well for settings in the past, but so do people's clothing and the types of technology they use. Using everyday items that have changed over the years, such as gaslights, candles, a hand powered can-opener, giant keys, or even a handkerchief, can start to clue the reader in quickly.

For future settings, depending how far into the future, showing the technology also works well. Tapping a thumbnail communicator, vocalizing to an omnipresent computer (that can do more than play music or tell you a joke), having lipstick that changes color, or even something simple like having someone call a cellphone quaint can give a good idea that the story takes place sometime in the future. The more alien-seeming the technology is to us, the further into the future it will likely seem.

Now why, you may ask, would I focus on these little things rather than say, "Just tell the reader this takes place in 2231?" Well, you can do that, and it works fine. We've all seen short stories, movies, and even novels that start with something like:

Arizona Territory 1864
or
Somewhere on the edge of Orion's Belt

Those are viable options, but they don't necessarily engage the reader's imagination. Don't expect that little hint will carry the reader's imagination very far. Arizona Territory 1864 makes me think of empty prairie. But that's all, until you give me more to go on. Somewhere on the edge of Orion's Belt just makes me think of a bunch of stars out in space, near the edge of a swirling galaxy. It's a start, but not a very good one. They need more.

The other extreme would be a 45 page treatise on the history of the settlement of the Arizona Territory as a precursor to a story about a gunslinger who falls in love with a woman from the Navajo Nation. That tends to ruin the story. No one wants to read the history of the Arizona Territory. Except historians, who are already looking it up instead of reading your Western Romance.

Now that sounds like an obvious example, but less is more if the end goal is engaging the reader and not losing them with too much unnecessary detail. And it applies to a place that most people can't seem to carry it over to—science fiction and fantasy.

No one wants to read a 45 page treatise on how Orion's Belt was settled just so that they can get to the laser-blasting rescue of a princess.

The same applies to that 19-book epic you have been working on since you were five years old, *The 14ᵗʰ Kingdom of the Star of Äzü*. If you need to tell the story of the first 13 Kingdoms, then maybe that should be the book for you to write instead. If you need to write the history of the Wayfin people in their original song-like language, more power to you, but don't make it a requirement for the start of your story about the boy who would be king and the scepter he pulls from the stone unicorn's head.

Don't get me wrong. I'm not saying the history is not important to your story, I'm saying don't allow the history to overwhelm your story. There are Tolkien fans who want to read every bit of history he ever wrote about Middle-earth. But if he would have started with that, instead of it all becoming supplementally available later, no one ever would have finished The Hobbit, and none of the rest of it would ever have been published.

Also, remember, you can't just slap a two-hundred year old date on a story about a kid playing computer games and expect people to believe the story took place two-hundred years ago. An extreme example, I know, but sometimes writers try to shoehorn a story they've already written into a call for stories that will fit into a certain kind of anthology. It doesn't work.

And it irritates the editor.

Don't Write The Way You Speak

Okay, maybe this breaks my personal rule about poetic license and letting a writer tell a story the way they want to, but some of us are not as verbally eloquent as others. The advantage of writing is that we get to choose our words and try to minimize misunderstandings.

Writing is an art form, and I don't like to impinge upon the way someone expresses themselves, but I do want to point out that if the reader can't understand what you are saying you have not expressed yourself to them.

There is a fundamental disconnect between writing and speaking. We don't speak the same way we write. This is something I mention several times in this guide because it is true. Examples of these kinds of problems will show up in the things I've listed in this guide. Some of the things we say to each other every day, and understand perfectly when we hear them, can get lost when written down. Inflections we use in our voices don't translate well to the page. Misplaced modifiers, while usually perfectly obvious when used in a real-world context, don't translate well to the written word.

How do you directly translate from the spoken to the written word? You don't. Instead, you interpret the ideas into the new medium of communication in such a way that they will be understood correctly.

Many authors have used various solutions to try to overcome this obstacle when translating our spoken words to our written ones, some with more success than others. I want you to be aware of this issue so that when you read what you've written, you keep in mind whether someone else will know what you meant.

This does not always apply to dialog. You most certainly do want your characters to sound like real people, and even your narrator (the "voice" telling the story) sometimes needs to sound like a real person, but for the most part, most stories are written with an invisible narrator. (Meaning you don't know who is telling the story, and it doesn't matter, as long as they stay invisible.) When the narrator unintentionally comes to the front of the reader's imagination, it can be devastating to the story.

For example, here, now, I am "talking" to you. If you've known me for any length of time you may imagine you can hear my voice saying these words.

The words I am choosing to write here reflect my personality and my opinions as I discuss these issues, so I am fine with that. In fact, that's what I wanted. I wanted to sound friendly and helpful. But, if you go back to the snippet of a story example I gave for the manuscript formatting, I would hope you hear none of my voice in there at all. (If you have ever met an author who has a very distinctive voice, perhaps you have become blessed/cursed to always hear his/her voice when reading their works. That is not what I mean here.)

Let's look at the opening of the story I used as an example for formatting:

"I am here. Do you remember me?"
The gentle voice roused the old woman enough to flutter her eyelids. Rheumy, faded blue eyes searched the hospice room, but saw only the blur of subdued colors.
"Over here." The voice spoke with a rich, yet subtle accent.
The woman struggled to turn her head, her thin white hair wispy against the pillow. A large, dark maroon-colored blur contrasted against her normally bright room.
"Margie. Do you remember me?"
At the sound of her name, Margie felt the world come into focus in a way it hadn't in years. Her vision was still blurred, but she knew where she was and why she was here.

Did you hear any of my particular *right here, right now, I am talking to you* narrative voice in there? I hope not. My general snarky-ness would ruin that kind of story. Any part of the story that was not inside quotes is part of the narrative voice. If the narrative voice speaks colloquially, but it is not intended to be a character in the story, things can get messy.

Example:

"I am here. Do you remember me?"
The old lady finally woke her tired butt up. She was old. Really old. Like older than Betty White. She was looking around with her older than dirt eyes but only saw the red shape of a horse. Ha! Instead of being ascared, she was laughing, on account of she knew she was nuts. There weren't any horses in her hospital room! Which was green. And small. Green, cold, small and echo-ey. Plus she was alone.
"Over here." The horse sounded like a horse, if a horse could talk, you know with bbbbbbb sounds and snorts and stuff.
That weak old woman was too-too tired, but she turned her tired, tired, messed-up-hair covered head anyways so that she could try to see what was what. There was for sure a horse there! And it was for sure red!
"Margie. Do you remember me?"
Responding because of knowing her own name, because she was Margie, that old woman suddenly knew she was Margie. Alls of a sudden

she didn't feel drunk and stupid no more. Right? She knew who she was again!

Okay, maybe that's not too bad. (Yeah, right.) But maybe that could be an interesting way to write that story, too. And maybe that's not really the way you, or anyone you know, talks. But did you notice the narrative voice is now a character in its own right? You can't help but notice it. You know it's not the old lady narrating. You know it's not the horse. But you don't know who it is or what the heck kind of thing the voice is going to say next. And it is definitely no longer invisible. If the author had no intention of the narrator being a character in the story, then this story won't work.

A story should only be told like a campfire story when the writer wants it to sound like a campfire story. Otherwise, the narration can become too distracting.

Writing for entertainment is an art. It is the art of painting pictures and emotions in the reader's mind, of bringing a story to life. A very important part of the art form, one that many people fail to recognize (professionals included) is the ability to *not* put an image in someone's mind. The ability to hide a thought, an idea, a recognizable setting or object in plain sight of the reader, and not let them see it until you want them to, if at all, can be very important.

The narrative voice is one of those things. (See the section on **Narrative Voice** for more about this.)

Don't write the way you speak. Unless you intend for the reader to notice. Because they will.

Point of View

There are entire books written on this, so consider this a crash course that left out a bunch of stuff and mainly applies to fiction writing.

There are two separate things that can be referred to as the Point of View (POV). One is the POV of a particular character. Much like you or I, each character should have their own POV (whether or not you choose to present it to the reader in the story). This can be either their opinions, thoughts, and desires, or it can be what they physically should actually be able to see from where they currently are located, if they were real.

The other kind of POV is that of the overall story. This is called the narrative point of view. That POV is based upon who is telling the story and how it is presented. Sometimes it is a character, sometimes it is the narrator. Sometimes both. Sometimes it is the narrator telling the story from within the confines of a character's POV. See also **Narrative Voice.**

Problems arise when the reader can no longer tell whose POV is being used, whether that is a confusion between characters or between a character and the narrator. This can happen when seeing different characters' POVs presented too closely together. Many new writers jump back and forth from Andy's thoughts to Mary's thoughts in one paragraph, or sometimes even in one sentence. That is called head hopping, and it is the reason the 3rd person omniscient POV has fallen out of favor in the last few decades, to be replaced by the 3rd person limited POV and 1st person POV. You can read more on **Head Hopping** in the next section.

Another problem is when writers use multiple kinds of POVs within the same story. Mixing up characters' points of view is one thing but changing the overall point of view a story is written in can be disastrous. More on this in the section **Narrative Voice**.

Here's a rule that works: Stick with one type of POV per story. Stick with one character's POV per chapter, or at most one per scene.

Yes, there are writers who play with breaking that rule. I don't recommend it. Even when the author pulls it off successfully, there are readers who don't want to read a story written that way, and just because they were successful doesn't mean you will be, too.

Here is a **summary of the types of POVs** a story can be written from:

1st person – the story is told from a character's direct point of view. In other words, the narrator is a character in the story. Generally easy to spot as the narration is full of "I" and "my." Usually the character telling the story is the main character, but not always. The reader is limited to knowing and seeing the things the character knows and sees (or is willing to tell the reader).

I woke up, got up, brushed my teeth, combed my hair, and ate breakfast. I felt great! As I set out for work, I knew this was going to be a great day.

There are three subcategories for 1st person POV that I know of. Some will argue that these are still just 1st person POV, but I do think there is an argument for these styles to be distinct:

1st person peripheral – the story is told from a character's direct point of view, but it is actually about a different character. In other words, the narrator is not the main character. An example of this would be Dr. Watson being our narrator in the stories about Sherlock Holmes. A limitation of this is that the narrator does not always know where the main character has been or what they were doing.

1st person omniscient – much like the 1st person peripheral POV, the story is told from a character's direct point of view, but it is actually about a different character. The difference here is that the narrator knows everything the main character does. An example of this could have God as a narrator, or perhaps a story about a writer who is telling a story about characters they know everything about.

1st person omniscient limited– as with 1st person omniscient, the narrator would be able to "see" everything but would perhaps be limited to knowledge of events and not have knowledge or access to the thoughts or feelings of the character the story is about. Examples of this could be narrated by a lesser god-like figure, such as Death, who can see everything someone does, but does not know their thoughts, or perhaps a scientist who develops a device to be able to watch anything that has transpired in the past.

2nd person – the story is about "you." Kind of. This POV isn't used much. The narrative voice is telling you about, well…you. This was how the *Choose Your Own Adventure* books were written.

You woke up, got up, brushed your teeth, combed your hair, and ate breakfast. You felt great! You set out for work knowing this would be a great day.

3rd person –There are different kinds of 3rd person POVs, and there are times when authors have mixed them (with varying degrees of success). Generally, 3rd person POV can be identified by the use of "he" and "him" or "she" and "her" as personal pronouns. The different types of 3rd person POVs relate to the restrictions the author places upon the narrator

3rd person objective – the narrator tells the story in a neutral way. The narrator does not give the character's thoughts or feelings. Think of it as perhaps a story told like a history book.

He woke up that morning, brushed his teeth, combed his hair, and ate breakfast. Then he set out for work.

3rd person limited – the story follows a character from their point of view. The narrator is (generally) outside of the story and merely relating it to the reader. The reader is limited to knowing or seeing only the things the character they are following at that time does, witnesses, feels, or thinks. This does not mean there is only one character in the book the narrator follows, but the narrator only follows one character at a time. See **Head Hopping** for more.

He woke up this morning, got up, brushed his teeth, combed his hair, and ate breakfast. *I feel great,* he thought, and set out for work feeling sure this would be a great day.

3rd person omniscient – the narrator of the story knows (or seems to know) everything about the story, from the history of the store the character walked into to the thoughts in the shopkeeper's head.

He woke up this morning, got up, brushed his teeth, combed his hair, and ate breakfast. *I feel great,* he thought.

The bird that had awoken him was an English Sparrow that had recently escaped the clutches of his neighbor's cat. The cat had been rescued from an illegal farm that made fake Chinchilla fur coats. He didn't know it, but had that cat not been rescued, he would currently be wearing slippers made from its fur.

Unaware of any of that, he set out for work, feeling sure it would be a great day. But he was wrong, as we shall soon see!

This knowledge of everyone and everything possessed by a 3rd person omniscient narrator is what leads to the downfall of many a new author's story. Many of the stories we read as children were written in 3rd person omniscient, and many still are, but to be told effectively, the author needs to know how to handle the dreaded issue of head hopping.

For more on that, and other mistakes with POVs, please see **Head Hopping** and **Narrative Voice**.

Head Hopping

Head hopping is when an author writes the narrative of the story in a way that hops from the point of view of one character to another within a single scene. This may be in regards to what the characters are feeling, thinking, seeing, or sometimes even doing.

If not handled well, the story becomes nearly unreadable. This is why so few people want to read 3rd person omniscient stories today. This is also why one of the first bits of feedback you are likely to get on your story is "You are head hopping."

Here is an example from my (then in progress and still pretty rough) book, *A Whiskey Jack in a Murder of Crows*, before I was convinced by others that I needed to change it:

Jack renewed his interest in the smudge he had been cleaning from his table as the warden turned back to face the rest of the bar. He felt her gaze fall on him and sensed her approach. He sighed to himself. Cops unerringly seemed to know who didn't want to talk to them.

"May I join you?" Her voice was softer and gentler than it had been with Charlie and Merle.

Jack looked up at her and carefully tried to wear a friendly smile. "Uh... sure?" He gestured to the chair across the table from him and wished his voice hadn't made him sound so unsure of himself.

She carefully placed her hat at the edge of the table and seated herself with her back to Charlie and Merle, but Jack could tell she was watching them in the reflection off the windows.

"What can I do for you, uh... Warden Durante?" Jack did his best to keep his tone pleasant and even.

"Please, call me Archer."

"Of course, all your friends do." Jack's smile had faded enough that he knew it wouldn't convince anyone it was real, let alone the warden, so he let it go. "Are we friends?" he asked her.

She contemplated him for a long moment and the practiced smile left her face too. "That's what I came over here to find out." She leveled her gaze at him. "You smell like a cop."

An involuntary smile sprouted and he chuckled. "So do you."

She smiled back, but hers was cold. "But there is something not right about you. Want to tell me what it is?"

Her cold smile froze his into a grimace. "Not really. Why don't you tell me what's not right about me?" She didn't like his answer, and he noticed she had tensed up just as fast as he had. The air between them suddenly became very dangerous.

Archer stared coldly into his eyes. Her instincts had been right. There was something wrong about this man.

Notice I hopped from Jack's thoughts to Archer's and then back again. Although at the time I thought the transitions were smooth and clear, in hindsight I can see where the reader starts to lose track of who is having the thoughts. (Also note all of the **Eye Talk, Face Talk, Talk Talk**. Please see that section for more on that issue.)

Generally, if you start in a certain character's POV, you need to stay in it throughout the story. If you are going to head hop, you should only do it when switching to a new section or chapter, to make sure the reader knows the POV has changed and whose point of view you are representing. At least that is what you will be told.

Romance novels seem to head hop all the time. Thriller novels seem to change characters' POVs all the time. And it seems like there is always someone trying to write multiple 1st person POVs in the same story.

What should you do? You should know the types of POVs, and the problems with head hopping, and then you should make up your own mind. Know what the differences are, know what the rules are, understand them, and then find ways to break them that work. Study how other writers (successful ones, not the other writers in your college class) handle it in their books. Decide what techniques they used that worked, and which did not, and apply that knowledge for your own use.

Caution! Looking for examples in self-published books can be dangerous. Many of them have not been properly edited.

Above all, when you break the rules, you really do need to be open, receptive, and understanding if an editor or beta reader tells you it didn't work. Because maybe it only worked for you. Any maybe you want it to work for others.

The last thing you want to do is confuse your reader to the point that they give up on your story and maybe never read another one written by you. If you break these rules, do so in a very clear, understandable way that adds to the story, not one that detracts from it. See **Narrative Voice** for other **Point of View** mistakes to watch out for.

Narrative Voice

The narrative voice is the way the story is presented. There are many ways to present a story. Sometimes a story, or part of a story, is presented as a series of letters, newspaper articles, diaries, clips of audio recordings, or some other similar presentation of data. This is called an **epistolary narrative**. Examples would be *Dracula*, *Bridget Jones's Diary*, and *Carrie*.

Usually though, the narrative voice is presented from a point of view. (Please see **Point of View** for more on this.) This POV may or may not be that of a character involved in the story. The type of voice an author chooses to use to tell that point of view greatly affects nearly everything else about the story. It sets the tone, the mood, the seriousness and earnestness of the story, as well as things like "can the narrator be trusted to tell me the truth?" The Unreliable Narrator cannot be trusted to tell the truth and (probably) needs to be a character in the story to some extent, while a 3rd person objective POV would nearly always be expected to accurately relate the events of the story. The narrative voice the author chooses sets the stylistic precedent for the rest of the story.

This includes how that narrative voice "speaks."

Imagine the movie *A Christmas Story*. Can you hear Jean Shepherd's voice (the narrator's voice) in your head as he says, "You'll shoot your eye out!" It fits that story very well, doesn't it?

Now imagine everything else about the movie is the same, but Jean Shepherd's voice has been replaced by comedian Gilbert Gottfried's. (He did the voice of Iago in *Disney's Aladdin*, and the voice of the Aflac duck for a while.)

Does that change the tone of the story for you?

Remember that Robin Hood movie, where Kevin Costner kind of, sort of started out with an English accent but gave up ten minutes in and switched to American? How well does that work in a story where the narrative voice is 90% of the voice the reader "hears?"

If you start your narrative out as though it is being told by an 18th century Londoner, and later it fades into 20th century surfer dude, it ruins the effect of the narrative voice. (Unless, of course, that was exactly what you were going for!)

Those examples tend toward the idea of the narrator being a character. But that is not always the case. Going back to the idea of 3rd person POV stories, what kind of narrative voice do you expect as a reader?

(I'll take a guess and answer for you!) You expect words on the page that describe the characters, their thoughts and dialog, settings, actions, and anything else that needs to be told. You might think, as there is no one actually telling the story, that the narrative voice is kind of a blank, bland thing. But it is not. It is the glue that holds everything together and makes it look the way the author wants it to.

Let's imagine we are watching a play. Now imagine a background set, built up for the actors to perform in and around. How could those backgrounds have been created?

They could be actual buildings, being used on a street corner, outside, in a city block, like a movie set. This could make the play very realistic.

Or they could be artistic, stylized drawings of the buildings. Or poorly done (but with lots of heart!) finger paintings created by children. How would those settings affect your opinion of the play you are watching? Not quite so realistic anymore, but nice maybe? Sweet?

What if the sets were cardboard boxes, torn off in approximate shapes of buildings and then held together with duct tape? Or what if they were expensive sheets of brass and copper made to look like they were cardboard boxes, torn off in approximate shapes of buildings and then held together with duct tape?

Did those images change the play you were imagining happening around the set? Of course they did. And we never said anything about what the play was at all.

The background set has almost nothing to do with a play, and yet, it has everything to do with how we interpret it.

The narrative voice is much the same way.

The wind blew her hair. She pushed the horse forward, and she was gone.

The gentle breeze teased her tresses. She nudged her steed forward, and the woman faded away.

The air swirled, twisting and knotting her hair. She kicked the animal to make it move, and she vanished.

Those all say the same thing, but they all say it in different ways. As an author, choosing which of those ways (or any of a million other ways) to express the narrative voice sets a tone for the story. (See the section **Don't Write The Way You Speak** for more on this.) Just by choosing the correct words or descriptions, an author can make a fantasy story sound different than a science fiction story, or a western, or a murder mystery.

And it's all done with an invisible character called the narrative voice.

Once the narrative voice is established, writers have to be careful not to break away from it. Typically, a reader wouldn't expect, halfway through the story, for the previously invisible narration to suddenly act like one of the characters by using a description like:

It was a particularly beautiful sunset. One I quite enjoyed.

If that sentence ends up in the story, the narrator has somehow become an actual character. If that character hasn't been explained to the reader, its sudden appearance doesn't make any sense and ruins the flow and continuity of the story.

The sunset over the village was a sight to behold.
vs.
One would find the sunset over the village a sight to behold.

Note the narrative voice in the second example. The voice has a characteristic of dialog. When One talks about what One does or does not like, then One is usually talking about Oneself. Which means that the narrator is a person telling the story.

If that is the way you want to narrate your story, that's fine. But don't use that sentence halfway through the story that wasn't started that way. Just as with the previous example, suddenly using this style of narration in the middle of a story seems to turn the narrator into a character that the reader was not previously aware of. And it is confusing.

Unless you are doing something tricky, and really think you can pull it off, messing with the narrative voice after it has been established is bad juju.

Point of view and vocabulary usage aren't the only things that comprise the narrative voice. The tense used can affect the story just as much, not only in whether the whole story took place in the past, but also in the way the story feels when you read it.

There are many choices to make in the narrative voice when you are establishing it in a story, and each of them will affect the story as a whole. Be deliberate in your choices and use them in a consistent manner that benefits your story rather than detracts from it.

Some of the mistakes I have seen are:

—**Writing the story in 1st person POV and not telling the reader a name, sex, or any description of the main character (who is the narrator).** While this can be done on purpose (and I have done it on purpose), it causes a stress for the reader as they to try to figure out who the main character is. See the section on **Location/Setting**, specifically the idea of **white room syndrome**, and apply that to the main character. The reader has nothing to work with when imagining the character.

—**Writing a story in 1st person POV and then moving beyond the confines of the story.** For example, the story is a message in a bottle. The reader is basically reading a diary of what the main character has gone through. Then the main character puts the story in the bottle, sends it off, and someone finds it, allowing us, the readers, to read it. But then, somehow, without a good way of explaining how it is possible, we, the readers, get the *rest* of the story of what happened *after* the story was put into the bottle.

A good reason to know more would be a follow up expedition that found the body, possibly with more diary pages. But some writers forget to do this. In fact, some writers continue the story in 1st person POV even *after* we are out of diary pages.

This completely ruins the suspension of disbelief for me.

—**Remember, in the 1st person POV, the main character generally can't die** without the story having been conveyed through some form of vessel, such as the aforementioned diary. This "inability" to die can prevent tension for some readers. Sometimes writers ignore this, kill the character, and keep on telling the story from the ghost's point of view.

—**Remember, in the 1st person POV, to tread lightly around the idea of who the character is telling the story to, and how they are communicating it.** Most authors ignore this, and most readers are okay with ignoring it for the sake of the story, but if the author messes that part of the story up, it will quickly fall apart.

—**Late entry POVs, or adding a new point of view late in the story.** In a sweeping epic like George R.R. Martin's *A Song of Ice and Fire*, POVs die out and are replaced all the time, but most of us don't write that way. Most of us write a story about a very few characters, with other characters tagging along for support.

If I write a book about a little girl training to be an Olympic gymnast, and you are thoroughly engrossed in her story, but then about halfway through, I switch to telling the story of an old man who owns a restaurant, you are going to be confused. If I stay with the old man, and don't come back to the girl, you are going to be upset.

If I switched to the girl's mother's POV, you may be more understanding. You are getting a different perspective on the story of the girl. But a random old man? At that point the reader will wonder who or what is the story about? Will those story lines collide? If so, why didn't I know about the old man right from the beginning of the book?

This can apply to many different things: adding a villain out of the blue, suddenly bringing in a hero who can solve all the problems, or the appearance of an ex-girlfriend who had never been mentioned in the first 150 pages of the book.

These kinds of things feel like a betrayal to the reader, like the author wasn't up front about what the story was about, or the author didn't think the story through, so a deus ex machina was created to save the ending. (A *deus ex machina* is a contrived ending that resolves an impossible situation. See the section on **deus ex machina** for a full explanation.)

—While the rest of the story is written in 3ʳᵈ person limited point of view, slipping into 3rd person omniscient just for a moment, the narrator points out something that the character didn't or couldn't see. This is the one most new writers get called out on.

Gem ran into the forest at full speed, never seeing the bear trap her foot missed by mere inches.

I have also seen this mistake made in the 1ˢᵗ person POV, but not as often as writers tend to notice the character can't see things they didn't see.

I ran into the forest at full speed, my feet barely missing the unseen, invisible bear traps in the dark.

This can also apply to things the characters do. It makes no sense for them to know what they don't know.

Sammy didn't notice a smirk had crossed her face as she hid in the closet and watched them dance.

If Sammy didn't notice it, and no one else is there to see it, who noticed it? Again, this would be slipping into the omniscient POV, and writers have even done it while writing from 1ˢᵗ person POV.

—While the rest of the story is written in 3ʳᵈ person limited point of view, the main character (focus of the POV) leaves the room, but the narrative stays to describe the reactions of the people still in the room. Again, this is slipping into the 3rd person omniscient POV.

I hate these people, Jake thought as he tossed back the last of his beer. Standing, he felt the anger in him rise up uncontrollably. He slammed the mug down on the bar as hard as he could. Feeling the shards of breaking glass slicing sharply into his hand, he bellowed. "To heck with you all!"
People all around the bar stopped and stared at him.
Whatever, he thought, and grabbed his white suede jacket, heedless of the blood flowing onto it.
Jake kicked the door open on his way out.
A man in red was the first to say anything after Jake left. "Did he say to *heck* with us?"
"Yeah," said a waitress who had stopped in the middle of the floor, tray of beer still in hand. "And he must be pissed, 'cause that's a thousand-dollar jacket!"

So here is the problem with that last example: If we've been following Jake the whole story, why didn't we follow him out the door, too? Why the sudden switch to 3rd person omniscient instead of 3rd person limited?

I think the last two problems I mentioned can be attributed to watching movies and television, which is a completely different medium. In those, the viewer is a non-participating observer and what is observed is controlled by the camera. Cameras often show us the dangers that characters aren't aware of because it builds the suspense for the viewer.

After seeing it visualized in so many stories, we writers begin to include it in our stories. Is this a bad thing? Sometimes, sometimes not. It depends upon the rules we have set for our narrative. If the narrator is supposed to be focused on Jake and his feelings and point of view, why step out of that for only one or two sentences to try to squeeze in some tiny tidbit of information that probably doesn't add anything to the story?

If that little part was so important, you should be able to find a way to present it within the rules you have set for yourself.

Why set those rules at all, you might ask?

For the reader. So they can follow your story and know what to expect. So they can spend their energy understanding and enjoying the story, not trying to figure out what you meant.

People often say (most) movies are filmed from the 3rd person point of view, but they generally are not. Generally, a movie is filmed from the viewer's point of view. While similar to various 3rd person POVs, it is different. It is more like a limited omniscient POV, but then there is no guarantee that a viewer will see what the camera saw, even when their POV is restricted to be within that. Video is a very different medium, and, like attempting to translate our spoken language into written language, some things don't translate well.

For more on the Narrative Voice, please see the sections **Don't Write the Way You Speak**, **Point of View**, **Head Hopping**, **Shifting Tenses**, **The Passive Voice**, and **The Generic Pronoun**.

Shifting Tenses

Past, present, and future tenses affect the tone, and therefore the feel, of your story in subtle ways. The tense you write in is part of the narrative voice, and a part of your story, and as such needs to be established early on. Also, it needs to be consistent, so you don't confuse your reader.

Generally, a story needs to stay in the tense it starts in. The main exception being flashbacks, or points in the story where you are revealing events that happened prior to the current events in the story. You can change tenses in a story, but you need to be certain that the reader is aware of what you are doing. This especially applies during flashbacks.

In writing, the change of tense from present to past is typically done along with scene or chapter breaks. The break in the story clues the reader that something is going to be different now. And then hints in the narrative, which usually include a change in tense, are used to allow the reader to recognize the time shift.

Television shows and movies often use a technique of showing the picture in a haze or a fog to let the viewer know that the story is now in a flashback, a memory, or a dream. Without that visual cue, the viewers could easily get lost or confused. The absence of the use of this technique is often intentional, such as to catch viewers off guard in horror movies or making dreams seem real until they are revealed to be only dreams.

This same technique, not telling the reader a scene is a dream, is something many new writers attempt and fail at.

Not that it can't be done successfully, but the written word is a different media than motion pictures. It takes more effort on the part of the reader to understand the story. If the reader doesn't like the story, or they keep getting confused, they will stop putting in the effort. This is a big difference in the mediums.

One of the ways to make a reader stop reading is to betray their confidence. When a writer creates a dream sequence, or some other falsehood of story events, the reader often feels cheated once that falsehood is finally revealed. Sometimes this is exactly the effect the writer wants, but if it is done poorly, this type of storytelling upsets the reader and ruins the story for them.

Sometimes this isn't intentional, and that's where the real problems come in.

Mom had been dead for over twenty years, but seeing my daughter acting all grown up brought back so many memories. I watched her take the cake out of the oven. Mom poked it with a toothpick to make sure it was done. She sat it on top of the stove and looked at me proudly.

In the above example, you may have realized that "she" and "her" referred to "my daughter" and that the one sentence about "Mom" was a flashback. I could see how someone could consider that a stylistic form of writing, but it was confusing. What if the whole story were written like that? Would you get tired of trying to figure out whether the author was referring to Mom or the daughter every time?

What if the memories were constantly intermixed this way, but weren't consistently related to Mom and the daughter?

Finally ready to go, I put on my tennis shoes. Dad wore slippers. The morning was warm, bright, and welcoming as I stepped out onto the stoop and began stretching. Mom said it was a wonder he didn't kill himself. Jogging with him was fun. I went out into the hall, nodding at

Mrs. Greely, and then my shoes crunched gravel as I dodged the lunch hour traffic.

Notice how the flashback in this example confuses everything. We aren't sure which characters are present or what the location is, and then even the time of day gets confused. This makes the story terribly difficult to follow.

I know this example is a bit extreme, but it is based on real examples I have seen more than once. Things like flashbacks and memories need to be carefully set apart so that readers can easily understand what is going on.

Finally ready to go, I put on my tennis shoes.
Dad had always worn slippers.
I had a quick memory of stepping out onto the door stoop at my parent's home. The morning had been warm, bright, and welcoming as I had begun stretching. Mom was ranting that it was a wonder my dad didn't kill himself.
Jogging with him had always been fun.
I went out into the hall, nodding at Mrs. Greely as I passed, and then my shoes crunched gravel as I dodged the lunch hour traffic.

Notice I clearly established everything that wasn't happening *right now* as something in the past. That makes everything much easier to follow for the reader. A big part of how I wrote everything as in the past was by shifting tenses. Things that already happened were reported in past tense, things happening *now* were in present tense, but I also separated out the time differently with new paragraphs to add yet another clue for the reader.

Some stories are written entirely in the past tense. While this is fine, a flashback can become very confusing if the whole story is already a flashback. I have read stories written in the past tense that went on to have a flashback, while already in a flashback. This can be very confusing for the reader, and sometimes even the writer. (For more on flashbacks, see **Continuity Errors Matter** and **Scene Breaks**.)

In many ways, the narrative voice is established by the tense the author uses to tell the story. One of the problems inexperienced writers have with shifting tenses is that they are often not aware they are doing it. This issue can carry on beyond timeline events and become a problem with the narrative voice itself.

Jorge threw the knife at her chest. She had caught it and thrown it back. He was dodging in the nick of time, but catching his foot on the leg of the table, he had fallen down. Her laughing voice haunted his dreams as she loomed over him, preparing to have come in for the kill. It was all over for Jorge.

It certainly was all over for Jorge. At least as far as I was concerned. I can't read that mess, and I doubt you can for long either.

Notice how tenses shifted from past to present. That could be written either as one or the other but mixing them ruins it. (Okay, maybe it was ruined to start with, but let's stay on point here.) On top of the shifting tense, the phrase "haunted his dreams" messes everything up. Does that mean he lives on, and this is only a memory? Or is it just a really terrible use of a cliché? (See **Less Filling** for more on **Clichés**.)

Jorge had thrown the knife at her chest. She had caught it and thrown it back. He dodged but had caught his foot on the leg of the table and fallen down. Her laughing voice had haunted him as she had loomed over him, coming in for the kill. It was all over for Jorge.

That one is okay. It's not good, as it is all past tense, specifically, it is in past perfect tense, which removes a lot of the immediacy for the reader. Writing in the simple past tense makes the scene much more enjoyable, and it is how many things we read are written.

Jorge threw the knife at her chest. She caught it and threw it back. He dodged but caught his foot on the leg of the table and fell. Her laughing voice was haunting as she loomed over him, coming in for the kill. It was all over for Jorge.

There are also the past continuous and past perfect continuous tenses to contend with. Those would look something like this:

Jorge was throwing the knife at her chest. She was catching it and throwing it back.

and

Jorge had been throwing the knife at her chest. She had been catching it and throwing it back.

When you use tenses like those, it should be limited and used for a reason. Writing entire stories in those tenses don't work well. Now, for posterity purposes, I am going to touch on what present tense means. It means the action is happening right now. However, as with past tense, there are four different kinds of present tense. Present simple, present continuous, present perfect, and present perfect continuous.

I don't want to go into all of these, as that is a whole English class as far as I am concerned, but the fact that there are four of each shows you how a writer can tend to get confused and slip back and forth between some of them.

If you are not familiar with them, please look them up and become familiar with them so that you can avoid confusing mistakes.

Why are there so many tenses? Because we use all of them to describe the things around us. We need to be able to communicate how and when things happened in relation to one another.

In that sense, we frequently mix tenses in order to correctly communicate what we are trying to say. But when we incorrectly mix the tenses, things get confusing. For a writer, this happens when we establish the tense we are going to write the story in, but then incorrectly shift tenses to convey the relationship of events to one another.

Here is that example again, in present continuous tense. I have seen stories written in this tense, and it is very difficult to read.

Jorge is throwing the knife at her chest. She is catching it and throwing it back. He is dodging but catching his foot on the leg of the table and falling down. Her laughing voice is haunting him as she is looming over him, coming in for the kill. It is all over for Jorge.

Stories can and have been told in this tense (not enjoyably, in my opinion), but hopefully this example helps you to see how some writers can begin to get confused and mix the tenses together improperly. Used properly, switching to this tense can create a "frozen in time" moment, like Neo dodging the bullet in *The Matrix*, but you don't want to stay with that feeling of being in that frozen moment for the entire story.

The best way to avoid the problem of accidentally shifting tenses is to understand what tense you are writing your story in and stay with it.

Please see **Because "As" is Also…** for more on the use of *as*.

The Passive Voice

In the last few years, writers have heard a lot about the passive voice. One of the problems many of us face in avoiding it is that we grew up reading books written in passive voice, so it seems natural to write that way for us.

Basically, the argument against the passive voice is this: it's not as exciting to read.

Generally, that is true, but many people tend to treat this like a dog with a toy. Once they have it in their teeth, they won't let go.

While I certainly don't recommend always writing in passive voice, it's silly to think that you should never use it. Like any part of our language, it exists for a reason, and there are times to use it. People don't usually continue using parts of the language that have no purpose.

Identifying it is a difficult undertaking for many and there have been several methods offered up, like looking for the words *was* or *by*, or pretending zombies are involved. (Yeah. That last one is not mine, and I don't know where to give credit, so look that one up on your own. For some people that one is helpful.)

I find it easiest to think of the passive voice as the opposite of the active voice. The difference basically breaks down to whether the subject of the sentence is acting or being acted upon.

The dog bit the postman.

This is active voice. The dog did something. It was being active.

The postman was bitten by the dog.

This is passive voice. The postman was not being active. He didn't do anything. Something was done to him.

The difference between the two sentence is that the subject of the sentence was being active instead of being acted upon. Notice the word *was* and the word *by* in the second example. That is why people look for those when trying to identify the passive voice.

Generally, you do want to avoid the passive voice, as the use of the active voice makes your story more engaging, especially in action scenes, but please don't think you have to get rid of the passive voice entirely. It does have its uses.

Sometimes it just doesn't make much sense to use the active voice. Sometimes the passive voice serves the purpose of leaving out unknown subjects or emphasizing the subject being acted upon:

The church was built in the Edwardian Era.

This sentence emphasized the church and when it was built but downplays who built it. Maybe we don't know who did it, or maybe we don't want to say. We could say:

Someone built the church in the Edwardian Era.

Although this is no longer the passive voice, notice how this sentence structure puts the emphasis on *someone* and makes you curious about who the someone is. That completely changes the intent of the sentence.

Here are some times when using the passive voice is appropriate:

—When the person/thing performing the action is unknown.
—When the person/thing performing the action is unimportant.
—When the person/thing performing the action is abstract.
—When the person/thing performing the action needs to be de-emphasized.

—When the person/thing being acted upon is most important.

The use of words that modify the verb can help clue you in that the passive voice is being used. Some of them are:

are, am, been, being, by, of, is, was, were

To get rid of the passive voice, a sentence generally needs to be restructured in a way that changes the subject of the sentence to be active instead of acted upon.

On a side note, the use of past tense is often considered use of the passive voice. It is not. People who believe this can fall into the trap of writing in the present continuous tense in an attempt to avoid the passive voice. Please see the section on **Shifting Tenses** for more on that.

Distinguishing Narration From Thoughts And Messages

When reading, it can sometimes be tough to tell which ideas are the narrator's and which are a character's. While it is generally not an issue with a 1st or 2nd person point of view story, this becomes important when writing in 3rd person points of view. (See the sections on **Point of View**, **Head Hopping**, and **Narrative Voice** for more.)

There are two types of speech and thoughts: direct and indirect.

In dialog we write a direct statement like this:

"I love you," he said.

This tells us the character spoke these words out loud.

An indirect dialog statement would be:

He said he loved her.

The same applies to thoughts. A generally accepted way to indicate direct thoughts is simply to italicize the thoughts of the characters, rather than put them in quotes as you would dialog.

I need to hurry, **she thought,** ***or I'll be late!***

This is a common enough convention that using quotation marks to indicate thoughts will most likely confuse readers. (See **Thoughts Or Spoken Words?** for more on this.)

"I need to hurry," she thought, "or I'll be late!"

Generally, readers will interpret this as spoken aloud, even if the character is alone and even if the dialog tag is "she thought."

Another way of showing thoughts is by including them in the narration, as indirect thoughts.

She knew she had to hurry, or she would be late.
or
She thought she would be late, so she hurried.

When done this way, italics are not needed, and would actually confuse the situation.

Remember, not all thoughts have to be given directly. In fact, writing all of a character's thoughts directly can lead to a strange story. However, you do need an indication for the reader when you are switching from narration to thoughts, just as when you are switching to dialog. Failing to clue your reader in will leave them confused and make your story difficult to read. Here is an example of what I mean:

The mountains at the end of the valley were little more than hills. They look like anthills. The green on them was lush and reminded her of home, but the color is all wrong. They should be brown this time of year. I miss home.

Knowing what point I was trying to make, I am sure you can pick out the narration from the thoughts, but if you hadn't known I was switching back and forth, and thought that was all going to be narration, how comprehendible would that paragraph be to you?

Even adding in italics doesn't fix the problem of mixing direct thoughts into the narration. The thoughts, at some point, need to be tagged, just as dialog does, with pronouns and identifiers. Treat a character's thoughts as a new idea that gets its own sentence to keep them separate and identifiable.

This also applies to things like notes, newspaper articles, television reports, or anything else that should be separated out from the narrative voice. If those things don't have their own independent ideas presented as such, they unintentionally blend into the narrative creating confusion.

Jedidiah stumbled exhaustedly up the front stairs to his house as the sun set. He picked up the newspaper that had been delivered after he'd left for work and continued on into the bathroom for his first restroom break of the day. Two homes in Bakersfield burned down. Firefighters responded within minutes but were unable to control the blaze. Jedidiah finished his business and began thinking about dinner.

Notice how jarring the information from the newspaper was to the narrative of the story. It almost sounds like Jedidiah had a really rough time in the bathroom, and it almost sounds like the fire was part of his day. And it doesn't sound like he's reading the newspaper.

It is just as important to separate written things out from the narrative as it is thoughts, and it is just as simple.

Jedidiah stumbled exhaustedly up the front stairs to his house as the sun set. He picked up the newspaper that had been delivered after he'd left for work and continued on into the bathroom for his first restroom break of the day. *Two homes in Bakersfield burned down. Firefighters responded within minutes but were unable to control the blaze.* **Jedidiah finished his business and began thinking about dinner.**

The above is an example of a style I have seen several times, and a way I have encountered the mistake before. Personally, I would rather separate the newspaper headlines out into their own paragraph, give them a tag, and then change their wording, and maybe even their font, to sound more like actual headlines. This would let you know for sure Jedidiah was reading and not a part of the action.

Jedidiah stumbled exhaustedly up the front stairs to his house as the sun set. He picked up the newspaper that had been delivered after he'd left for work and continued on into the bathroom for his first restroom break of the day.
The headlines were discouraging.
TWO HOMES BURN IN BAKERSFIELD. FIREFIGHTERS UNABLE TO CONTROL BLAZE.
Jedidiah finished his business and began thinking about dinner.

Scene Breaks

Scene breaks are something many writers don't think about—at first. Then they start to think about them a lot. Scene breaks can represent many different things. The passage of time, a change of viewpoint, a change of setting, or just a break in the action so the reader can catch their mental breath. (See **Marking Scene Breaks** for more information on how to signify them.)

Occasionally I encounter a writer who doesn't use them at all. Depending upon the story, that can be all right, but imagine reading a novel with no chapters. There is never a natural break to pause and put the book down. While some people would think that's a great idea, as it is often taught that the writer always wants to keep the reader engaged, it simply isn't true. It's exhausting for the reader. (See also **White Space**.)

If you find yourself using phrases like "Later," "Shortly thereafter," or "A short time later," you probably need to consider using a scene break to indicate the passage of time instead. It isn't always necessary, but it needs to be considered. The use of those phrases can be stylistic. They can make your story feel like an old-fashioned fairy tale. But if that is not your intention, or if you are using them too often, it can make your writing feel stilted or outdated.

Scene breaks are also useful for avoiding head hopping. (See the section on **Head Hopping** for more information.) When you find you need to write another character's point of view, you should use a scene break to let the reader know something has changed, then show them there is a new point of view being used.

A change of setting can be either with a passage of time, as in when a character falls asleep and wakes up, or a change in location. If a character is going home from work, you might want to follow along with them in the car from one place to another. If you want to skip the boring car ride, but still stay with the character, it can be done with or without a scene break. It's not hard to say something like:

Charlie left work, drove home, and plopped down on the couch.

This was a quick scene change with minimal fuss that didn't need a scene break. It could also have been done with a scene break:

Charlie left work at exactly five o'clock.

\#

Dropping onto the couch just in time to see the news, Charlie was glad to be home.

Either way works fine, and you should use whatever best fits your story.

Changing settings with different groups of characters takes a bit more finesse. If you aren't using scene breaks, it can become very confusing as to where the story is taking place and which character(s) the reader is following. It can be done, but it can also be done so poorly as to ruin the story.

"Goodnight," Charlie said to the night guard, who was just coming on duty.

"Goodnight," the guard answered.

Mary walked up to the barista and asked for a latte. It was going to be a long night for her.

Charlie unlocked his car and got in.

Mary paced impatiently while waiting.

The car started hard, but finally turned over.

"Hi, Mom!" Billy ran into the kitchen and gave Nancy a big hug. Tears formed in her eyes as she squeezed his little body tight.

"Did you miss me?"

"You know I did!"

Traffic was terrible, and Charlie had a hard time even getting out of the parking lot.

The coffee was terrible too, and Mary wished she hadn't stopped at all.

As you can see, this seems like you can follow it at first, but then it becomes a chore to keep up with it, and the different places and people start to blend into one. The advantage this example has is that it is short, and you know I am jumping around because I told you I was going to. As scenes get longer, it is harder to keep things straight in your mind. If I spend longer than a sentence or two with each character, suddenly it becomes jarring when I do switch.

The only time I would attempt something like this example is if I felt it was of the utmost importance that the readers know what each character was doing at that exact moment, and I definitely wouldn't try to maintain it for long.

Each scene, the one with Charlie, the one with Mary, and the one with Billy and Nancy, deserves to have its own paragraph, at the very minimum, so that the reader can keep the characters, the settings, and the actions organized in their mind as they read. The longer each scene is, the more jarring it is for the reader to suddenly be switched to the next one without warning.

New Idea, New Paragraph

Just as there are run-on sentences, there are run-on paragraphs. Many people who have had a story edited by me have seen "new idea, new paragraph" repeated so many times I am sure they grew to hate it. I sometimes consider setting that phrase up as a hot key macro so that I can enter it with a single keystroke, but the truth is I always need to give an explanation with it anyway.

New paragraphs should occur when there is a new action, new idea, new description, a new person speaking, etc. Some paragraphs can be pages long. Some can be one word (for emphasis).

Paragraphs are a grouping of sentences arranged by a similarity of ideas. When the idea changes too much, you need a new paragraph. Some things can stay together, like a mechanic using tools while talking about dinner, because they are simultaneous, but most things don't happen at the same time. Even if they do, you need to pull the reader's attention back and forth between them to keep everything clear and in focus.

A common mistake is not using a new paragraph when switching from the description of something to an action.

Example:

It was a beautiful sunset, full of golden hues fading into orange and then darkening into purple. The sky above, filled with dark clouds, made the deepest purple Hugh had ever seen. The arrow missed his head by inches. With a start, Hugh leaped for his horse and kicked it into action, racing for the safety of the castle.

There should have been a break for a new paragraph as soon as the description ended and the action began:

It was a beautiful sunset, full of golden hues fading into orange and then darkening into purple. The sky above, filled with dark clouds, made the deepest purple Hugh had ever seen.
The arrow missed his head by inches.
With a start, Hugh leaped for his horse and kicked it into action, racing for the safety of the castle.

Just as a sentence is comprised of like ideas, so is a paragraph, and when you begin an unrelated idea (or one not closely enough related) you need to move on to the next paragraph.
You wouldn't write (or at least I hope you wouldn't!):

Margie had to babysit, and the rocks the astronauts found on the moon were given away as tokens of goodwill.

The ideas are just too disparate. (Unless you had found some way to work that into the story, then good for you!)
In the same vein, you shouldn't leave dissimilar ideas in the same paragraph:

Margie had to babysit. It was Tuesday and Joey always had to watch the kids on Tuesdays. The smell of the pumpkin pie on Thanksgiving was what she lived for. Joey needed new brakes on his car.

This is an extreme example to try to make my point. Why would those sentences ever even be near each other in a story? Hopefully they wouldn't
Here is an example that is more realistic:

Jenny folded the laundry and carried the basket of clean clothes up to her room. After putting them away, she sat on the corner of her bed and cried.
A car pulled into the driveway and caught her attention. The driver got out, and Jenny's heart skipped a beat.
Could it be…?

In the first paragraph, I am describing Jenny's actions. In the second, I am describing something that happens that has nothing to do with what Jenny was doing. In the third, I hint at Jenny's thought reaction to the thing that happened. Her thought is a new action and has no effect upon, and is not part of, the other thing that happened.

In each paragraph something new, different, and separate happens, so I break them apart into new paragraphs on their own.

Did the paragraphs need to be broken up that way? Maybe. It depends upon how you write them, and how closely related you make the ideas appear.

Here is an example where I keep them all in the same paragraph, because they become interrelated.

Jenny folded Marshall's clean clothes and carried them up to the bedroom, wondering if she would ever see him again. As she put socks in the drawer, she heard the sound of his car in the driveway. Could it be...?

Okay, not perfect, but hopefully you get the idea. The more closely related you can make the ideas, the better they work together in one paragraph. Personally, I like to break them up more than that. (For more on why, see the section on **White Space**.)

Here are some examples of new ideas that need to be broken off into new paragraphs:

—**Anytime a new character speaks:** You don't want multiple characters speaking in a single paragraph unless you are trying to show a bunch of people talking over each other.

—**Anytime a new character acts while a different character is speaking:** When a character is speaking, and another character speaks, interrupts, or does something, those actions need to be broken off into a separate paragraph, unless you are very carefully handling the way you show it in the narrative. See **Breaking Up Speech With Actions** for more on that.

—**If there is a change in time:** If you have a passage of time, you must be very clear about it. Breaking the time change off into a new paragraph of its own helps make it stand out.

—**When you contrast ideas:** If you write two sentences about why ceramic is better than steel, then you decide to write two more sentences about why steel might be better after all, they usually work best in separate paragraphs as, while related, they are contradictory ideas.

—**If there is a change in action:** If the action is closely related, you may not need a new paragraph. Such as the above example where Jenny is doing laundry. Washing clothes, drying clothes, folding clothes, and putting away clothes could all be considered parts of the same action. But what if we started with cleaning house instead of doing laundry? We could say doing laundry, making the beds, dusting, sweeping, mopping, and doing the dishes are all part of cleaning house, and then keep them all in the same paragraph.

But if we start out by saying Jenny is cleaning the house, and then move into describing the washing and folding of jeans, t-shirts, and socks, we have changed the focus of our idea.

If we start with the larger action and then focus in upon the smaller ones, the ideas, while related, have changed and we need to break off into a new paragraph.

Sometimes it's a lot more obvious:

Carol finished writing her essay, stood up, stretched, and decided to make dinner.

She was using scissors to cut the lettuce for a Caesar salad when the cat ran in.

Carol knelt to pet her beloved kitty. It hadn't been home for two days.

"Where have you been, Mr. Tinky?" she asked, relief heavy in her voice.

The cat meowed as if it understood.

Picking Mr. Tinky up, Carol carried him back to the living room so she could hold and cuddle him.

Another extreme example, I know, but notice how I started a new paragraph with each new action that wasn't closely enough related to the previous.

—Sometimes just because: Reading is exhausting. If you find you have a paragraph that is verging on being the length of the entire page, you might want to break it up simply to give the reader a rest. For more on why, see the section on **White Space**.

Eye Talk, Face Talk, Talk Talk

At first, everything seems all right. You are describing what your characters are doing as they talk or listen to each other. But soon, an editor points out that your characters glanced, glared, stared, winked, or rolled their eyes at each other twenty times in one chapter. That's what I call **Eye Talk**.

Then you realize your characters had also been glaring, leering, grimacing, grinning, smiling, smirking, and frowning so much that the muscles of their faces should have spasmed and locked up by now. That's what I call **Face Talk**.

I am guilty of both of these and nearly always have to go back and take out this stuff. My characters tend to look down, look up, look at, look off…the list goes on. I have to work to get back to the plain old Talk Talk that should have been there in the first place.

It's fine for characters to do any or all of that stuff but keep a close watch on how often they do it. They don't need to glance sideways at each other every time they speak. Your characters do not need to smile repeatedly to show they are not angry. If they stare too much, you readers might start to wonder if it's a contest of wills. In fact, if any of these are used more than once or twice (maybe three times) in the entire book, readers will start to notice.

In other sections I mention writing tools that need to be used invisibly. Overuse pulls these actions out into the spotlight and makes them stand out. No longer invisible, they begin losing effectiveness and become counterproductive by distracting from the story.

This mistake often accompanies the problem of **Impossible Dialog Tags**, where characters do things like chuckle words at each other. Even if you are not incorrectly using words like giggled, sighed, snorted, and breathed as dialog tags, be sure you are not overusing them as conversation fillers.

People have mercilessly made fun of E. L. James and Stephenie Meyer for these sorts of things. While it may be true that, as successful authors, they were laughing all the way to the bank, I suspect the comments cut deeply. If you are fortunate enough to write something as popular as their stories, you may not want to receive the same criticisms.

In case you missed it, go back to the section on **Head Hopping** and read the uncorrected excerpt from my book *A Whiskey Jack in a Murder of Crows* for an example of too much Eye Talk and Face Talk.

And please note; I've learned from those mistakes. (I hope.)

Talking Heads

Talking heads are characters who just talk to each other. They don't do anything. Like television news station anchors. They just talk. Nothing happens.

Some writers have been known to go on for pages with just two people talking and nothing happening. This becomes boring very quickly. Sometimes entire books have been written this way.

This is what a lot of stage plays are like. Two people talking, nothing happening. Why do you think children hate plays? Nothing happens.

It is very rare that a conversation will be worthy of forgoing all action. It's even more rare that a character needs to deliver an extensive soliloquy. Be careful if you think you need to do this.

Also, beware of the info dump. This much conversation is likely nothing more than an extended info dump. (See **As You Know, Bob… It's An Info Dump** for more on this.)

Misplaced Modifiers

Misplaced modifiers are a problem nearly all writers stumble over from time to time. Experience will make those mistakes happen less often, but they occasionally happen anyway. Part of it goes back to our speech patterns as compared to our formal writing patterns. (Please see **Don't Write the Way You Speak** for more on this idea.) But the larger problem I have seen is with newer writers who think they are writing elegantly (my word, not theirs) when they are actually just being confusing.

There are different kinds of modifiers, therefore there are different kinds of misplaced modifiers. Modifiers can be words, phrases, or clauses that modify other words. A misplaced modifier is one that is improperly placed in the sentence so that it either modifies the wrong word or it is unclear what it is modifying.

A simple example would be:

He drank his iced glass of tea.

Most readers will instantly think that meant iced tea, not iced glass, but it says iced glass, so that is what it means.

He drank his mug of iced beer.

Although mugs are often frosted or iced, beer itself usually isn't.
A more complex example is the famous joke:

I knew a man with a wooden leg named Smith.
What was the name of his other leg?

The joke is that we know the man's name is Smith, but the misplaced modifier has made it appear that the wooden leg is named Smith.
Another old joke:

I bought the car from a salesman with a comb-over.

Here the problem becomes does the salesman have a comb-over, or was that the currency used to pay for the car?
How do you correct those sentences?

I knew a man named Smith who had a wooden leg.
or
I knew a man who had a wooden leg. The man's name was Smith.
or
I knew a man, with a wooden leg, named Smith.

and

The salesman I bought the car from had a comb-over.
or
I bought the car from a salesman who had a comb-over.

These problems tend to arise from writing and speaking informally and can usually be recognized by a proofreader even when the author has missed them. More complicated examples can be more difficult to spot.

"Hello, Dear," John said, kissing her in his underwear as she walked in the door. Mary kissed him back halfheartedly closing the door behind her.
Exhausted, she sat with one arm crossed over the other on a barstool. She sighed.
Feeling at home for the first time in weeks in that office had left her vulnerable to the interns' machinations all around the board room.

There are several misplaced modifiers in that example that make the entire passage very confusing. Was she in John's underwear? Did she halfheartedly kiss him or halfheartedly close the door? How exactly did she sit on that barstool? She feels at home...in the office? While at home? And what did the interns leave all around the board room?

You can (mostly) read this passage and understand what is going on, but at the same time, it is a mess. Sometimes writers don't realize that they are blending their descriptions together. It is better to write short, clear, concise sentences that get the meaning across accurately than it is to muck about with complex sentences that don't make sense.

Grabbing his wallet, Frank ran as fast as he could, racing past the clueless guard playing Cotton Candy Critters on his smartphone and kicking open the back door.

The above modifying clause, at the end of the sentence, is too far away from the subject it is meant to be associated with and too close to one it is not, creating confusion. It reads as thought the guard is playing on his phone and kicking open the door instead of Frank kicking open the door.
Another common type of misplaced modifier is the dangling modifier. This is one that doesn't have anything to point at.

Mary was tired. Trying to sleep, the curtains were pulled tight and the lights turned off.

There is no subject in the second sentence. We don't know who was trying to sleep, or who closed the curtains and turned off the lights. Some will argue that the previous sentence may have answered those questions, and that it was Mary, but that still doesn't make the second sentence correct, and sometimes authors make this mistake without attaching it to a prior sentence that enlightens the reader.

Please see **Because "As" is Also…** for more on the use of *as* with modifiers.

Contrasting And Conjoining Things That Are Not There

Contrary to some opinions, starting a sentence with a conjunction (and, but, if, or, etc.) is an acceptable thing. But some writers tend to forget that these are *conjunctions* and as such they still need to conjoin ideas. (See what I did there?)

There is, however, a problem with starting a new chapter or scene or story with something like:

And they hoisted the mainsail.

The word *and* implies something happened prior to the mainsail being hoisted, but the author didn't give that information, so there is no reason for the conjunction to be used there. There is nothing being conjoined, or associated with hoisting the mainsail, so the sentence should be:

They hoisted the mainsail.

Some people are not bothered by starting with *and*. I'm not too bothered by it as the opening line of a story. I find it a bit artsy. Maybe a bit trite. But it's not technically correct. And is a conjunction. It should be joining two things, not be the start of something. For me, the real problem comes when writers use sentences like that in the middle of a story.

Susie and Jamie ran through the woods laughing and playing until they were exhausted. Finally, resting in the shade of a great oak tree, Jamie confessed her love for Susie as the flittering shadows of the leaves played across their faces. And the dog ran up, barking loudly.

What did the dog have to do with anything? Nothing. It didn't deserve the *and*. There was nothing before the *and* that the dog needed to be added to. The dog was a new, separate issue. I have seen new writers do this many times when what they really wanted to do was something like this:

Susie and Jamie ran through the woods laughing and playing until they were exhausted. Finally, resting in the shade of a great oak tree, Jamie confessed her love for Susie as the flittering shadows of the leaves played across their faces.

Just as Susie was leaning in for a kiss, the dog ran up, barking loudly.

The implication of the irony or disappointment, or whatever that people often imply in spoken language when they say something like that doesn't translate well to the written word, particularly not to narrative text. (Please see **Don't Write the Way You Speak** for more on this idea.)

The issue of contrasting something against nothing is a similar one.

Weaver got out of bed, brushed her teeth, and got dressed. But she made coffee and headed for work.

Why is the *but* there? *But* implies she had a reason not to make coffee *but* she did anyway. I have seen this mistake with *yet, however, besides, more likely, because, as,* and other terms that should only be used in a situation where two or more things are being contrasted. (See **Poor Contrasting** and **Because "As" is Also…** for more on this.)

Because "As" is Also…

The word *as* can be a problem because *as* is so many things. Writers often make mistakes with the punctuation around it and accidentally change the meaning from what they intended to something quite different.

But let's start with the basic problem.

What is *as*?

It can be used as a conjunction, with a preposition, with an adjective, with an adverb, with a pronoun, to show simultaneous actions, and probably other things I've missed (like the fact it is also a noun[49]). If you look it up in a good dictionary, you'll find double digits worth of definitions.

Because it is used so many ways, doing something simple, like putting in a comma, can drastically change the meaning of a sentence containing the word *as*.

This can be a problem, because, as we all know, you always need to use a comma before a conjunction when combining two sentences, right?

Wrong. Not always in the case of *as*.

When used as a conjunction, the word *as* can have one of several different meanings, and the use (or not) of a comma will change those meanings. Here are some of the things *as* can mean, when used as a conjunction:

at that time
because
determined by
during that time
for the purpose of

---

[49] It is a type of Roman coin.

in comparison to
in that way
like
since
that
though
with the result of

And here are some examples of how a comma changes them:

Susie and Jamie brushed their teeth, as their mother told them to.
or
Susie and Jamie brushed their teeth as their mother told them to.

The first sentence means Susie and Jamie brushed their teeth because their mother told them to. The second sentence means they brushed their teeth at the same time their mother was telling them to do it. But it's not always that simple.

He smiled as she smiled.
or
He smiled, as she smiled.

The first sentence means he smiled at the same time she smiled.
The second sentence means he smiled the same way she smiled.
Or does it? I mean, without more context, it's confusing, right? Let's try again.

Susie brushed her teeth as well as Jamie.
or
Susie brushed her teeth, as well as Jamie.

The first sentence means Susie brushed her teeth in a manner that was just as good as the manner in which Jamie bushed. But what does the second sentence mean? Susie brushed her teeth, and she also brushed Jamie? Susie brushed her teeth at the same time as Jamie? Susie brushed her teeth and so did Jamie?

Like with the previous set of sentences, the second sentence is an example of when you probably need to write a different sentence and clarify your meaning. Rewording the sentence or adding more detail can easily fix it.

Now let's take a look at the use of *as* with a preposition:

She worked as a nanny to pay for her car.
or
She worked, as a nanny, to pay for her car.

Do you see any difference in meaning between the two sentences? I do. But the difference is cosmetic. I see a difference in emphases. When you set *as a nanny* apart, I feel you are bringing attention to it. Beyond that, a comma is probably not a big deal and editors will likely tell you to cut them.

Here is *as* with an adverb:

He smells as fresh as a daisy.

Any commas inserted into that sentence will make it nonsensical.

While a "writing style" can be important and may make some writers feel they need to phrase things in a certain way, clarity for the reader is usually more important. Sometimes a confusing sentence can be understood by the context around it. But sometimes it cannot. Why risk it?

Here are a couple of rules of thumb to help you keep your meanings straight and try to keep things clear for readers:

Never use a comma to interrupt a simultaneous action, even when it is a conjunction.

Avoid substituting *as* for *like* in a comparison.

Still having problems? If you are not using a simultaneous action, then consider what the *as* is being used for. Is it a conjunction? Can you break your sentence into two sentences to fix it? Can you replace *as* with *because* and fix your sentence that way?

"As" is mentioned in several sections of this guide. In particular, certain aspects of *as* apply to the sections on comma use, as well as **Run on Sentences**, **Shifting Tenses**, **Misplaced Modifiers**, **Contrasting And Conjoining Things That Are Not There**, **Poor Contrasting,** and **Breaking Up Speech With Actions.**

Autonomous Body Parts

Autonomous body parts are parts of the body that do things on their own accord. I have also heard this referred to as **actions by disembodied body parts** and **animate body parts**.

This is something that some readers never notice, and other readers despise.

His eyes searched the darkness.

This makes it sound like his eyes left his head and went searching for something in the darkness.

Her eyes followed him down the street.

This sounds like her eyes chased him down the street like puppy dogs.

Their feet ran up the driveway.

Did their feet have little feet that they used for running?

His fist shook in anger.

Why was his fist angry, anyway? Do fists normally get angry?

Her nose wrinkled at the thought.

When did noses start to have thoughts?

His arm instinctively shot out and caught the snake by the back of the head.

Why does his arm have instincts?

These are but a mere few examples of the many possibilities. I hope they give you an idea of why some people dislike this type of description so much and why other people don't notice it at all. Done properly it can focus the reader's attention on certain details, but done poorly, it creates a comically poor effect.

Cherie's eyes rolled.
vs.
Cherie rolled her eyes.
vs.
Cherie exasperatedly looked up at the ceiling.

A simple change may slightly affect the feel of the story, yet it can make all the difference for a reader who can't stand the thought of eyeballs bouncing across the table like dice in a craps game.

The eye-rolling example is one of the most difficult to get around, which is why I chose it. It is a common expression with few synonymous terms, hence my use of the adjective to express the meaning I am trying to convey.

The idea of misplaced autonomy can also apply to other things the character is doing. Sometimes writers forget the character is the one who is in control of things, and they make it sound like those objects have a will of their own.

The sword lashed out and removed his head from his neck.

The motor revved impatiently as they waited.

Choosing when to write things poetically, and when to write them literally, is part of the writer's job. I personally feel there is a time and a place for both, but many people strongly dislike writing that gives the appearance of autonomous body parts or inanimate objects.

Be aware of your choices so that when readers or editors get upset that your characters always have roving eyes, wandering feet, or falling faces, you can defend yourself, or at least be prepared to tolerate their criticisms.

CONTINUITY ERRORS MATTER

Juggling characters, props, scenery, and events can be difficult. As a writer you hold all of these things in your mind, trying to fit them into the right place like jigsaw puzzle pieces. You don't want to mention something too soon, and yet you don't want to forget to mention it at all. And sometimes we goof. Sometimes we mention things three times, or we take them out entirely, except for that one line of dialog about it we missed.

Readers have the advantage of only knowing the things you tell them, when you tell them, so they know whether something made sense when they read it. This is part of the reason why writers really can't effectively self-edit, and it is an important function of an editor and beta readers.

There are a few types of continuity mistakes I have seen repeatedly, so I wanted to put them in a section of their own to bring them to your attention in the hope that you can avoid making them.

Deus Ex Machina

The phrase **deus ex machina** is Latin for "god from the machine." Although the etymology relates back to the Greek tragedies and their propensity to use the gods to resolve an inescapable situation (the actors playing the god would be raised or lowered to the stage using a machine, hence "god from the machine"), in common usage it means any sort of plot device that suddenly, and without warning, fixes an unsurmountable problem. (Because the "god from the machine" usually intervened and fixed the story, with magic, for no reason other than it pleased the god to do so.)

This is usually regarding something out of the character's control or that comes out of nowhere and is considered by many to be a poor or lazy way to solve problems or wrap up a story that has no real ending.

Sometimes this is a thing that can make sense, such as the ending of H.G. Wells' *War of the Worlds*, where humanity is saved from extermination when the aliens become infected with Earth's tiniest organisms and die. But usually (unless used comedically), this technique irritates readers as it introduces something that easily fixes a problem in a nearly magical way that had never been foreshadowed and often makes no sense.

An example is *Superman* (the 1978 Christopher Reeve version) spinning the Earth backwards to save Lois Lane's life. The ability to turn back time and change anything negates any real danger in the story and was never hinted as being possible until it happened.

Many new authors make this mistake with silly things like the main character pulling out a weapon and killing the bad guy when the fact that the main character carried a weapon was never mentioned before and there were many places in the story when that weapon would have come in very useful had the main character known they had it at the time. See **Magically Appearing** for more on this idea.

More famous instances are things like when Dorothy accidentally finds out water melts the Wicked Witch, or nearly anything that randomly showed up on Batman's Utility Belt in the 1960's television show. (Like the Bat Shark Repellent, or the Bat-Magnifying Lens, or anything else that nearly magically showed up right when it was needed instead of being built in advance in case it was needed, or built after they knew they needed it.)

Out Of Sight, Out Of Mind

When secondary characters linger in the background without doing anything for too long, readers tend to forget they are there. Unfortunately, so do authors. It is jarring to the story when one of those characters suddenly comes back into the story and does something important, like saving the main character's life.

This can feel like a deus ex machina although the writer planned the story out and there really wasn't one, and it can make some of the secondary characters feel like mannequins that only come to life when needed. It can also bother a reader to never know what happened to a character left in a bad situation.

Characters, even minor ones, need to feel like real people to the reader. If the writer only uses the character at pivotal moments when the character is needed, it can seem like that character does not exist outside of those moments.

This idea also applies when making scene changes. Unless the scenes are very quick, you need to remind the reader who is there every time you come back to a scene. You can't expect a reader to remember all five characters who are present at the pizza shop after you've spent a chapter in Billy's backyard and a chapter in flashback since the last time you mentioned the gang at the pizza shop.

Magically Appearing

I have seen stories (yes, plural, this didn't only happen once) where soldiers (or guards) step in at the end of a story to arrest people. The authors assumed the reader would know the soldiers were lurking in the background the whole time, because of the setting.

But readers don't do that. We don't assume certain people or things are present just because of the setting. It is the writer's responsibility to tell us they are there. Otherwise, they aren't there.

This may seem counter-intuitive, as saying the characters are in the forest implies that there are trees and maybe squirrels, and using that implication is crucial to establishing setting. But that doesn't mean the reader will also assume there is a logging encampment with men actively working all around. When that tree falls and kills someone, it will come as a surprise if you've never mentioned the chainsaws and cries of "Timber!" up until that very moment.

The same rule applies to stories that mention the soldiers (or whatever) in the first couple of paragraphs and then never mention them again until the end of the story. The writer must keep reminding the reader those characters are there, or we forget.

Characters as far as continents away at the moment of a story's climax often inexplicably return instantly so that they can participate in the congratulatory celebrations and happy ending with the ensemble cast. Teleporting people and things to be back with the main character, without explanation, is rarely a good thing outside of science fiction.

This can apply to things like weapons, special abilities, medicine, phones and anything else that could end up being a deus ex machina.

The reverse is also true. If you mention someone has a whip on their hip, don't allow your characters to be challenged by difficult obstacles a whip would be helpful in getting past without them trying to use that whip.

An example of this for me was the Jonah Hex movie. Hex has the power to temporarily raise the dead and talk to them, which he does at the start of the movie, and again late in the movie, but he never bothers to do it with any of the other dead characters who could have answered the questions the movie centered around.

Probably because that would have ended the movie after only ten minutes or so, but the movie was ruined for me because of that anyway.

Taking Too Long To Speak Up

Background and secondary characters have a tendency to speak up about something long after they should have. Remember to treat them like real people who do and say things all the time, not just at the precise moment you are ready for them to have an epiphany or an opinion. Having a background character make a comment about something several pages later than they should have can make the story feel forced.

If a character is disgusted by all of the blood on the ground after the big fight, but never said a word two chapters ago when that other guy was beheaded and arterial spray covered everyone in the group, that is taking too long to speak up.

As stated in **Out Of Sight, Out Of Mind**, characters, even minor ones, need to feel like real people to the reader. If the writer only uses the character at pivotal moments, it can seem like that character does not exist outside of those moments.

The Third Hand

Romance readers complain about the third hand all the time. One hand in her hair, one on her lower back, and one…somewhere else. It seems like an obvious mistake, but it happens all the time. Even in other genres.

When a character has a sword in one hand and a shield in the other, it can be confusing to the reader when the character picks their enemy up and slams them to the ground and then hits them in the face with the shield and stabs them through the heart with the sword.

Remember to keep track of what your characters are doing and how they do it as well as what they are holding, or not holding, and how that will interfere with what they are doing. A character busy flying a jet pack controlled with dual sticks, one for each hand, won't have a third hand to hold and shoot a pistol.

Unless they are an alien. Or a robot, I guess…

Grafted on arm maybe?

The Bag Of Holding

The bag of holding is a fictitious magical bag that is larger on the inside than the outside and never gets heavier, no matter what you put into it. Readers and editors are often disturbed by characters who can carry unlimited amounts of useful stuff in their myriad of pockets. While this is great in video games, it doesn't go over so well for us true believers reading about the adventures of our personal heroes.

This idea can apply to things like cars that never run out of gas, people who never need to eat, sleep, or go pee (although most stories generally leave out the excretory functions, and I'm just fine with that), torches that never burn out or use up oxygen in closed spaces, batteries that never die, guns that never need reloading (and if they do, the cache of bullets never runs out), or the sun never goes down and the day lasts impossibly long.

All of these things can ruin the suspension of disbelief for a reader who is paying attention to details. I can't count the number of times I have held my breath waiting for a character to deal with something I felt was a worrisome constraint that the writer forgot to ever acknowledge again. Seriously. If you say someone is dying of thirst or has to pee so badly they feel their bladder is about to burst, I can't hardly concentrate on the rest of the story while I wait for them to get relief.

Going Back To The Future

Mistakes in the timeline are the first thing I think of when I think of continuity errors, but not all of them involve time travel. Writers need to be careful that flashbacks are clearly marked and not taken for mistakes in the timeline. (See also **Scene Breaks** and **Shifting Tenses.**)

There are many ways writers have shown flashbacks in their writing. Sometimes a book starts in the past and then moves to the present, sometimes chapters alternate between time periods. It is not necessarily a bad thing to tell a story out of order, but it is confusing unless the reader knows you are doing it. Whatever you choose to do, make sure the reader can easily follow the timeline so they don't get confused or distracted trying to figure out what happened/what is happening.

Writers make mistakes in this area the same way movie editors do. When fixing, updating, and correcting stories, a part gets moved around or cut out completely and suddenly you have a scene wherein someone is holding the magic ring before it had been discovered, or a character references something that never happened.

One movie, that I won't name because I was told I was mistaken and it is not worth watching again to find out, had someone die in the middle of a battle, then, after two quick scenes of other people fighting, showed that person fighting and killing enemies. A later scene showed his body dead on the ground and everyone mourning his loss.

Something like that can happen quickly in a movie and most people won't notice, but it will stand out in a book if a dead character is speaking, or if the cause and effect chain is broken, showing the effect before the cause.

There is a different kind of time-slip mistake writers sometimes make without realizing it as well. It can be hard to describe simultaneous actions, especially when mixing them with descriptions or background information. This can lead to a writer "jumping back in time" to describe an action that the reader already thought happened.

The tavern door flew open. Blue Bart and Red Bob stood in the entrance with menacing snarls on their faces. Blue Bart was the first in the door, making a beeline for the bar, his eyes on the barkeep the whole time.

"Gimme a bottle!" he growled, pulling a long knife from his belt and slamming it down on the bar top. While the bartender went for the bottle, Blue Bart turned around to lean against the bar and began glaring at the rest of the room like a starving dog warning them off a bloody bone he'd found and intended to keep to himself.

"Whaddaya lookin' at?" he bellowed. Everyone in the tavern pointedly looked away.

Red Bob, being more of an elephant than a dog, broke the tavern door off its hinges as he followed Blue Bart in like a chick after its hen, not even bothering to look around, but trusting Blue Bart would get them where they were going.

So, here's the problem. Did Red Bob stand in the doorway and watch Blue Bart for thirty seconds before following him in, as the story makes us feel he did, or did he immediately follow him in, staying very close to him, as the text says? Did his tearing off the door happen while Red Bob was still walking up to the bar, or after Red Bob yelled at everybody?

Writing the scene that way makes the reader feel like they have slipped back in time to find out what Red Bob did while Blue Bart was doing his thing. Sometimes it is not a big deal, but sometimes a writer will go more than the paragraph I went before jumping back in time. I have seen it be pages. At that point, you should probably be using a scene break and re-telling the scene from the other character's point of view so that the reader understands the narration has jumped back in time.

Consistency In Made Up Words and Names

This tends to be a problem in Fantasy stories more than Science Fiction or Horror, but it happens in all genres. When an author invents a name for a person, place, or thing, there is often an element of the spelling that can be easily changed. And very often, that element does get changed.

I don't mean just a typo on the name, which happens. I have seen authors, even in professionally published books put out by big, mainstream publishers, suddenly change the spelling of a character's name halfway through the book (or even flat-out use a new name—but that's a different problem).

If you decide to give a city a lovely name, like Chryssells, you need to continue to spell it that way through the entire book (series). If you suddenly switch the spelling of the name to Chryssals, it really throws off the reader.

Many of us readers, myself included, tend to skip over made-up names. I look at the shape of the word when I read, rather than waste time trying to figure out how to pronounce it in the character's native Gargolian language.

To me, the shapes of Chryssells and Chryssals are similar. I might notice the difference or I might not. If you have accidentally changed the name of the city, and I notice the different spelling, I may never realize you meant the same city. I may think you are referencing a new city. If I don't notice the spelling change and you actually have two cities with similar names, I may never notice there were supposed to be two cities. For this reason, I recommend trying to keep made-up names clearly differentiated from one another.

An early example of confusion, for me, due to similar names, was in *Star Wars*. Luke came from Tattoine, where the first part of the movie takes place. Under duress, Leia confesses the rebel base was hidden on Dantooine. When I first saw the movie, I didn't hear her say, "Dantooine. They're on Dantooine." I heard "Tattoine" and thought the Death Star was headed for Luke's home planet. Totally different story there.

While this was an auditory problem of the names sounding alike to me, I probably would have noticed the difference in writing, but I might have taken it for a typographical error. (Which I actually did when I read the book. Because I had heard it incorrectly in the movie!)

Sometimes an author accidentally changes the spelling of a character's name, even the main character. Bryan to Brian, or Cheryl to Cherall, while sounding alike when spoken aloud, both have a change in the shape of the letters that is large enough I probably won't be able to re-program my brain to accept this is still the same character.

This idea also applies to spellings for the names of creatures, or anything else, for that matter. Don't start out with Vampyre and switch to Vampire unless you are going to make a distinction between the two somehow. (Yes, it is all right if the only distinction is in the dialect of a speaking character, but make sure your reader can follow what you have done.)

PROBLEMS WITH DIALOG

Many new authors have problems with dialog. Not only with how characters talk to each other, but also with punctuation, dialog tags, identifying speakers, and whether characters are speaking or thinking.

Dialog is a major part of most stories, and the only part of others. There are many techniques writers use to achieve various effects, but before you can successfully pull off those wondrous moments that will never properly translate to the movie screen, you need to know the pitfalls. (Also see **Punctuation in Dialog**.)

Identifying Characters

It is important to quickly identify which character is speaking, especially at the start of a story. The longer a writer takes to identify a character, even if all the other characters have been identified, the more confusing the scene will be for the reader. Calling a character "he" or "she" for three pages, or even a whole chapter, does not identify the character and frustrates a reader.

If the writer has some reason for hiding the identity of the speaker, details about the speaker still need to be given out so that the reader can identify them in their minds as a mystery character instead of a **Talking Head.**

You should never make a reader try to figure out who is talking. It should always be obvious, even as a mystery figure. (See also **Pronoun Problems**.)

Multiple mystery figures should have something identifying about them so that they can be differentiated from one another as well. Just because you don't want the reader to know who that character is right now, doesn't mean you don't want the reader to be able to attribute those actions to the character when their identity is revealed.

The lack of identifying features can also cause a confusion in mystery characters. I have read a story where one mystery character ends up being the hero, while the other is a villain, but as there were no identifying attributes, a horrible evil deed that was done was never clearly specified to the reader as not being committed by the hero figure. It is possible this was intentional, however it soured the redemption of the character for me, as I never ascertained if they were guilty of that crime or not.

To Said Or Not To Said, That Is The Question

Some people feel that the only dialog tag that should ever be used is *said*. (See also **Punctuation in Dialog**.)

"Hi!" he said.

There are a couple of reasons for this line of reasoning. *Said* is often considered to be an invisible word, much like the word *the*. People generally don't see it when they are reading it, therefore it does not disturb the flow of the story. (Although they notice if it is missing!) Another reason is, by only using *said*, you will avoid using any impossible dialog tags. (See **Impossible Dialog Tags** for more.)

Personally, I don't like the idea of only using *said*, but that is a stylistic choice you must make for yourself. What you do need to watch out for is the overuse of the word *said*. If you use it too much, it is no longer invisible and will seriously detract from your story.

"Hi!" he said.
"Hello," she said. Her reply was demure.
He said, "I think I love you." He looked away.
"So, what are you so afraid of?" she said.

Even in that short bit, I got tired of the word *said*. And yes, some people prefer *said* over *asked*, feeling that using a question mark already implies a question and following the question mark with *asked* is redundant.

As I said, it's a stylistic choice and you will need to decide for yourself.

Leaving Out Dialog Tags

If you read the last example (in **To Said Or Not To Said, That Is The Question**), you might have wondered about the overuse of the word *said* in every line of dialog. Well, some people think it should always be there, every time a character speaks. I wholeheartedly disagree.

Leaving out dialog tags is a good way to speed up the pacing and control the flow of the story, especially when you are leaving out all of the other description as well. (See **Pacing** for more on that idea.)

"Hi!" he said.
"Hello," she replied.
"I think I love you."
"So, what are you so afraid of?"
"I don't know."
"I think I do."

Generally, characters take turns speaking, so if you have them continue speaking only when it would be their turn to speak again, it is easier for the reader to follow. Actions included with the dialog can add cues as to who is speaking, especially if the dialog continues for any length, or if more characters are involved.

"Hi!" he said.
"Hello." Her reply was demure.
"I think I love you."
"So, what are you so afraid of?"
"I don't know." He looked away.
She stepped closer. "I think I do."

Hopefully you didn't have any problems following who was saying what. A mistake often made by writers learning the craft is putting actions in but not keeping them immediately identified with the character. When that happens, things get confusing.

"Hi!" he said.
"Hello," she said. Her reply was demure.
"I think I love you."
"So, what are you so afraid of?"
"I don't know."
He looked away.
"I think I do."

When I left *Her reply was demure* on the same line as the rest of "her" dialog, the reader knows it belongs to "her." By starting a new paragraph after the action, I signaled a new action was happening. As that action was more dialog, the newness is implied to be a new character speaking, so the reader knows *"I think I love you"* was spoken by the other character, "he."

By putting the *He looked away* on its own line, I have confused the order of the back and forth, and now it is impossible to tell who said, *"I think I do."* Had I left it on the same line as "his" other action, it would still have belonged to "he."

"Hi!" he said.
"Hello," she said. Her reply was demure.
"I think I love you."
"So, what are you so afraid of?"
"I don't know." He looked down.
"I think I do."

I wouldn't recommend going more than four of five lines of dialog without tags or actions to remind the reader who is who. The longer it has been since the reader knew who was speaking, the easier it will be for them to get confused.

The thing to be wary of is making sure the reader knows exactly who is talking. Even when there are only two characters this can be an issue, but when there are four or five, it becomes a problem for even the best writers. That would be a time you need to make sure you have clearly identified all the characters and that the reader is intimately familiar with the voice patterns of each of them.

"Oh d-d-dear, what are we going to d-d-do now?" asked the stuttering little pig that was in no way related to a character created by A. A. Milne.

"Don't worry… I'm sure someone will come along…or not," replied the gray donkey in a deep, slow voice.

"Stheee? Thatsh exactacicatly why we shoulda bouncthed over it all!" The stripy one jumped up and down in frustration.

"Ahem." The feathery creature with big eyes puffed up his chest in self-importance. "While expressing your frustrations may make you feel better, it does not aid in resolving our predicament."

"Our predicacament? We have a predicacament? Whaths a predicacament?"

"Whatever it is…I'm sure it's a bad thing…for sure."

"I find it terribly hard to believe none of you know what a predicament is!"

"P-p-please, c-c-can't we—"

"Listhen, smarty-panths. I'm gonna bouncth you so—"

"Oh no… More trouble… Again."

Hopefully when I dropped the dialog tags you were still able to follow which character was speaking based upon their speech patterns, even when the order changed This is an extreme example done so it wouldn't take a whole book to build up your familiarity with the characters, so I hope you'll be forgiving.

Use of Verbs And Adverbs With Dialog Tags

"Tom Swifties" became a joke, literally. Originating with (or at least becoming painfully noted in) the Tom Swift series of books, this idea came about from the authors' severe overuse of descriptive verbs in dialog. Eventually used intentionally for humor, the use of the verbs was apparently an attempt to avoid overuse of the word *said*.

"I might as well be dead," Tom croaked.

"I decided to come back to the group," Tom rejoined.

While this may be humorous, it is also distracting. There are times when an author wants to write this way, but for most stories these will detract from the experience the writer wished to convey.

The same applies to verbs used in dialog tags that aren't meant to be humorous. They can detract from the story for many different reasons. These are often called *said bookisms* and are words used to replace *said* in dialog.

The use of alternative verbs has fallen out of favor in the last decade, but was quite popular prior to that, which is why so many (of us older) new authors are confused when we're told we are doing it wrong. We grew up reading the alternate verbs in our favorite books. Whispered, croaked, roared, sighed, etc., were all perfectly acceptable once.

But now they're not. (For some.) Later that will likely change again.

I consider this a stylistic choice, but I wanted to bring it up to make you aware of it. Here's the general reasoning behind not using the alternative verbs: the use of these words makes for lazy writing. Instead of using the dialog to *show* how characters are speaking, this is *telling* how they speak.

Some verbs are still generally acceptable, such as asked or replied, but this will come down to the preference of the editor or publishing house, and many writers choose to forego the descriptive words anyway, because they can be redundant.

This is the area wherein some call the writing lazy. Many feel that the dialog and the context of the story should imply how the words are being spoken. And there is some truth to that. Some *said bookisms* replace ideas in a story that would have had more impact had they been shown instead of told.

Here is a quick list of things I think easily demonstrate this idea. As you read them, consider this: as a reader enjoying a story, would you rather *realize* these things in the story you are reading or have them *told* to you?

"I love you," he lied.

"You're the only one I'll ever love," she jested.

"Those were the best of times," he remembered.

"Did you finally get it this time?" he nagged.

"It happened when it was dark outside," she hinted.

Obviously, the list of verbs that can be used goes on and on, but I hope this helps you understand that realizing someone is lying is a lot more fun than having the author tell you.

Another major problem with the use of the verbs is redundancy and repetitiveness. (See the **Pro Tips** section on **Redundancy** for more.)

"Please," he pleaded.

"Can I help you?" she asked.

"I have gathered you here to hear me speak," he orated.

"Take this," he offered.

"I am better than you!" she boasted.

"This is unforgivable!" she ranted.

This redundancy often applies to the use of adverbs in dialog tags as well. The use of adverbs can be considered even more problematic, as they *tell* even more than the use of verbs did, and they are often even more repetitive.

"I'm home!" she said loudly.

"Who?" he asked inquiringly.
"Me!" she hollered with gusto.
"Who?" he whispered quietly.

As a general rule of thumb, avoid the –*ly* words in dialog tags. (For more on this, see **–ly** words in **Less Filling**.)

As a side note: I used some of the examples of Tom Swifties from the Wikipedia page on "Tom Swifty," but there are entire websites devoted to this humorous art form should you desire to amuse yourself for a while. Tom Swifties are considered an art form by some people. If you enjoy them, you may wish to look further into them.

Impossible Dialog Tags

When using alternative verbs in dialog tags, there is another problem writers need to avoid. A problem that goes beyond the redundancy and *telling* mentioned in the previous section. That problem is the Impossible Dialog Tag.

Occasionally writers get carried away with their use of verbs, adverbs, descriptions, and actions in dialog, and they end up creating something that just isn't possible.

"Come here," he smiled wickedly.

On the surface, this looks all right, but this is saying he smiled the words, and people can't smile words. We could mouth the shape of the word, but we can't smile them. This can be easily fixed by changing the punctuation.

"Come here." He smiled wickedly.
or
"Come here," he said as he smiled wickedly.

There are many people who feel characters cannot laugh words. Or hiss them. Or chuckle, bark, growl, huff, or pant them. I disagree with some of that. I do think you can growl words, or moan them, or sing them. I think you can hiss words that have soft vowels. I think that if you can shout a word, you can bellow it.

You will need to decide for yourself and review these types of dialog tags on a case by case basis with your editors, but many commonly used expressions really just don't work.

We cannot leer words. That is a facial expression. As are glower, squint, smirk, pout, scowl, and wink. We can't use those expressions to say words. We can make those expression with our faces while speaking, but the expressions don't actually make the words.

Most actions inappropriately used as dialog tags can be easily fixed with punctuation that separates the action from the dialog.

"Hello. How are you?" she waved.

This implies she used sign language or hand signals. While this may apply to some stories, for most it just doesn't work the way the author intended, and the action needs to be separated.

"Hello. How are you?" She waved.

It's easier to see why this is true in some other examples where the meaning of the action is not as easily intermingled with the action of speaking.

"Where were you?" she slammed the car door.
(In Morse code, perhaps?)

"I'm angry!" he beat on his chest.
(Like a war drum, sending messages across the jungle?)

He opened the door. "Who's in charge?" he stepped out onto the sidewalk.
(Morse code again? Or a secret code he developed with Sammy Davis Jr.? Wait. Did that reference just date me? Am I too old? Did you have to look up Sammy Davis Jr.? *sigh*)

"But I need you," his eyes pleaded.
(See **Autonomous Body Parts** for more on this idea.)

Sometimes authors try to use actions as a dialog tag, but it doesn't work very well.

"I volunteer," one of the soldiers raised his hand.

The speech and the action are two separate things and really need to be broken apart.

"I volunteer." One of the soldiers raised his hand.

Breaking Up Speech With Actions

Although, in **Identifying Characters**, we looked at how actions can identify characters in dialog while not using dialog tags, we have also seen how incorrect placement of that action confused the identification of the character speaking and could create **Impossible Dialog Tags**.

"I really don't know what you're talking about." Amy lit a cigarette and blew out a cloud of smoke. "I was here all night long."

"Right." Pepe looked over his glass at her as he took a sip of the whiskey. "And everyone saw you."

"They did! You can ask them!"

Done properly, the actions still act as identifiers for the characters. But done haphazardly, the story becomes a jumbled mess.

"I really don't know what you're talking about." Amy lit a cigarette and blew out a cloud of smoke. "I was here all night long."

"Right. And everyone saw you," Pepe said.

"They did!" Pepe looked over his glass at her as he took a sip of the whiskey. "You can ask them!"

Even though I identified Pepe with a dialog tag, and even though it was Amy's turn to talk, putting Pepe's actions inside of her dialog confused the exchange. If the reader isn't paying close enough attention, and sometimes even if they are, it becomes easy to confuse which character is speaking.

If you absolutely must have one character's actions occurring during another character's dialog, there is a way around this: write the actions in a way that shows them being observed or reacted to by the speaking character.

"I really don't know what you're talking about." Amy lit a cigarette and blew out a cloud of smoke. "I was here all night long."

"Right. And everyone saw you," Pepe said.

"They did!" Amy insisted as Pepe looked at her over his glass of whiskey. "You can ask them!"

Actions during dialog very much need to follow the rules set out in the section on **New Paragraphs**. Anytime a new character speaks or acts you need a new paragraph, or you will confuse your reader. In the last example, Pepe's actions are included as part of Amy's actions, or more specifically, from Amy's point of view, to prevent this confusion.

Please see **Because "As" is Also...** for more on the use of *as*.

Words Not In Your Character's Vocabulary

When I was young(ish), my mother took me to see *Flash Gordon* (1980) at the movie theater. Five minutes into the movie, which was a genre she should have very much enjoyed, she stopped having fun.

"Oh. It's going to be *that* kind of a movie."

What stopped her in her tracks?

Ming the Merciless asked what "plaything" Klytus has to offer today. The response was something along the lines of "an obscure planet, the inhabitants call 'Earth'." Seconds later, Ming pushes a button labeled EARTH QUAKE.

Now how did that button get labeled with the name of an unknown planet? That instantly ruined the movie for my mother. The same thing will happen with a lot of your readers.

It is, for example, difficult to get away with using the word humane in a story with no humans. Wizards from a magical realm, or people in a pre-industrial word, shouldn't know about DNA, nuclear fission, or PTSD. Or, at very least, not in those terms. On the off chance they acquired the knowledge somehow, they would have a different word for it than we do.

Why would someone, a hundred years before Humphry Bogart lived, tell someone not to bogart something? In a world where Franz Mesmer never lived, why would people refer to hypnotism as mesmerism? Why would people in a time and place far, far away, be concerned about chauvinism, when not only could they never have heard of Nicolas Chauvin, but in reality, we ourselves have bastardized the original meaning (similar to blind devotion) to nearly the exact opposite?

An **anachronism** is something (or someone) that is outside of its correct time period. The term is also applied, in fiction, to things from our world that show up in worlds they should not be in.

Most writers know better than to include a cell phone in a Western, but sometimes they forget to pay attention to the terms they use for other things.

Don't have an 18th century cowboy call a wagon a taxi, and don't have a 15th century peasant offer another peasant a Kleenex after a sneeze.

Even terms that could be correct need to be considered. It doesn't really matter that the word compute has been around since the 1600's; your readers will see it as a computer and think it is out of place.

If you were writing a modern-day story about modern gangsters, you wouldn't use terms like flapper, dame, or moll to refer to a female character. You likewise wouldn't use those terms in a Victorian Era Fantasy, even if it were about cutpurses, sneakthieves, and blackguards organized into something that looked like a 20th century crime syndicate. Use the same caution with our modern vocabulary.

Be careful how you present the worlds you create, or you will shatter the illusion you are trying to grant the reader.

Thoughts Or Spoken Words?

This is closely related to the topic discussed in **Distinguishing Narration From Thoughts And Messages**. Just as some writers have problems clearly delineating a character's thoughts from the narration, some tend to mix those thoughts in with spoken dialog in a confusing manner. One of the best ways to keep thoughts clearly marked is to put them in italics. Failure to indicate thoughts differently from speech can cause serious problems with the story.

Some authors feel the need to put both thoughts and dialog in quotations and then indicate they are different through the use of dialog tags. This doesn't always work out so well in terms of clarity.

"John, come over here!" Phil called. "John will do a good job," he thought.

Until you get to the end of that sentence and read the dialog tag, you don't know that the second half is a thought and not spoken aloud. If the dialog tag is left off, it makes no sense at all.

Even if you break the sentences into separate paragraphs, following the rule that a new idea or new action requires a new paragraph, this is still hard to follow.

"John, come over here!" Phil called.
"John will do a good job," he thought.

Does the pronoun *he* belong to Phil or someone else? (See **Ambiguous Pronouns** for more on this.) If you replace *he* with *Phil*, the text suddenly becomes very repetitive.

"John, come over here!" Phil called.
"John will do a good job," Phil thought.

No matter how I play with the idea of putting thoughts in quotation marks, I cannot find a way that I feel is not confusing. However, italics clears the confusion right up.

"John, come over here!" Phil called. *John will do a good job,* he thought.

Sometimes authors choose not to use quotation marks or italics. While admittedly less confusing than the use of quotation marks, it still creates a situation where the reader is not always sure what is the narrative voice and what is an actual direct thought by the character.

"John, come over here!" Phil called. John will do a good job, he thought.

This also forces the author to add the thought tag every time someone thinks something, otherwise it will look like part of the narrative, and it will seem to have an odd narrative voice. (See also **Distinguishing Narration From Thoughts and Messages**.)

"John, come over here!" Phil called. John will do a good job.

Imagine trying to write the next example, and retaining the feel of her comment, while using quotation marks.

"I love you." *Sort-of,* **she thought.**

This is a complicated expression of dialog. My point is the expression of thought can be experimented with in many ways, some to a much greater degree of success than others. I feel the italics work best for thoughts. It even allows the thought tag to be left off while still conveying a clear understanding to the reader.

"I love you." *Sort-of.*

PRONOUN AND PROPER NOUN PROBLEMS

The use of pronouns and proper nouns can be a confusing issue for many of us. A noun is a person, place, or thing. Specifically named nouns, like Robert, Judy, Texas, or Great Wall of China, are proper nouns. A pronoun falls somewhere between the other two. A pronoun can substitute for a multitude of other nouns, including proper nouns.

And thus begins the confusion!

While there are multiple types of pronouns (demonstrative, indefinite, interrogative, reciprocal, reflexive, relative, object, possessive, subject, and probably a dozen others I don't know or have forgotten), I am only going to deal with the common usage errors regarding the most common pronouns, such as he, she, his, hers, they and theirs.

Hopefully the examples I give will help you navigate some of the many pitfalls I have seen writers fall into.

(I resisted all the **pro**noun jokes. Aren't you proud of me?)

Ambiguous Pronouns

An ambiguous pronoun, sometimes called an unclear pronoun reference, is one that does not clarify which noun it has replaced. Ambiguous pronouns are by far one of the most common problems I have seen as an editor, so this section will be a little longer than most. Even experienced writers and editors make these types of mistakes, especially when making edits where they may inadvertently create them when removing other text.

Jimmy went to meet Bobby at the school, but he didn't know he was going to be late.

The ambiguity of *he* in that sentence means the reader doesn't know if: Bobby didn't know that Jimmy was going to be late, Jimmy didn't know Bobby was going to be late, or if Jimmy didn't know that Jimmy was going to be late.

Replacing one of the pronouns with a proper noun can mostly clear up the meaning of the sentence.

Jimmy went to meet Bobby at the school, but he didn't know Bobby was going to be late.

But that doesn't always work. It is still difficult to tell if the pronoun that is left was meant to replace Bobby or Jimmy.

In cases like this, it is best to break the sentences apart, or restructure them, unless you are sure the context has left no room for confusion.

Jimmy went to meet Bobby at the school, but when he left, neither he nor Bobby had known that Bobby was going to be late.

Sometimes the ambiguous pronouns are even more insidiously hidden:

"Jaqueline and I went down to the train station to pick up Molly, Mary, Margaret and Mildred. She really needed the extra help!" Judy said.

While it is fairly easy to identify that *she* refers to Jaqueline in this example, many writers get carried away and put too many things between *Jaqueline* as a proper noun and *she* as a pronoun, and then it is not so clear.

"Jaqueline and I went down to the train station to pick up Molly, Mary, Margaret and Mildred. Molly had two suitcases, Mary had three, and while Margaret had only one, Mildred made up for it with six of them! She really needed the extra help," Judy said.

Now the pronoun *she* seems to point to Mildred, who had six suitcases. But what if it wasn't supposed to? What if the suitcases were added in later, when the writer did edits to the story, and the story really needed *she* to still refer to Jaqueline? Then things get confusing.

Sometimes the reader can tell the pronoun is pointed at the wrong proper noun, based upon situational awareness. For example, what if Jaqueline were the only one capable of casting a magical spell, and the reader knew it.

"Jaqueline got into an argument with Molly at the well. Molly tried to throw her into the well! Mary, Margaret and Mildred were there, too. Mary and Margaret were laughing, while Mildred just stood and watched. Finally, she couldn't take it anymore and turned her into a toad!" Judy said.

Now things have gotten confusing. Who couldn't take it anymore, and who got turned into a toad? If the reader knows that only Jaqueline can do magic, they can narrow down that Jaqueline turned someone into a toad. But was it Molly, or was it Mildred who became amphibious?

Generally, a pronoun points back to the most recent person, place, or thing mentioned, so moving the pronoun farther away from the noun it is replacing, and inserting other nouns between them, increases the chances of confusion.

I dropped my phone on the glass table and it broke.

Which broke? My phone or the glass table? By placement of the noun and the pronoun, it should be the glass table. But this is still confusing, so it would be much easier to understand if we rearranged the sentence.

My phone broke when I dropped it on the glass table.

The glass table broke when I dropped my phone on it.

Here is an example of the hardest to spot type of ambiguous pronoun:

They saw Shelly down at the zoo where the friendly monster exhibit was set up. She looked like a goof with her phone in one hand and her camera in the other as she took a bunch of selfies with it.

So, does "it" refer to the monster exhibit, the camera, or to the phone?

Another place writers make this mistake is at the start of a new paragraph. When telling the story from a certain character's point of view, the writer tends to hold in their mind the idea that everything comes from that point of view, but an ambiguous pronoun can quickly throw that off.

Hugh dodged the thug's fist and rolled away, scrambling to his feet. Two more bruisers walked in. He recognized these two. The shorter one was Charlie, a real tough cookie. The taller man was Gerald.

He stumbled as he prepared to attack. This would be over quickly, one way or another.

Who was stumbling? Hugh or Gerald? Writers often get caught up in telling their story and lose track of the pronouns when they start new paragraphs. This especially happens in conversations with people of the same gender.

> **"Do you think he's going to ask you out?" Kitty raised an eyebrow.**
> **"Oh, I don't know..." Twisting a curl in her hair, Rachel feigned disinterest.**
> **"I think you do!"**
> **"Maybe."**
> **The doorbell rang and she got up to go answer it. It was Kevin, and he looked mouthwateringly good.**
> **"Can I come in?" he asked.**
> **Blushing, she stepped aside. "Of course."**

In the author's mind, it is very clear who answered the door, but the reader is dying to find out! Was it Kitty or was it Rachel? Now that there is a "he" and a "she" in the scene, and the other "she" was left behind in a different room, sometimes authors forget they need to throw in a proper noun every now and then as an identifier. Sometimes there can be a couple of pages(!) of exchange between the two characters before the reader finally finds out which woman got up and is now fawning over Kevin at the door.

These kinds of mistakes apply to more than characters. They can happen in nearly any situation.

> **The dragsters were lined up on the starting line as the judges took their places. The powerful V-12 motors had enough power to make them roar like beasts.**

So, did the judges take the place of the dragsters at the starting line, and did the V-12 motors make the judges roar like beasts?

Most of the time readers, and even editors, are forgiving of these kinds of mistakes, because we can easily sort out which nouns the pronouns are substituting for. But sometimes the sentences go wonky when the pronouns don't obviously point back to the correct subject or object. Be careful with your writing and be aware of this issue.

Mom Or mom? When To Capitalize

When do we capitalize mom, dad, sweetheart, sheriff, and hotdog man? Some writers I know have been vexed by this for years, even though it's usually quite simple.

Is it a name or not?

Names are proper nouns. They specifically identify something or someone as unique or different than the others. Nouns merely state what they are, in general.

"My mom is home," Jamie said.

This shows that "a mom" is home, even though Jamie also identified exactly which one with *my*. Mom is not capitalized here because we still have not identified the individual. Think of it as an elected official. Having identified the "office" they hold, we still haven't identified the person.

"Mom is home," Jamie said.

Jamie is no longer identifying which mom is home, Jamie is now identifying a person. That person's name, at least for Jamie, happens to be Mom.

I suspect some of the confusion sets in with the idea that Mom is not Mom to everyone. Only to Jamie. More confusion comes with capitalizing the first word of a sentence. Seeing that first letter capitalized may lead some of us into thinking mom (or dad, or sheriff, or something else) is always supposed to be capitalized. But a large part of the problem with titles is that they are treated differently by writers who work for political offices than by writers who write formal prose. Paperwork that comes out of government offices tends to capitalize all titles, while general literature typically capitalizes the title only when used as part of the name.

For our purposes, I'll stick to the way it usually appears in general literature.

"Go get the sheriff!"

Sheriff does not need capitalized, as, even though there is likely only one sheriff in town, we have not used it as a name.

"Go get the sheriff of Custer County!"

As in the example "My mom is home," the sheriff has been specifically identified, but not the specific individual who occupies that office.

"Go get Sheriff Jones!"

Now we are specifically identifying a person and using Sheriff as part of that person's name, just as if you were saying, "Go get Mom!"

This can get a little confusing as we don't say, "Go get Sheriff!" We usually separate out the title from the individual, but we might say something like "Go get the mom!"

We do however say things such as "Go get Mother Jones."

"Good morning, Sheriff," the deputy said, nodding his head as he

approached.

"Good morning, Deputy." The sheriff raised his cup of coffee in greeting.

When addressing each other, the sheriff and the deputy used each other's titles as a proper noun, or as names, thus requiring them to be capitalized.

Titles can be confusing. While we do capitalize things like Mr. President or Your Majesty when directly speaking to the person, we don't capitalize titles such as sir or ma'am.

"Yes, ma'am."
"No, sir."
"No, my lord."
"Yes, my lady."
"Hey, mister! You forgot your change!"

Those types of titles are given out of respect but don't actually represent a status or a position, so they are not capitalized.

Another manner in which many writers find themselves challenged is choosing to use a noun as a proper noun. Once a specific name is established for someone or something, it becomes a proper noun and is then capitalized. This is how nicknames work.

I rapidly walked around the corner and almost bumped into a hotdog vendor. He seemed nearly as surprised as I was.

Nodding a quick apology, I stepped around him. I needed to get away from my pursuers.

A black sedan appeared at the corner ahead, and I knew that escape route was lost to me. I turned back only to find Hotdog Man holding a gun pointed at my belly. He was one of them.

As soon as the hotdog vendor stopped being a random person and received the name "Hotdog Man" as an identifier, Hotdog Man became a proper noun and could be capitalized. This does not mean I can't call him the hotdog man, or just hotdog man, it just means I have nicknamed him Hotdog Man, and that is who he is to me, so it gets capitalized. Not all writers do that. Continuing to call him hotdog man is valid, but to me, it is less personal in the text. I feel the choice of capitalizing it makes Hotdog man seem more real, more of a real character, a specific person, who may or may not be mentioned again, rather than merely part of the generic background of the story.

The last thing I want to bring up is terms of endearment.

"Honey, I'm home!"
or

"Yes, dear, I love you too."

Like with "Mom is home!" having the pronoun at the start of the sentence means it has to be capitalized, and probably causes confusion. "Honey" is not the person's name, and it's not a nickname either. It is a term of endearment, so it should not be capitalized.

How do you tell if something is a term of endearment or a nickname? Ask yourself, would someone else call them that when referring to them while talking to you? Would you call them that when referring to them while talking to someone else?

Imagine a child coming home from afterschool activities and excited to talk to their father. They walk in the door, see their mother and ask:

"Hi Mom. Is Honey home from work yet?" Billy asked.

It doesn't work because Honey is (probably) not the father's name, and the child wouldn't refer to their father that way. (I dunno. Maybe in today's world they would. But I hope you get the idea.)

But something like this would make more sense:

"I would have gotten away if it hadn't been for Hotdog Man's fancy style buns," I said, nodding toward the glowering man.

It works for me to call him that because it was a nickname and not a term of endearment.

A place where people get confused with terms of endearment is when the lines get blurred. Jim Dear and Darling, the humans in Lady and the Tramp, have no other names. That is what they call each other, and they are obviously terms of endearment, but Lady (their dog) has no other names for them. She never hears them called anything else. So that is what she calls them, too. And she is not using them as terms of endearment, so they become actual names and have to be capitalized. (Not to mention they are used as actual names in the story, but again, I hope you get the gist of what I mean.)

Changing Identifiers

In the previous section (**Mom or mom? When To Capitalize**) I talked briefly about Hotdog Man. He was a background character we knew little about, and were not likely to learn more about, who had, at least for the moment, become important enough to need more of an identifier than the brief mention of him being a hotdog vendor.

In that example, what if two more thugs show up to battle our hero and the encounter erupts into a free-for-all action sequence? How do we identify the three new characters our hero just met and doesn't know the names of?

I swatted the gun from Hotdog Man's hand, but two more thugs were already upon me. The first thug punched at my head, but he was too slow. The second one was faster, kicking my leg out from underneath me, sending me to the pavement.

If this is going to be an extended fight scene, how long can we call the men the first and the second until it becomes too confusing?

Sometimes writers will name them things like "thug one" and "thug two," but those still leave the reader dealing with blank characters who have little to no description or identification.

Hotdog Man probably already has a mental image you have granted him even though he was never described beyond being a hotdog vendor. That's because most of us have seen hotdog vendors in some form, and we can fill in that blank. But the two thugs? What do they look like to you? Agent Smith from *The Matrix*? Anonymous gangsters from *The Untouchables*? Gangbangers from *Boyz n the Hood*? Or did they just look like any other person on the street?

The lack of description leaves the thugs too open for interpretation. Worse, it can make things confusing for the reader as they try to tell them apart—especially if they turn up again later in the story. So, adding more description, and using it as an identifier, will help.

I snarled and looked up in the face of the guy who had kicked me. He grinned at me with gold teeth, and I knew right then I wouldn't stop until I'd knocked those nuggets down his throat.

Now we have easy ways to identify two of the three men. Anytime I mention hotdog or gold, the reader will know which person it was. The absence of description can now apply to the third man.

Before I could get up, Thug Number Two put a penny loafer up my nose and sent me into a partial backflip. Then Weinerman was holding me down while Ritchie-Snitch grinned gold in my face.

I used two new identifiers, but because they are closely related to what I had used to previously name the characters, you could easily tell who they were. This is another place where a writer needs to be careful.

Did I go too far with *Ritchie-Snitch*? Was that a reference that dated me, or worse, excluded my younger audience? What if I hadn't added the *grinned gold* part? Would you have known which thug it was then?

If a writer tries to use the identifier as a description, before already establishing that description in some way, it can become very confusing to the reader.

I got a lucky kick in, right on Purple-pants' zipper, sending him to the ground curled up like a fetal pig. A quick head butt to his buddy and I was up again, the odds a bit more even.

By suddenly using *Purple-pants* as an identifier, I've lost the reader. Which one of those three guys was Purple-pants? Maybe the third guy, Thug Number Two? Maybe. Maybe Hotdog Man was in a clown uniform. Who knows? Now the fight scene has become confusing for the reader and may end up staying confused for the duration.

Note: I don't have to stop calling the characters things like "the man with the gold teeth" or "the man in the purple pants" (no capitalization) just because I give them other nicknames such as *Goldtooth* or *Purple-pants*. Although the nicknames may just be an identifier I created, I am using them as proper nouns, and proper nouns need to be capitalized.

Another problem I have encountered is when authors switch to identifiers that don't make sense to the reader. If you are talking about a demon from hell and you call it demon, Satan-spawn, monster, and cursed one, the reader will probably follow your line of descriptions. The reader will probably even follow along if you call it *she*, especially if you have indicated it has a female appearance. But if you suddenly call it *the woman*, you will lose them.

The beast towered over Angelina. It looked like a giant bat fused into the damned body of a curvaceous woman. The cursed creature snarled and its serrated fangs glistened in the torchlight as black wings opened and closed agitatedly behind it. The demon spawn leaned in for the kill, and Angelina could smell its brimstone breath. But then it hesitated.
The woman turned and walked away instead.

Did that confuse you? The demon is going to eat the woman, but the woman just walked away, and the demon let her? Or did I just use a poor identifier for the demon because in my mind it has a woman's body, so I called it woman?

Be careful when deciding to use a new identifier to describe something, or you can confuse the reader.

If you do decide to say something like I did in that last example, you need to consider a few things first. Did the demon actually look like a woman? If so, did you say that right away, so that the reader will think it does too? Have you introduced the creature enough to have humanized it to the point where the reader might accept you calling it a woman? In that case it may work. But if you wait three pages, and you've described the wings, horns, and tail, and then write, "The woman turned her back to me," the reader is still going to get confused.

In the writer's mind, the demon may look like a woman, but *woman* is not the kind of description that fits it well. The reader will better understand your characters when you use identifiers that have been well established.

The Generic Pronoun

Throughout this guide, you may have noticed I keep referring to "you." Let's think about that for a moment. Who exactly is *you*? I mean, you know who you are, but do I? How could I? I can't, and I don't. In that sense, I am using the pronoun *you* generically, to apply to anyone who may read this.

Another generic pronoun is *they*, as in, "They say the beaches in Hawaii are lovely." Who are *they*? It doesn't matter, it was used generically.

Another word used in this situation is *one*, as in, "One would find the beaches lovely in Hawaii."

I point these out because you shouldn't use them in your narrative unless you have established your narrative voice in such a way that allows it.

Wait just a minute, Sam! You've been using you *and* your *all the way through this guide!*

Yes. Yes, I have.

I intended my narrative voice in this guide to be approachable and friendly, so I often chose to use *you* and *your* instead of *one*, or *writers, authors, people*, or other pronouns that would end up making this guide sound stuffy or pretentious.

I wanted to point this out to you because unintentionally using these generic pronouns in a narrative can ruin the illusion you have created in your story. It "breaks the fourth wall" and can lessen the experience for the reader.

This can sneak into the narrative without writers realizing it when they use colloquialisms, or sayings, or start to write the way they speak. This doesn't usually matter with a 1st person POV narrative, it is what a 2nd person POV narrative is all about, but it can be jarring when it shows up halfway through a 3rd person POV narrative.

The wind whipped the snow so hard you couldn't keep your eyes open.
or
The sewer was so rank your eyes burned, and your nose watered.
or
It was the kind of thing that made you want to curl into a ball and die.

All these can be fixed by removing the generic pronoun and replacing it with the point of view of a character in the scene.

The wind whipped the snow so hard Bob couldn't keep his eyes open.
or
The sewer was so rank her eyes burned, and her nose watered.
or

It was the kind of thing that made Biff want to curl into a ball and die.

If the narrative hasn't yet established characters in the scene, such phrases, which were really observations, should be rewritten into factual descriptions.

The wind whipped the snow into sheets of deadly ice crystals.
or
The rank sewer emanated noxious gases, repelling creatures for miles.
or
It was the kind of thing that made entire civilizations give up and crumble away into history.

See the sections on **Don't Write the Way You Speak** and **Narrative Voice** for more about this.

I DO NOT THINK THAT WORD MEANS WHAT YOU THINK IT MEANS

There are some words that are repeatedly misused. The mistake can cause a chuckle or ruin a story. Some people don't mind, others can't stand it. As a writer, words are your trade, so you owe it to yourself to have the best command of them you can.

One of the biggest "invisible" problems writers can have is homonyms. Homonyms come in two different flavors. Homophones and Homographs.

Homophones sound alike, have different meanings, and have different spellings (too, two, to). (They are sometimes (rarely)referred to as heterographs.) Sometimes they are phrases or groups of words, such as "I scream" vs. "ice cream." When that happens, they are called **oronyms** or **eggcorns**. (More on eggcorns below.)

Homographs are spelled the same, but pronounced differently, and have different meanings ("Time to *wind* your watch" or "Feel the *wind* in your hair").

Homographs aren't usually a big problem for a writer, other than they sometimes stop us in our tracks as we try to figure out why what we just wrote doesn't look right. But Homophones can slip past even the best of writers. For some reason, our brains occasionally put the wrong one out there, and then we need a proofreader to find and fix them for us.

I often see "I'm over *hear*!" or "Did you *here* that?" Those are generally just an honest typo that needed another set of eyes in order to catch it. Most of us easily know the difference between *hear* and *here*, but some words can stymie us and need to be mastered before they ruin our stories.

This especially applies if you use dictation software, which will be more than happy to make the mistake for you.

While there are online services that will allow you to run checks on your text for homophones, they generally just highlight everything in their dictionary that is a homophone, and you have to go through one by one manually and see if you used the correct word. And those type of checks definitely won't help you with problems caused by other things, like malapropisms, eggcorns, and mondegreens.

Also known as a Dogberryism, from the character Constable Dogberry in William Shakespeare's *Much Ado About Nothing*, a **malapropism** is the use of the wrong word in place of a word that sounds similar. While this is often used for comedic effect, such as when the famous Yogi Berra said, "Texas has a lot of electrical votes" (instead of electoral votes), the unintentional use of a malapropism can make you sound ignorant and ruin a story for the reader.

The same can be said, but maybe even more so for **eggcorns,** which are generally near (meaning not exact) oronyms (the name comes from the mishearing of the word *acorn* and thinking what was said was *eggcorn*), and

mondegreens, which are what happens when people mishear or misunderstand common phrases or song lyrics (such as "bathroom on the right" instead of "bad moon on the rise").

A general term for the incorrect use of words, especially those that sound alike, is **Acyrologia.**

By now, you may be wondering why I chose to dump so many terms and details on you. I did it because there is one more I want to bring up, and, for me, it is the biggest problem. The one that is most likely to ruin a story for me. Okay, I admit, it will ruin the story for me every single time.

I spent a long time trying to research the correct term for it, and the closest I was able to come was **Cacozelia.** Which doesn't fit what I want. Cacozelia is when someone uses "big" words, or foreign words, to appear educated or snooty or whatever. Great. Fine. Whatever. We can all do that and pretend to be haughty.

Except when we can't.

A writer who attempts that in their writing, but unknowingly falls victim to malapropisms, eggcorns, and mondegreens, ends up with something that is, well, generally unenjoyable and unreadable. So don't do it. Stick with words you know instead. Not only your writing, but your story as well, will be much better for it.

And if, like me, you find yourself making the same mistake over and over again, consider adding it to your **Final Checklist**.

If you take nothing else away from this section, heed this: always be willing to look up anything you are not 100% sure of. If you can't find it, you've probably got it wrong.

Following is a list of some of the most commonly misused words and related mistakes I have seen.

a (an) vs. the

I suppose it's fitting I start this off with proving the last sentence I wrote was wrong. These are by far NOT the most commonly misused words I have seen, but I have seen it, and it hurts when you come across it.

Most people don't even know what parts of a sentence *a*, *an*, and *the* are.

They are all articles. They help identify nouns.

A and *an* are indefinite articles. *The* is a definite article.

What does that mean?

It means when I say, "a banana" or "an apple," I could be talking about any of the bananas or apples. It doesn't matter which one. "Hand me a banana." It was indefinite.

When I say, "Hand me the pear," it means, specifically, *the* pear. It was definite.

This seems obvious, especially if there is only one pear in the bowl of fruit, but there are subtle implications here.

What if there is a bowl full of pears, and I say, "Hand me the pear"? At that point you are going to start trying to figure out which pear I thought was special enough that I was asking for it specifically.

In writing your stories, saying something like "A cop walked up" implies this is a minor character, or there are several officers around. Changing it to "The cop walked up" increases the importance of the officer. She is the only officer there, or she is about to be important to the story.

Imagine you are writing this scene:

A firefighter, a cop, and a postal worker walk into a bar.
The fireman says, "Hot enough for ya?"
The cop says, "Say that again, and I'll ice you."
A postal worker says, "I'll send it special delivery."

(Okay, I can't make up a joke. Forgive, please, and move on with the example.) Did you see what happened in your mind with the indefinite article *a* used with the postal worker? We envisioned a firefighter, and then a cop, and then a postal worker walking into a bar. Having established those characters, they are set in our minds. Then *the* firefighter speaks, then *the* cop speaks, then…what? Some other random postal worker who was already in the bar spoke up? It sure didn't feel like *our* postal worker, who we had already established was there. It felt like some other person had magically appeared.

Watch for accidentally doing this with characters you identify with multiple pronouns (like sheriff, judge, or reverend), as well as with objects you are introducing for the first time.

"Shut up!" she snarled and pulled out the gun, pointing it at me.

This seems like it works, but if it is the first time a gun is mentioned, it comes off really strange. We didn't know a gun was there, so how could this be *the* gun? The reverse is true. What if the whole story revolves around a magic gun and at the very end, this showdown happens:

"Shut up!" she snarled and pulled out a gun, pointing it at me.

When *a* was used, instead of *the*, suddenly there was no way the reader would think it was the special magic gun. It had to be some new gun, right?

a lot vs. alot

This, unlike many of the other problems on this list, is easy to deal with. **Alot is not a word.**

It just isn't. Don't use it. This will come up a lot, so you need to know it. (See what I did there?)

Allot is a word, but it is unrelated. It means to assign or distribute something.

adverse vs. averse

I am averse to adverse situations.

Adverse generally means something is not good, whereas **averse** is related to aversion, which is a strong feeling of dislike.

accept vs. except

Accept generally means to receive something, or to approve of it (albeit not always willingly).

Except is pretty much the opposite of accept. It usually means to not include something.

The place writers most often make mistakes with these words is with the phrase "present company."

"Present company excepted."

When most people speak these words, what they mean is "I just said something unpleasant about everyone, but I didn't mean to include you people I am currently talking to." They are leaving them out of that grouping. The present company is the exception to the generality just stated.

"Present company accepted."

This is not the phrase writers usually intend to use. What the use of *accepted* in this phrase means is: I approve of the company around me. I am okay to have these people here.

I remember the differences this way:

The "X" in except reminds me of scissors cutting something out from everything else, setting it apart, and making it the exception. The "A" in accept makes me think, "Ahhh! I want that! I will accept it!"

affect vs. effect

This is a really tough one a lot of people have problems with. I had written a bunch of cutesy, smartass sentences and examples for this (which, in a fit of pique, I deleted and then wished I hadn't), but it is so confusing I was afraid of messing people up if I wasn't straightforward enough.

First, before we get to the hard part, let's get the alternate meanings out of the way.

Affect is the word you use when describing someone's countenance (expression on their face) or their emotional state.

"When I told him, he maintained a flat affect."

Effects can be used as a synonym for possessions.

"They catalogued all of the victim's effects before returning them to his family."

Those meanings are fairly easy to differentiate and remember. Unfortunately, the other meanings are, well, not so easy.

There are many different usages for both *affect* and *effect*, both as verbs and nouns (and adjectives if you use *effective* and *affected*), and if you aren't sure which you need, I strongly recommend you use a thesaurus and figure out which has the synonyms that would correctly fit in place of the word where you are trying to use it. Don't be lazy and skip this. If you do your editor might not catch it, but it will feel like every one of your readers do.

Some **affect synonyms** are change, assume (to take on), alter, influence, and inspire. Some **effect synonyms** are outcome, response, consequence, cause, create, carry out.

Meanwhile, here are some examples to get you started down this rabbit hole.

Affecting things tends to cause **effects**.

"I want to effect change" means I want to start making a change.

"I want to affect change" means I want to change the change.

The movie affected me. It made me sad.
The effect of the movie was to make me sad.
The explosion had no effect on the wall, but it adversely affected our eardrums.
The delay affected our plans, but once we effected the plan, the special effects were used to spectacular effect and affected the crowd deeply.

Some things have an effect on things
Some things affect other things.

afterwards vs. afterward

This problem applies to an entire group of words: **afterward, backward, forward, upward, downward, inward, outward, toward**, etc.

Generally putting an *s* on the end of the word is British usage. American usage tends to not use the *s*. The biggest issue is that you need to pick one way or the other and stick with it. Don't use *toward* in some places and *towards* in others in the same story.

afterward vs. afterword

Afterward: This is an indication of time relation.
We went out to dinner afterward.
As with *backward*, *toward*, or the other __*ward* words, it can have an s on the end or not. Again, it's up to you, but be consistent.

Afterword: This is notes or comments on a story, not more of the story itself. Think of it as it is spelled: things written after the words. Unlike *afterward*, adding an *s* to the end of *afterword* does change the meaning to plural. (See also **Epilogue**.)

albeit vs. all be it

This is one of the terms we get wrong when we write it the first time after hearing it for years. The word **albeit** came from the words *although be it*, and generally can be used in place of the words *although* or *even if*.

Which is quite a different meaning than *all be it*, which sounds like a strange game of tag to me.

all ready vs. already

All ready means something is prepared.

"We're all ready to go."
"The supplies are all ready to be packed up."

Already means previously.

"They already left."
"I already packed the supplies."

To contrast:
"The cars are all ready at the starting line," means the cars are started and revving their engines, waiting for the signal to go.
"The cars are already at the starting line," means you don't need to wait for the cars to get to the starting line, they are there.
If you make this mistake often, add it to your **Final Checklist**.

all right vs. alright

You are going to have to make a judgment call on this one, but at least you will know what you are getting into, right?

One of the things many of us heard in school is: "**Alright is never all right,**" meaning that you should never use the word alright—just like "Ain't ain't a word."

For many people that is true.

For others **alright** is an acceptable contraction of all right.

But for some people, very much in the minority as of this writing, *alright* has come to take on a different meaning than *all right*. They feel *alright* means acceptable, or adequate, while *all right* means correct, or accurate.

Examples:

"She seems alright."
"The measurements are all right."

Whether to use this distinction, as well as whether or not *alright* is all right, is a choice you will have to make, but as with anything, be consistent in your usage, especially within each body of work.

all together vs. altogether

Some sources I have seen say these words are synonyms for each other. They are not.

All together means as one, or in a group. It is the opposite of one at a time. Some synonyms are: collectively, jointly, and en masse.

"Get ready and go all together."
"It was really cute when they sang all together."
"Let's bring them all together, and then we'll deal with it."

Altogether means *as a whole*. Some synonyms are: entirely, fully, absolutely, and thoroughly.

"That was altogether a terrible experience!"
"Now we have altogether new problems."

A common phrase, used as a euphemism for nude, or unclothed, is being **"in the altogether."**

alloneword

Okay. That's not a typo. It's not right either, but I wanted to get your attention. I wasn't sure where in the book to put this section. It needed to go in the section about misused words, but it also needed to go in the section about hyphens. On top of that, it is big enough, and problematic enough, to be its own section. But really, I finally decided this boils down to not knowing the meaning of a word, as the hyphenated version of a compound word can have quite a different meaning than an open or closed version.

Putting this section here, in this otherwise alphabetical list of words, was a tough choice, but I decided to do what I always do and break my own rules. (This one is breaking the consistency rule, but at least I stuck it in alphabetically and alongside other common problem compound words!)

There are a lot of compound words that confuse many writers. We use them in everyday language but not always in formal writing. When writing fiction, we often discover we are writing a turn of phrase we've never seen in print before, and often we don't realize it wasn't a phrase after all, but an actual word. (See the introduction to this section, **I Do Not Think That Word Means What You Think It Means**, for more on that idea.)

There are three kinds of **compound words**:

Open - this means they are separate words such as ice cream, South African, living room, hot chocolate, and make up.

Closed - this means they are one word (which is what the rest of this list deals with) such as sunglasses, drugstore, daytime, baseball, and shortchange.

Hyphenated - this means they are two words joined together to form a new idea. Sometimes these are new ideas (see the section on the **Hyphen** for more on this) and sometimes they have been around long enough to become part of the language, such as self-respect, get-together, left-handed, and mind-boggling.

I thought I would throw together a short list of some compound words that I've seen cause problems (or at least caused me problems) just in case you needed a reference point on some of them. This is by no means even close to a complete list! These are just words that I, as a fiction editor, have come across most often. (Well, sometimes only once, and other times only in my mind.)

Sometimes it doesn't matter how you write them because the words mean the same thing whether they are written as closed, open, or hyphenated compound words, but sometimes the compound word has a completely different meaning than the two words separated!

Remember, the dictionary is your friend. If you don't know a word, look it up.

The following is a list of words that mean something different if you break them up, or words that are generally considered a misspelling if broken up. This list is not meant to be comprehensive.

Afterthought	Foreleg	Scapegoat
Anybody	Foresee	Somebody
Anyhow	Forklift	Someday
Anything	Fortnight	Somehow
Anywhere	Furthermore	Sometime
Awestruck	Ghostwriter	Somewhat
Backhand	Handmade	Somewhere
Backlog	Headquarters	Southeast
Backtrack	Hereafter	Southward
Bedroll	Hereby	Southwest
Bellyache	Herein	Spoilsport
Bodyguard	Hereinafter	Straightforward
Bookworm	Heretofore	Storeroom
Brainwash	Hereupon	Superstar
Breakthrough	Homemade	Takeaway
Bypass	Howbeit	Therefore
Candlelight	Insofar	Throughout
Counterclockwise	Inasmuch	Throwback
Daydream	Keyhole	Underbelly
Eastward	Lifeblood	Upside
Elsewhere	Lukewarm	Westward
Everlasting	Meanwhile	Whatnot
Everybody	Moonstruck	Whatsoever
Everyday	Moreover	Whenever
Everyone	Nevertheless	Whereas
Everything	Nobody	Whereto
Everywhere	Nonetheless	Whereupon
Firsthand	Northeast	Wherever
Foolproof	Northward	Wherewithal
Footprints	Northwest	Whoever
Forefather	Noteworthy	Whomever
Forefinger	Notwithstanding	Woebegone
Forehand	Nowhere	
Forehead	Overview	

bare vs. bear

The surface meanings of these words are generally not a problem. Most people know a **bear** is an animal and **bare** means naked.

A bare bear has no hair.

Where people tend to get lost is in the other uses of the words.

The bare bear knew his endeavor wouldn't bear scrutiny, and staying would bear no good, and he could no longer bear the worry of the need to bear more weight upon his own back, so he decided to bare his soul and bear toward his neglected and bare bear cave before everything came to bear down upon him.

Okay, enough silliness. **Bare** means naked. This can be interpreted as *not much*. Things that are *bare* can be naked, empty, exposed, or barely something.

The room was bare. (It was empty, naked of furniture.)
The plains were bare. (Naked of animals, or maybe plants.)
That piece of junk is barely a car. (Naked of what it needs.)
He bared his soul. (Exposed it, or made it naked, so it could be seen.)

Bear means everything else. It can be used to mean heading (direction), support, load, carry, and others.

He chose to bear west toward the coast.
She had a heavy load to bear.
The tomato plant bears fruit.
He chose to bear his head high.
Their sins bear heavily upon them.

The one that seems to confuse most people is the common phrase involving the teeth. Do you *bear* your teeth, or do you *bare* your teeth? Well, both, actually. The problem comes with what you mean and how you intend it. Also, in that its usage has been muddied for a long time and has changed over time. Most sources will say that **"bare your teeth" is correct**. This means you make them naked and show them.

But if I bear my teeth, that means I am carrying them. Which I am, so that's not wrong, if that's what I meant. Especially, I suppose, if they've been knocked out and I am now carrying them with me in a bag.

Now here's the nasty one. A lot of older writing contains things like "The snarling dog beared its teeth." Is this wrong? Yes and no. Either way, I don't recommend using it. Modern standards don't care for it, and the support for reasons to use it are weak.

Here are my reasons not to use it: the word bear also means to produce. Kind of. So, if you say, "the snarling dog produced its teeth," you would be correct, wouldn't you?

Maybe, maybe not. The problem is there are two meanings for produced. One is *presented*, as in "here you go, here are my teeth, see?" In that case, the usage might be right. The dog did bring its teeth out of hiding, thus producing them.

But what about "the snarling dog created a set of teeth?" That's one of the other meanings of *produced*. It doesn't work as well. No one expects the dog to go back to its workshop and make the teeth, so obviously this use of *produced* is not a good synonym for *bear*.

What about "the snarling dog gave birth to a set of teeth"? That one is even more iffy, right? There is a poetry to saying that, though. I mean, the reader knows the dog didn't lie down, have uterine contractions, and bring a set of teeth into this world through the miracle of birth, but the reader can also see the metaphoric meaning here. And that may be how some of those writers, years ago, had intended it to be.

But most readers today won't understand it that way.

Use of the word *bear* as a synonym for *produced* is generally accepted as limited to giving birth of some sort. Such as "to bear a child" or "to bear fruit."

Some dictionaries also list definitions of *bear* to include *to show*, which brings people into this argument from a different place, but again, it ends up being an imperfect synonym. When *bear* is used as *to show*, it shows something by way of implication rather than literally showing it. Such as "bears a resemblance."

In any example of this usage I was able find, the word *carry* (or a form of that word) was a stronger synonym than *show*, so "the snarling dog beared its teeth" still seems to fall back to the dog carrying its teeth.

That is why I will always use it as **"The dog bared its teeth."**

Be wary of the also-confusing typo "barred its teeth," which again, could sometimes be considered correct but probably isn't.

began vs. begun

Began is the past tense of begin. **Begun** is the past participle of begin. The problem here is that *begin* is an irregular verb, so it conjugates oddly in the present perfect and past perfect tenses.

The easiest way to remember which to use is **begun needs a helping verb,** such as have or had.

They began working on Monday.

They will *have* begun working on Monday.
They *had* begun working on Monday.

bemused

Bemused does not mean amused, in an amused way, or entertained. **Bemused means confused.**

If something the jester says bemuses the king, the king will not be amused about it. The king will be irritated that the fool was trying to make him look a fool.

Kings like to be amused, not bemused.

blond vs. blonde

Many languages have what is called grammatical gender. This is basically the assigning of gender to nouns in the language. For example, in Spanish, an apple, or *la manzana,* is a feminine noun, and as such is spoken of, or written of, with feminine traits. Meanwhile a banana, or *el plátano,* is a masculine noun and is spoken of, or written of, with masculine traits. This also applies to things that are not (or never were) alive, such as *el vestido,* a dress, and *la corbata,* a necktie. (Of interesting note, in Spanish, the dress is a masculine and the necktie is a feminine. I included this to show guessing grammatical gender doesn't always work out so well.)

This idea often confuses people who speak languages, such as English, that do not typically assign grammatical gender to nouns. We do still have some in English, such as actor and actress, and waiter and waitress, but they all (that I know of) apply to living things which actually have gender, such as people, cows, horses, etc. (I have been told Old English used grammatical gender assigned nouns.)

With that in mind, consider this:

Blonde is the feminine form of the word blond in French. Using it to describe a male makes little to no sense to them, or it could possibly be considered as an attempt at humor.

Common American usage is to stick with *blond,* but if you must use *blonde* remember that word means a female blond.

could have vs. could of

There is a common mistake here that derives, once again, from the spoken language being different than the written one. This mistake comes from what people think they hear each other say and then mistakenly repeat incorrectly.

The correct term is "**could have.**" The problem comes in with the use of the contraction *could've*. People hear that spoken, and it sounds like "coulda" or "could of," so then they write it that way.

This mistake applies to **could've, must've, should've,** and **would've** as well. They should be (when not contracted): could have, must have, should have, and would have.

could care less vs. couldn't care less

A lot of people say they could care less when they actually mean they **couldn't care less**. When they say they could care less, they imply that they actually do care, because there is room for them to care less.

decimated

Although it has fallen into common usage as meaning mass destruction, decimated originally meant nothing of the sort. **Decimated meant one in ten destroyed**, not nine out of ten.

Only a few short years ago, were you to have a general declare his troops decimated the opposing army, you would actually be having him say he ruined 10% of their forces. If your general were to say something like he only lost one in four of his men while decimating half of the enemy's army, he would actually be saying he lost 25% of his men to destroy 10% of 50% of the enemy forces, or only 5% overall. Not really much of a victory after all.

This is why so many people don't like the modern usage of *decimated* to mean destroyed. Be prepared to come under attack for using this word no matter which way you go with it.

every day vs. everyday

Every day means each individual day.

Every day that goes by is one day we are closer to death.
Lizzie goes to school every day.

Everyday means ordinary.

"Why don't you just wear your everyday clothes?"
He's just an everyday kind of guy.

farthest vs. furthest

Farthest is used in talking about physical distances that can be measured.

He threw the ball the farthest.

Furthest is used when speaking metaphorically, about something that cannot actually be measured, or about time. (Which I feel can be measured, so I don't know who made up this rule. A scientist grammarian who knew time was relative and therefore not measurable, maybe?)

He has gone the furthest into madness.
We cannot go any further back in time.

gray vs. grey

This comes down to an American or British preference. American usage leans toward gray, while British leans to grey. Mostly it is important to be consistent in your usage. Don't switch back and forth.

imply vs infer

To **imply** something is to show a hidden meaning, to drop hints about something.
To **infer** something is to find meanings, or to pick up on something someone else was implying.

inflammable

Inflammable does not mean fire-proof or resistant or non-flammable. It means the exact same thing as flammable.

ironic

Ironic isn't just when a bad thing happens at a bad time. In fact, it doesn't have to be a bad thing at all. It also isn't merely something unexpected.
Something is ironic when there is an unexpected outcome that is close to, if not the opposite of what was expected. Good, bad, or indifferent.
There are several types of irony, the main ones being Verbal, Dramatic, and Situational. I'm not going to go into deep detail here, so please, if it interests

you, look them up. You may get some cool story ideas out of them.

Verbal Irony is basically sarcasm. When you say something that is the opposite of what you really mean, like telling your brother "Nice shoes," when he shows up barefoot.

Dramatic Irony is when the audience or reader has information a character doesn't, and we enjoy the tension/humor of them making choices that don't make sense or are the opposite of what they would have done if they would have known that information.

The final (major) type of irony is **Situational**. This is what most people are referring to when they say something was ironic. It is when an outcome of something is pretty much the opposite of what was expected. The typical example of this is when a fire station burns down, but this could be something like having that rubber band you're getting ready to shoot your sister with break and hit you in the nose, or finding out all of the things a time traveler did to try save the world are actually what destroys it.

irregardless vs. regardless

Many people say *irregardless* is not a word. Irregardless of what they say, this one has been around since the late 1700's and people still say it isn't a word. How many people have to use a word before it becomes a real word? How long do they have to use it? Irregardless, whether you choose to use it is up to you.

I certainly would stand my ground if I chose to use it in dialog, but I wouldn't use it in narrative. Like *decimated*, it's not worth the argument. It means exactly the same thing as regardless.

Kind of.

It means that the way people use it, anyway.

Irregardless is a double negative type of situation, which is why so many people don't like it.

With regard to something means paying attention to it or giving it consideration. *Regard-less* means with no regard. See? Less regard. *Irregard*, were it actually a word, would mean the same thing as regardless. The prefix *ir-* basically means *not* or *negative*. So, when you add *ir-* to regard, you get "no regard." When you add *−less* to regard, you get "no regard." When you add *ir-* and *−less* to regard, you get "no regard no." So basically you are right back to *with regards.*

Irregardless would actually mean the opposite of regardless. If it were a word.

it's vs. its

It's is not a possessive, it's the contraction for *it is*. (That's fun! I should use a word in its own definition more often! Oh, wait. I ran into that problem with *affect* and *effect*. Never mind. That sucked.)

Its is possessive. This is confusing because an *apostrophe s* almost always means possession, but not here. You need to remember this one is the exception to the rule.

Examples:

It's a nice day today. I should decide what it's going to be used for. Today is its birthday. I wonder what its name is?

lay vs. lie and laying vs. lying
(Also known as the crash-course in English irregular verb conjugation and intransitive verbs.)

Okay. There is no pop quiz on this at the end, but you'll feel like I was planning one by the time you get there. I decided that I should explain this completely, rather than just giving examples, because I think being able to understand it makes it easier to remember.

Lay is a problem for people because it is an irregular verb. That means when we conjugate it, it does not change the way most verbs do.

Let's start with a simple verb and conjugate it:

Smile becomes:

I smile, I smiled, I am smiling, I have smiled, I will smile

Pretty simple, right? Most of us are fairly good with standard conjugations. Now let's do the same thing with **lay**:

I lay, I laid, I am laying, I have laid, I will lay.

See how the word changed in a non-standard way? We don't just add *–ed* to it and move on like we did with *smile*. We have a whole new word we have to use. But that wasn't too hard, was it? You recognized that word right away! I knew you had it in you! Good job.

Gee, Sam, that was *easy, but you didn't answer the question about when to use* lie *instead of* lay.

Okay. I admit, it's not fair of me to put words in your mouth. Er…on the page for you? Never mind.

Notice that above, where I used *smile* as an example, *smile* is an intransitive verb. That means it doesn't use a direct object. I can't smile a ball. I can't smile you. But I can make myself smile.

Lie is kind of the same thing.

While some verbs are intransitive only, many verbs can be used as a transitive or an intransitive verb.

Example:

I eat.
I eat pizza.

The first example is intransitive. I eat. It does not have an object. It is an action that I perform but doesn't have to say what I perform it on to make sense. The second example is a transitive verb. I eat pizza. It is an action that I perform on something.

The verb *to lay,* which means to place something, conjugates irregularly for past tense and becomes *laid,* also conjugates irregularly when used as an intransitive verb. At that point, *lay* conjugates to become *lie.*

When I lay myself down, the conjugation is *lay,* because there is an object for the verb to transform in some way (hence the term *transitive verb*). Just as I lay a book down, I lay myself down.

But when I lie down, I do not tell you I am going to do it to myself. It is implied with a reflexive verb that points back to me.

If I say, "I'm going to go lie down," you don't ask me *what* I am going to go lay down, because you should know, I am going to lay myself down. There is no object for the verb to transform so the verb is intransitive.

Hopefully that explains how *lay* becomes *lie.*

And hopefully we all know that to not tell the truth is to lie, and we can just leave that there and move on.

Unfortunately, just when you thought I had gone too far with this whole thing and we were done, you were wrong.

Here's the pop quiz:

Just kidding. But there is more, and it adds to the confusion.

When *lay* has been conjugated to its irregular transitive form of *lie,* and then is used in the past tense (meaning something that happened already), it turns back into *lay.*

Why? I don't know, he's on third, and I don't give a darn.

Seriously.

"I am going to go lie down."
Becomes
"I went to lay down."

So…

"Yesterday, I laid the book down." (past tense transitive)
"Yesterday, I laid myself down." (past tense transitive)
"Yesterday, I lay down." (past tense intransitive)

Hopefully, after following all the explanations of transitive and intransitive verbs, and irregular verb conjugation, you followed how that worked. If not, try this: Only a chicken can say they laid in bed last night. (Okay, any bird really. Or reptile. Or fish. Or the platypus. You get the idea.)

And now, on to the one that confuses everyone! *To lie* means to rest, or to recline, and, unfortunately, it conjugates irregularly for past tense as well, becoming, for goodness knows why, *lay* in the simple past tense.

The book lies on the bed next to me. (simple present tense)
The book lay on the bed next to me. (simple past tense)
The book had lain on the bed next to me. (past participle)
The book is lying on the bed next to me. (present participle)

For many writers, the confusion in whether to use *lay* or *lie(s)* is a confusion with the tense they are writing in. Remember, we tend to write in simple past tense, not present tense. See Shifting Tenses for more on this.

Bonus Example Commonly used idioms:
Hope lies within.
Therein lies the problem.

Neither *hope* nor *the problem* lay anything down, so we use *lie*.
Ready for the mind-rot?

"I was lying."

Does that mean I wasn't telling the truth, or does that mean I was reclining on a bed?
It means both. Same word for both meanings.

Lying is intransitive, meaning it does not need to have an object to act upon.
Laying is transitive, meaning it does need an object.

I was lying on the floor.
I was laying the rug on the floor.

As he lie on the floor, I lay a blanket upon him.
While he was lying on the floor, I was laying a blanket upon him.

A good way to help you remember is you can hear the word *lay* being said in the word when you *place* things somewhere, and you can hear the *lie* being told when you say you're staying home from work, sick in bed. (I'm going to *lie* down because I am ill.)
Oh, and just to be thorough:

"I have lain in the past" means reclined.
"I have lied in the past" means told untruths.

Whee! That was fun—not.

I hope your head doesn't hurt as much as mine, and that you made it through all of that all right.

literally

People have given each other enough grief over this word that I don't hear or see it misused much anymore, but I listed it just in case.

Literally means that whatever you are saying is exactly what happened. Not a metaphor for what happened, but exactly what happened. People misuse it as a replacement for figuratively (which was never actually used in that way as far as I know).

When you say, "That was the best thing ever!", you are making an exaggeration to prove a point (unless, of course, it was the best thing ever). This is a figurative use of speech. So is saying, "There were a million people in line for the bathroom!" Everyone knows that is an exaggeration. It is intended to be. It is supposed to make the person you are talking to think, "Wow! There must have been a lot of people there!" It is not supposed to make them think that a census taker counted the people in line and turned in a report that said there were exactly one million people in line for the bathroom.

Adding the word literally to those sentences changes their meanings. "That was literally the best thing ever!" means that there has never been anything that good, anywhere, before now. "There were literally a million people in line for the bathroom!" means there were 1,000,000 people standing in a line to use that bathroom.

Why is this a problem? First, because it's irritating to a lot of people. "So what?" someone may say, and then they could go on to argue that, in and of itself, the use of the word literally in this way is a figurative exaggeration. And they would be correct.

So why is it listed here? Because using it in writing is confusing.

Although you may have occasion to want to write a character who speaks in that way (using the word *literally* as a figurative exaggeration), you should never use it in the narrative voice of your story. It will sound stilted and odd, and it will confuse the readers.

Example:

Mary held Todd's hand as they walked up the grassy hill in the ruddy light of the sunset. Golden motes drifted lazily in the still, warm summer air, like fairies swirling around them. Todd glanced at her with a smile dancing across his face, and Mary beamed back at him. They were

literally **floating on air** with their love for each other and the perfect setting of this moment.

So, did the world suddenly become a magical place where people do actually float on air when they are in love?

The other metaphors seemed okay, didn't they? You didn't really think the dust in the air was made out of gold or that it had turned into dancing fairies. You didn't really think that Todd's smile danced around his nose like Fred Astaire. Did you think Mary shot a beam at Todd? Hopefully not. But as soon as I told you they were literally floating on air, you had to wonder if they were really floating.

This starts to cause confusion with the reader, and it ruins the use of other metaphors.

The only example I can think of, where you would want to use *literally* as a figurative exaggeration in narration, would be in a story told in the first person point of view. Even then you would need to make sure it was done in a way that let the reader know, for sure, that the narrator was using the word *literally* as a figurative exaggeration.

loose vs. lose

For some people this is just a common typo, for others, it is a common mistake.

Lose means you lost something.
Loose means you let something go, or something got away.

"Lose the horses!" means get rid of them and walk on foot.
"Loose the horses!" means release the horses, set them free, let them go running wild.

Loose papers would be sheets of paper that are not bound together in some way.
Lose papers would be something that informed you that you didn't win. Or perhaps it would be something an angry Russian would tell you to do.

The easiest way for me to remember: **lose lost an o because it was loose**.

ludicrous vs. Ludacris

This is a ludicrous mistake often made by people of a certain age.

Ludicrous means something like stupidly ridiculous.
Ludacris is the stage name of a hip hop artist and actor.

The way to remember is Ludacris' real name is Chris, not Crous.

nonplussed

Nonplussed does not mean *not impressed*.

Although it has been used that way by so many people for so long that even online dictionaries are starting to say it means things along those lines, nonplussed actually means nearly the opposite.

Nonplussed means confused or something more along the lines of "so bewildered he couldn't even talk."

So, when a character is nonplussed, and just stands there staring at another character, it doesn't mean they were unimpressed. It means the character is staring at the other person like that person just grew a second head and they have no idea what to say about it.

You can see why people learning this word from reading (like most of us do) could become confused even if the word were used correctly.

past vs. passed

Past indicates time. Passed indicates motion. Easy, right? You wish.

"I passed the time thinking about the past."
"It was past the time to think about the past."
"In the past, the quarterback has passed the ball past all of the receivers."

The problem is not only that *passed* and *past* are so similar sounding, but that *pass* can be used as a transitive or an intransitive verb. I can pass an object, or I can make myself pass. (Oooh… That sounds terrible. In more ways than one.) For more information on transitive and intransitive verbs, and how they confuse us in situations like this, see **lay vs. lie** and **laying vs. lying** to bring you up to speed.

So, when do you use *past* in the place where you thought you should have used *passed*? When there is a verb already there in place of *passed*.

"I passed the horse." becomes **"I walked past the horse."**
"She passed the park." becomes **"She drove past the park."**
"They passed the point of no return." becomes **"They went past the point of no return."**

These are all two different ways to write nearly the same thing, but notice the subtle difference:

"I smiled as I went past the point of no return."
"I smiled as I passed the point of no return."

Part of the reason we get into trouble with this is we don't write the way we speak. Colloquially, some of us often say things like "I passed past the store five minutes ago." But written out that looks strange and is redundant. I don't recommend doing it.

peaked vs. peeked vs. piqued

Peaked means reached its apex, or its highest point, or the best, or most, it will ever be.
Peeked means someone looked at it.
Piqued means to raise interest in, or arouse, either in a good way or a bad way.
Generally *piqued* is implied as a negative idea when used alone as a noun:
"I was in a fit of pique."
When used as a verb, *piqued* tends to be used as a positive idea, unless specifically stated as negative:

"His smile piqued my interest." (positive implied)
as opposed to
"Her smirk piqued my ire." (negatively stated)

Sometimes a writer is not sure which they mean: peaked interest or piqued interest. While very similar, they are different.

"Peaked my interest" means raised my interest to the highest level it's ever been at.
"Piqued my interest" means created an interest or captured my interest.

peal vs. peel

Peal is a sound. Specifically, it is a sound that seems to echo or reverberate.
Peel is the outside skin, or an action of removing/opening said skin.

You need to learn the proper way to peel off a banana peel.

The peal of thunder rolled across the mountains.

Bonus Thunder peals, lightning does not. Lightning is only the flash of light, or the actual energy itself. Thunder, which is the sound, peals. I know this is strange, as bells themselves can also peal, as well as be the ringing sound the bells make, but for some reason we have so strongly separated thunder from lightning that we cannot say, "the peals of lightning echoed across the valley," without people assuming you are wrong.

penultimate

Imagine the New York City Marathon. The race kicks off with a bang! The runners sprint outward, some to prove they are the best, others just to prove they can do it.

Around two and a half hours later, the first runner crosses the finish line, arms raised in victory, beads of sweat, mixed with tears, roll down their cheeks. That person is not the penultimate. Not even close.

Twenty minutes later the second-place winner runs up, grin wide on their face. They're not the penultimate either. They are closer, but still a long ways off.

About eight and a half hours later, 45,000 people have crossed the finish line. None of them were the penultimate either.

Eleven hours later, it's dark, nearly everyone has gone home, but one enduring individual is pushing themselves hard to achieve a personal goal. They know everyone else has already finished the race. They know they are dead last. But they refuse to give up. They refuse to admit they couldn't reach the finish line. Finally, slowly, deliberately, to the sound of a smattering of applause and shouts of encouragement, they stumble across that line and fulfill their life-long goal of running the New York City Marathon.

Guess what? That person wasn't the penultimate either.

The penultimate was the person who crossed the line an hour earlier: the second to last person to finish.

That's what **penultimate means. Second to last.**

It doesn't mean the best or even second best. It doesn't mean the worst or second from worst. **There is no connotation of value prescribed to this word.**

You can think of it as next-to-last, but it doesn't matter which way you were counting. Instead of the next to last racer crossing the finish line, it can mean "there is only one model newer," or "it's the middle film in the trilogy," (though no one uses it that way). But it doesn't mean ultimate, supreme, best, or hardly any of the other things most people think it means.

This confusion seems to come from the duality of the meaning of the word ultimate. While ultimate means last, it also means something along the lines of best. This probably came about because in contest situations, like, oh, I don't know, things that happen in coliseums with swords, the last contestant remaining is the best. All the lesser ones have been eliminated, so the final standing swordsman (or swordswoman) is the ultimate, and the one lying in the pool of blood at their feet was the penultimate.

The next time you try to convince me your character and their weapons can't be defeated because they are the penultimate warrior with the penultimate equipment, remember; what you're actually telling me is they are second best and armed with last year's models of weapons. Or, if you were counting things the other way, there is only one warrior or one weapon that is actually worse than they are.

prescribe vs. subscribe

A **prescription** is something the doctor gives you to take to the pharmacy. **"The doctor gave me a prescription for a placebo."**

A **subscription** is something you sign up for. **"I have a subscription for *Time Magazine*."**

To **subscribe** to something also means that you concur with that idea. **"I subscribe to the Theory of Evolution."**

You can **subscribe** to a magazine to receive it for yourself, but if you **prescribe** the magazine, you are recommending it to someone.

I **subscribe** to the idea that doctors can heal me, so I go to see what they would **prescribe** to help me.

You **subscribe** to an idea if you believe in it. You **prescribe** an idea if you think applies.

There are also **proscribe** and **ascribe**, but I have never seen anyone misuse these. This is relevant as things that are **prescribed by law** are set by, or established by law, not to be confused with **proscribed by law**, which has nearly the opposite meaning: banned by law.

To be thorough I am including **ascribe**. It means to give credit to. **"The Theory of Evolution is ascribed to Charles Darwin."** Or **"She ascribed his failure to the inclement weather."**

poisonous vs. venomous

This is one of those "drives people nuts" things. Some people can't stand when you get it wrong, but it is confusing. The problem is that both venom and poison are toxins. The difference comes down to this: how is the toxin delivered?

If you have to eat it, breath it, or get it on your skin, it is a **poison**. If something has to bite or sting you, it is a **venom**. So basically, if you only say animals are **venomous** and then, only when not talking about eating them, you should be fine.

If you eat something that has a toxin that makes you sick, that thing is **poisonous**. Even if it was an animal.

Is a rattlesnake venomous? Yes. It can bite you and inject a toxin. Is it poisonous? Maybe. Are you really going to eat the venom and find out?

Is a stinging nettle venomous because it injects you with toxins when you brush up against it? I don't know, but there really don't seem to be any results when you research venomous plants, so I would just assume that if it is a plant, it's poisonous.

pore over vs. pour over

This is a common homophone problem, especially in fantasies where wizards have giant tomes of information. To **pore** over something means to study it intently. To **pour** over something is to make a mess with liquid.

He pored over the book, looking for hidden answers in the text.
She poured lemon juice over the book, looking for hidden answers in the text.

A subtle but distinct difference!

rain vs. reign vs. rein

Rain – water that falls from the sky
Reign – to rule over
Rein – a strap used to steer a horse

If you can't remember which is which, look it up. Don't be lazy and get it wrong. If you are good at remembering things by mnemonics, try this: **Reign has a G, just like a King.**

secret vs. secrete

This one doesn't happen often, but when it does, it's a deal killer for me. A **secret** is, of course, something you don't tell anyone except your best friend, who then goes on to tell everyone for you.

For those of you who like to use fancy-schmancy words, yes **secrete** means to hide something, especially in past tense.

Before the soldiers came, the spy secreted the secret papers away in the night.

But **secrete also means to ooze disgusting stuff from body orifices.** No one likes it when the main character secretes. Especially not into his love interest's ear on a quiet moonlit night.

Technically, there is nothing wrong with using the word secrete when talking about secrets and such, but modern readers nearly always start to think about gooey stuff when you do. And it's easy to use it in a place where the comic effect is horrendous.

Example:

The king's and queen's love for each other often interfered with the royal duties. Anytime they became worried they weren't performing well, they would secrete themselves away in the royal dungeons. Sometimes together, sometimes separately.

You should give serious consideration to how your readers will interpret the word *secrete* before you use it. And then you should re-think using it. Maybe not even then.

Yuck.

shear vs. sheer

Sheer luck and **sheer cliffs** are common phrases. Unfortunately many of us confuse the spellings and meanings of *sheer* with *shear*.

Sheer means pure or total, as in "**sheer luck**," or steep or abrupt, as in "**sheer cliffs**." It can also be a noun relating to fabric or a ship.)

Shear means *to cut* or *to sever*, as in "**go shear the sheep**," or "**the bolt was sheared off.**"

sight vs. site

Site is an easy word. It is a place. That is pretty much all it is. A place. A work site. A web site (now usually one word: website). The site of a battle. An archeological dig site. The word site isn't used for any other meaning than a location, real or virtual.

Sight has more meanings. First, it is our ability to see. From there, it gets used in ways that relate to seeing.

The biggest confusion seems to be with when a site is a sight or not.

Tourists go sightseeing to see the sights.

That means they are going to see the things to look at, not go visit the sites.

A construction company supervisor will be going out to see the sites.

But that has a different meaning than what the tourists are doing.

Guns have sights, and you sight them in.

Sight is related to vision. If you can't see the g, you're not using your eyes.

than vs. then

Than is used for comparison.
Then is related to time.

"I will prove I am better than you, and then I will treat you to ice cream!"

The exception (Isn't there always an exception? Of course there is. That's why it's confusing!) is when we say something like "No sooner than…," or "No sooner (had I, or did I)(do something) than…"

"No sooner had I gotten in the shower, than the doorbell rang."

Notice that, although time is involved in this situation, this situation is also a comparison. It is a comparison of time, so we use *than*. People get confused in this situation because they feel as though they are somehow contrasting getting in the shower with the doorbell ringing, but it is actually a comparison of the times at which those events occurred.

that vs. who

People are *who*, things are *that*. This distinction is falling out of favor in modern usage, but purists insist.
As do I.

The woman who stopped by to visit.
The tree that blew over.

This is an issue that can add to your problems if you are struggling with ambiguous pronouns. (See **Ambiguous Pronouns** for more information.)

their vs. there vs. they're

Their is a possessive pronoun.
There is a place.
They're is a contraction for **they are**.

That is their car.
Their car is over there.
They're over there with their car.

A surprising number of us get these wrong. An even more surprising number of us refuse to be even the tiniest bit forgiving of someone else's mistake involving one of these homophones, even in this age of autocorrect failures.

If you don't know which to use, try using elimination to figure it out.

If you can substitute **they are**, then you need **they're**.

I would say that if you can substitute the word **here**, then use **there**, but the sentence structures don't always interchange perfectly, and I don't want to confuse anyone. So, if you don't want to do that, I would offer that maybe you could try to think of **there** as a kind of contraction for **not here**.

(**Not here = nothere = 'there = there**)

Their is a pronoun. *I* is a pronoun. There is an *I* in *their*. So...
"If I is in their, I is a pronoun, too!" (Silly, I know, but it works for me.)

use to vs. used to

Yay! An easy one! **Used to** is the past tense of **use to**, so anytime we say we used to do something, we are talking in the past tense, which means it is almost always *used to*.

"I used to walk that way to school every day."

Even when you are describing what something is used for, such as "A hammer is used to hit a nail." Because it was.

Unfortunately, as always, there is something that complicates this, which is why we all mess it up.

When did we not use to do something? When we never did it. And that is when we use "**use to**."

"I never use to walk home that way because I was afraid of bullies."

The negation in the sentence shows that action never happened in the past, so we don't make *use to* past tense.

Another usage is to say you will, or did, become familiar with something:

"You get used to it."

weather vs. whether

This is a straight up simple homophone, but I've seen it used incorrectly many times.

Weather is the climate
Whether expresses a choice between two things.

You can try to remember weather and rain both have an *a*. Or you can just add it to your Final Checklist.

who vs. whom

Both of these words mean the same thing. The usage of *whom* is considered archaic by some, pointless by others, and mandatory by sticklers. Whether you use it is up to you but stay consistent in your choice within each project.

Whom is the objective case of *who*. In other words, the word changes form depending upon how it is used. In English, the objective case only exists with personal pronouns. (I think! I could be wrong.)

The personal pronouns (subjective case) that change form are:
he, I, she, they, we, who, and whoever

They become (in objective case):
him, me, her, them, us, whom, and whomever

You and *it* do not change in objective case.

So, knowing that, we can decide whether to use *who* or *whom* by which case we need. Whee! I know, right? I still have no idea what any of that means or which to use. Basically, when you are substituting for the subject of a verb, you use *who*, and when you are substituting for the object of a verb, you use *whom*.

Here is the simple rule of thumb to get you through: **If you can answer the question with *him*, use the *m*.**

"**You gave the car to whom?**"

"I gave the car to he." vs. "I gave the car to him."

"Him" fits correctly in this case, but "he" does not. So "whom" was the correct usage.

"**Who lives in that house?**"

"He lives in that house." vs. "Him lives in that house."

"He" fits correctly in this case, but "him" does not. So "who" was the correct usage.

who's vs. whose

Just as with **it vs. it's**, the *apostrophe s* breaks the norm and does not mean possession, but rather represents a contraction.

Who's is a contraction for *who is* or *who has*, while **whose** is used as the possessive.

"**Who's going to the store with me?**"
"**Whose house are we going to?**"

One of the best ways I've heard to remember this is: If mine can't have an apostrophe then neither can his, hers, ours, theirs, yours, its, or whose.

your vs. you're

Your is possessive.
You're is a contraction for *you are*.

If you can substitute **you are**, then you need **you're**.

This generally seems to be more of a typo than a mistake. If you are having problems with it, add it to your **Final Checklist**.

I DO NOT THINK THAT WORD MEANS WHAT THEY THINK IT MEANS

Or maybe it does. Maybe it doesn't mean what I think it means.

Not too long ago, I came across a question on Quora (a website where people ask questions and other people answer them) that had me thinking about this. The question was something along the lines of "Who decided bad words were bad words?" The answer of course is that we all did. Every time someone uses a term in a way that is meant to insult someone else, they are moving that term closer toward being an offensive term.

Because of the way words have been used in the past, we have to be careful how we refer to some animals, such as roosters, cats, donkeys… The list goes on and on. We also have to be careful when we decide to give characters names like Dick or Peter. And then there are always the unintentional jokes about clams, tacos, sausages, pickles…

You get the point.

Sometimes this can be fun. It can be humorous. I laughed pretty hard the first time I read an old book that repeatedly used the term *ejaculated* instead of *said*. It ruined the story for me, but I laughed.

These things can be seriously offensive to some people, and we, as writers, have to watch out for those situations as best we can. Unless your intention is to offend, then…well, I got nothing. My intention is to entertain. I don't understand wanting to offend. I only use the offensive stuff as indicators of the types of characters I am writing and then only when the story calls for it. Or maybe to humorous effect.

But on top of all that, there are words that will apparently cause some people to immediately throw down a book. Or so they claim.

For example, Romance readers apparently hate the word moist. In fact, there are huge lists of words and descriptions you should never use if you write romances. Considering they seem to always be describing the same four feelings and six body parts, I can't imagine why they would want to limit any descriptions—they need all they can get. But nonetheless, there it is. (I'll let you look up those lists on your own. I went far enough here listing a few food euphemisms.)

These words are not necessarily genre specific. Leer is one of them. Some people seem to think the word leer means leaning over, tongue hanging out, drool dripping down, flat-out lust incarnate. So, they hate the word. Personally, I have never seen anyone (outside of a movie) do that. Men leer in much subtler ways. Women tend to leer even more subtly. But it doesn't have to be subtle. And just because some people think it is not a subtle word doesn't mean I have to think that it is an over-the-top word too.

But I do consider what other people will think every time I use it now. I make sure I give other clues to indicate that it is subtle. I do the same with moist.

(No, I don't. I was trying to be funny.)

Nazi, fecund, impacted, literally, glisten, ginormous, and retarded are words I have heard people tell me they actively hate, and they never want to see them in a book. I can't promise I won't ever use any of those words (well, I just did, so there), but I can say I will always think twice before using them.

I recommend you pay attention when you hear someone say they hate a word. See if you can find out why. Then add it to your list of words you will always think twice about using.

I probably shouldn't have to mention this, but I am going to just in case:

Any word even remotely resembling a racial, religious, or socio-economic slur should be on your list of things to reconsider five times before using, even in dialog when it fits a character. Some words that we think are normal actually (or are thought to) come from disparaging origins, and they continue to insult some people. (Terms such as *paddy wagon* or *gypped*.)

And then there are some people who are always looking for any excuse to be offended. Think twice before you give it to them.

Unless that was what you wanted to do.

Bonus Note Be careful when creating a new insult. You may unintentionally turn a word you once liked into a word you are no longer allowed to use. I bet frackers love what was done with that word.

PRO TIPS

The following are things that I think will help you improve your writing if you keep them in mind and use them with deliberation. One of the biggest mistakes we can make as writers is not being aware of what we have written. This doesn't mean all of these things are bad; it means that, like any writing rule, you need to understand it so you can decide when to apply it and when not to, to obtain the effect you want.

Sometimes these things will make a story more enjoyable to read, sometimes they will make it nearly impossible to slog through. Being aware of them allows you to determine, on a case by case basis, if you want to use them or not. Being aware of them can even help you fix a story that you were feeling went wrong, but you couldn't quite put your finger on why.

As you read through the Pro Tips section, keep the idea of filler words in mind and you may begin to see how many of these tips involve removing unnecessary filling from your story.

Software Assisted Writing

There are many software tools for writers. Some claim to make your story better, some claim to make your writing better. But all are fallible, so be cautious.

Many writers love Grammarly, ProWriting Aid, Autocrit and other programs that help with their text. These can help you weed out problems with passive voice, dialog tags, sentence variation, overuse of adverbs, and a ton of other things. But the danger of using them is that if you don't already know this stuff, you won't know when these programs are wrong, and they do get things wrong. Blindly following their suggestions will add mistakes into your text that weren't there before. Worse, they can stifle your voice as a writer, making you think you should or shouldn't do something when it would be perfectly fine for you to do or not do it.

Programs have to conform to someone's idea of what writing should be, in order to have rules to follow, but sometimes those rules are conflicting. That means the rules the program authors chose to follow may not conform to what the rules of your writing should be.

Remember, in the introduction, when I said you should follow rules until you figure out and understand why those rules exist, and then you should break the hell out of them? These programs might stop you from doing that. Worse, because of the mistakes they make, they can confuse you and prevent you from understanding the rules.

Along the same vein are programs that help with outlining/story development and character development. Two that come to mind, because I have a friend who teaches classes on them, are Persona and Contour. I have limited experience with the programs, but I want to caution that, as the text-fixing programs mentioned above can quash your writing style, these kinds of programs can limit your creativity. Not in the same way. They don't make "character development" mistakes as the others make grammar mistakes, but they can put you "in a box" that you have a difficult time thinking "outside of," and thereby restrain you from coming up with unique and unusual characters and plot structures.

I recommend you use all helpful software with caution. Use them as supplements to help you, not as substitutes for real learning from interactions with real humans who have real opinions and can give real feedback.

Less Filling

Some words taste great! Some are bland. The best way to water down your story is to fill it up with bland words. Some of the following words literally add nothing but word count to a story, yet many writers use them like they are going out of style. Which they are. So, you should stop using them.

that

One of the best examples of a filler word is the word *that*.

In many cases, the word *that* adds neither clarity nor meaning to a sentence. We writers seem to use it kind of like we use the filler sound *um* when we speak.

He asked her about the wedding, knowing that she hadn't planned anything yet.

She turned away from the family that she might never see again

Bobby put his hand on her elbow to let her know that she wasn't alone.

The big man took a deep breath, an action that Sue knew meant that he was ready.

In the examples above, note how no meaning in the sentence is changed if you remove the word *that*. I recommend always searching your stories for *that* and removing them if they are not necessary. Don't get me wrong, the word *that* has many uses. It can be a pronoun, an adverb, a definite article, an adjective, a conjunction, and maybe more. But although it occasionally changes the overall connotation or meaning of a sentence, I suspect you will usually find that *that* has been used as a filler word.

just

Another example of a filler word is the word *just*. (See more on the word **just** in **Meaningless Descriptors**.)

All around, everything was just silent. Everything was just concrete and asphalt as far as the eye could see.

Used as an adverb in this way, *just* adds no worthwhile description or contrast. At best it offers a weak change in the feeling of the sentence.

of

There are many different kinds of filler words. Some are filler only when used in certain ways, such as the word *of*.

Get off of there!

Why don't you go outside of the house?

In both of these cases, the word *of* is unnecessary, or redundant. While you may want to the leave the usage of the word *of* in dialog to represent how a character speaks, I recommend removing most instances from the narrative. (See the section on **Redundancy** for more on this idea.)

managed

Another word we often manage to turn into filler is *managed*. (See what I did there? Gosh, I love using things I tell you not to! Especially while telling you not to!)

He worked at the rope until he managed to free his wrists.
He worked at the rope until he freed his wrists.

Pointing out that a character *managed* to do something is redundant and slows the pacing of the story.

If you intentionally want to slow the pacing, this could be a good thing, if not, you may want to avoid the use of *managed* in this manner. (See **Pacing** for more on this idea.)

finally

Finally, we have come to what I think is the second worst offender of being a filler word. It is one I am always guilty of. Which is probably why I dislike it.

After putting on her makeup, Shelly finally finished getting ready for school and left to catch the bus.
Bobby went to bed after finally eating supper, doing his homework and watching a little television.

Finally is a word that contrasts things, placing something at the end of a list or at the end of a time period. Using *finally* without ending a list or a time period creates a filler word that doesn't mean anything, yet we often try to fit it into our writing when we shouldn't. (See **Vague Time Periods** for more about **finally**.)

and then, and (s)he, so then

She smiled and then she walked away.

I stood up and then I left the room.

The car stopped at the green light and then it drove off at the red.

I don't want to say you should never use *and then*, as it does have a place in writing, but overuse starts to make the story feel stilted and paced too evenly. A big problem with *and then* is when writers routinely start new paragraphs with it. See **Contrasting And Conjoining Things That Are Not There** for more on this idea.

Dirty looks flew across the room as they recognized one another. Tom saw the women exchange glances and knew he was in for trouble.
And then the hostess walked up to greet them, and she took their jackets and then offered ticket stubs in return.

I have also encountered the word *so* used this way, in *so then, so she, so they*, etc. The word *so* is a contrasting word and needs to have a causal relationship with an action when used this way, or it makes little sense. (For more on the use of **so**, see **Vague Measurements**.)

If you find yourself doing this on a regular basis, consider adding it to your Final Check List as a reminder to use the word processor's search feature to locate instances of it and break them up into separate sentences, especially when the *and then* isn't emphasizing an action.

Characters Who Are Always Surprised

Overuse of the term *suddenly* is a fault many of us writers accidentally picked up somewhere. There is a dual problem with using *suddenly* in our stories. First, most things that happen suddenly usually happen so fast that saying they happened suddenly slows down the telling of the action and is repetitive.

Suddenly, shots rang out.

She stood up and suddenly slapped him in the face.

Secondly, it makes characters seem surprised by everything, even their own actions.

All of a sudden, the sun went down, so she lay her head on the pillow and closed her eyes. Suddenly the phone rang.

He tipped his hat and nodded to the woman, and suddenly she smiled.

Walking back to the car, they suddenly turned and waved, smiling. Suddenly, all was forgiven.

Suddenly we found ourselves lost.

There is a place for the word *suddenly*, when it actually does add emphasis, so don't be afraid to use it, but be careful not to overuse it.

Ralph stared at the plate of food. She wasn't coming. Not tonight, not ever. Suddenly he became aware of the laughter of people dining around him, and he felt out of place.

Characters Who Never Finish Anything

He sat down and began to tie his shoes and then he started to stand up.

Starting to walk down the street, she began to hum nervously.

She started to go into the kitchen. The phone rang just as she began making dinner. She tucked the phone between her shoulder and ear and began talking to her mother as she stirred the stew.

He began climbing up on his horse as he spoke. "Captain, get the men ready. We leave at midnight."
"Yessir," the captain began. "They will be ready—"
The colonel started riding away. "They had better be."

At first, using *began* or *started* seems innocuous enough, but some writers use them constantly, and then, eventually, the reader realizes no one ever finishes anything they start. They just start to do something and then move on to the next action they are starting.

Once a reader notices this pattern to the writing, they cannot "unsee" it, and it ruins the story for them.

Putting Your Characters To Bed

Many writing coaches will caution against "putting your characters to bed." There are good reasons for this, but first let me explain that, for once, the writing coaches meant this literally. Don't put your characters to bed.

That doesn't mean don't let them get into bed and have sex, it means you should avoid having the narrative follow them into the bedroom, get ready for sleep, and then climb into bed and go to sleep.

Doing so creates a natural end to a scene or a chapter, but it also creates a natural place for a reader to put down the book and stop reading. And readers often do.

If you have managed to create a "sleepy time" feeling for the character, it has probably transferred over to the reader, and they will be ready to turn off the light and go to sleep themselves.

This can be a bad thing. If the reader puts your book down with a feeling like that, one that lacks suspense, drama, or curiosity, they may not find a reason to pick your book up again and finish reading it.

As far as pacing goes, this is bringing the story to a dead stop.

It's also the reason why *Goodnight Moon* has been a great children's book since it was written and likely will be available forever.

Clichés

While clichés can be used to the writer's advantage in some situations, just as stereotypes can, they can also detract. Generally, when a writer uses a cliché, they are missing out on the opportunity to make their writing better and more descriptive. Unless the narrative voice is one that should be using clichés, those common phrases are a lazy way out of explaining something to the reader. Remember, once upon a time, a cliché was a description of something that worked so well it was appropriated into everyday language.

An overuse of clichés can make a story appalling rather than interesting. Here are a few examples of the cliché phrases we often use:

A diamond in the rough
Head over heels
Heart skipped a beat
Just then
In the nick of time
Not a care in the world
Opposites attract
Read between the lines
Scared to death
Sent a shiver down his spine
Tail between his legs
Time will tell

In a character's dialog, these clichés, and others like them, are fine to use, if they fit the character and the situation, but they should generally be avoided in the narration. (See **Don't Write The Way You Speak** for more on that idea.)

While we are on the subject of clichés, I wanted to point out the other kind of clichés: the story telling clichés. There are some things that happen in stories so often that you probably shouldn't put them in your story. These are often called **tropes**.

In some old black and white movies, the woman would slap a man, who would then grab her and pull her in for a kiss. And then everything would be all right. That became a cliché and only works well in the movies. (Trust me on that. Don't try that at home.) When readers see some of these kinds of clichés in a story, it can ruin it for them.

Here are some examples to give you an idea of the things you should consider never using in your stories:

> **Heroine twists her ankle.**
> **Mystic native/old person who "knows impossible things."**
> **Earthquake/volcano destroys the island at the end.**
> **No one listens to the kid.**
> **Bad guy kills one of his men to prove he is a bad guy.**
> **Removing the bullet means they are okay now.**
> **Someone hit in the head to knock them out.**

I know we all do that last one, but the odds of it working in real life are almost zero, and when it happens three times in one story (yeah, I did that) you should have created a character with permanent brain damage.

A great resource on clichés is **tvtropes.org.** You can get lost for a couple of hours there looking into the things that have been overused or that you never realized all televisions shows do to manipulate your expectations.

A great place to see what kinds of stories have been overdone can be found on **strangehorizons.com**. Under their submission guidelines they have a list of "stories we've seen too often."[50] This can help you decide if you really want to write another story about a writer with writer's block.

Meaningless Descriptors And Weak Words

In writing, we tend to need a lack of ambiguity. When we describe things, either they are or they are not. They happened or they didn't. The characters think or believe something, or they don't. If we have too much gray area in our meanings, readers have problems comprehending what we are trying to communicate. Because of that, words we normally use for emphasis in our speech patterns tend to weaken descriptions rather than strengthen them when modifying descriptors in writing.

For example, one of my biggest foibles when I started writing was *seemed.* Here are some examples lifted from an early draft of my book, *Lucid Nightmares.*

> **He sniffed at the air, and the taste of dank rotten garbage that had exuded from the demon seemed to fill his mouth.**

---

[50] This has since been archived here: http://strangehorizons.com/submit/fiction-submission-guidelines/stories-weve-seen-too-often/

Did it fill his mouth or not? It *seemed* to…but is this a mystery? Did I want the reader to be guessing about this for the next few sentences? If not, then I needed to just say that it *did* fill his mouth, otherwise I have weakened the description. I have lessened the impact of the idea that the stench filled his mouth.

His good mood seemed to dissipate with the sunlight as the sun melted over the mountaintops.

Did his good mood dissipate or not? Again, is this something I am hiding from the reader? If not, I need to take the word *seemed* out of there as it weakens the description.

His good mood dissipated with the sunlight as the sun melted over the mountaintops.

This is a much stronger description, and it is much more accurate.

Julie seemed to hesitate for a moment before she looked back up the stairs at Jack.

That was the last example for *seemed*, I promise. You can see the problem here, right? Either she hesitated or she didn't.

Some other words and phrases with this problem are:

About
Almost
(It was) like
(It was) as if
(It was) as though

The reverse of this problem is also true. As readers, we need a lack of ambiguity, so the writer saying that something *is*, when it actually *isn't*, can be very confusing. (See the section on **Literally** for more on this idea.)

His axe glanced off the rock and hit the chain, severing it. Shocked, he stared at the broken bond. He was untethered for the first time in years.
Looking up, he felt as though he saw the mountains for the first time. No one else was around.
"Run and you die," the master's voice sounded in his ears.

Is this a memory? Or is this the master suddenly appearing and talking to him? Or did he magically get an earpiece the reader didn't know about before.

If this is a memory, it needs to be indicated as such in some way.

His axe glanced off the rock and hit the chain, severing it. Shocked, he stared at the broken bond. He was untethered for the first time in years.

Looking up, he felt as though he saw the mountains for the first time. No one else was around.

He recalled the words he had heard so many times before: "Run and you die."

He flinched as if the master's voice had sounded in his ears.

Vague Measurements

She was tall.
He was big.
They were small.
It was long.
There were a lot.

Those sentences mean next to nothing. The descriptors have no basis of comparison or contrast and are left useless as a result. We speak this way, but often the information is known to us or given in context.

When my son, who is 9 years old as of this writing, tells me someone is tall, I don't know if that means they were 5' 8" or 7' 2". I only know it means they were taller than him. When my 6' 8" tall friend tells me someone was tall, well… I know that person was *tall*. My point is that these words are subjective and for them to have any impact, they need to be put in perspective.

She was tall for a giraffe.
He was big as a thimble.
They were small for molecules.
It was a long trip. Four generations lived and died during the voyage.
There were a lot. They overflowed the planet and drifted out into space.

With a quantifier, those vague measurements become much more meaningful.

Here is a list of some of the words that have this issue:

big/small
short/tall/long
heavy/light
some/many

a few/a lot
a couple/a handful
a little/a bit

A problem I have seen with using these vague terms to indicate amounts is when much more specific amounts are used later in the story, and they don't come anywhere near the vague idea I, as a reader, previously had in mind. In chapter one the writer may say something like:

The children ran and played in the schoolyard with glee. A few played foursquare while some climbed on the monkey bars and still others played kickball.

Then in chapter four they say something like:

The children gathered around her, pressing close but not touching her, surrounding her in a sea of youth. Hundreds of frightened eyes looked up at her.

In chapter one, the idea I get is a couple dozen kids at the most. But in chapter three, with the descriptions of "a sea of youth" and "hundreds of frightened eyes," I am suddenly imagining at least a hundred students (or else we'd have less than hundred**s** of eyes).

These are simplistic examples but keep them in mind the next time you use nonspecific measurements. (See **Poor Contrasts** for more on this.)

Vague Time Periods

Just as with vague measurements, we often speak using vague time period descriptions that don't translate well into the written word.

**later/a short time later/after a while
often/rarely/frequently**

Without contrasting information, these words can mean anything from mere seconds to years or longer. It is important to remember not to use them without adequate contextualization and contrast.

Don't use these words in place of a scene break. (See **Scene Breaks** for more on this.) When a character finishes a scene and you feel the need to say, "a short time later she arrived at home," you should instead be starting a new scene with a scene break.

Indicating the passage of time with these vague time periods can dramatically alter the pacing of your story, as though we are fading out and then back into the action. This can lead to a loss of interest on the part of the reader who may put the story down and never come back. (See **Pacing** for more on this.)

One of the worst offending words in this category, because most of us don't realize we have used it as a vague description of time, is *finally*.

Monday morning came early. Wilber turned off the alarm and finally got out of bed.

To me, *finally* implies Wilber had been lying in bed for a long time, waiting to get up or resisting getting up, but the context doesn't support that. In fact, it suggests the opposite.

Many writers accidentally use this as a filler word, not realizing they are indicating the passage of time. (See **Less Filling** for more on this.)

Changing Focus

Once upon a time, a writer's first exposure to storytelling was someone telling them a story. Orally, in person, in real life. Eventually some writers' first exposure was to someone reading them stories that had been written down. Today, nearly everyone's first exposure to a story is to some form of playback of an audio/visual performance.

If you don't believe this affects the way those future writers think and approach storytelling, you either haven't thought about it or you're fooling yourself. (For example, the idea that people dreamed in black and white, not in color, came about during the time period when movies were in black and white. That idea has since, thankfully, been discarded.)

A major side-effect of this form of early exposure to storytelling (one of many) is new writers tend to think of their story in the manner they were first exposed to stories. In other words, they try to direct the reader like a movie director directs the cameraman filming a movie. Look at this, look over here, look up from this angle, look what's going on over here where the characters can't see, look at how they fight, notice the frost on the window—it means something.

While not all of that is bad, there are times when it is done poorly. One of the big problems occurs when the writer changes the focus they want the reader to concentrate on. This generally happens at three different places for new authors: first, when time passes, second, when switching characters, and third, when changing locations.

These generally are all times that call for a "scene change," a time when the writer should throw in a # (or whatever symbol you've chosen to use) so an editor will know the scene has changed and can put in a wingding or extra spaces or whatever the publisher is doing to denote a section break to make it easier for the reader to know what is going on.

In older movies, there were usually obvious times when the image would fade to black and indicate a scene change. This was likely a holdover from plays, when the same would happen while stagehands removed or added scenery. In today's video entertainment world, seconds are precious, and the director has a fear of losing the audience's attention, so you almost never see a fade out. Scene changes are done quickly, often jumping back and forth multiple times in a matter of seconds.

Because of this, I think, many new writers have a difficult time knowing when one is necessary. They imitate what they have seen, but just as our spoken language does not perfectly translate into our written language, the visual cues used in video productions do not translate well into the medium of text.

Poor Contrasting

so

She was so tall.
He was so big.
They were so small.
It was so long.
There were so many.

If you read the section **Vague Measurements**, then you probably already understand why the word *so* is a contrasting word that we use in everyday language but find little value in when we write.

The word *so*, when used by itself, offers no contrast at all, and therefore doesn't work as a descriptor.

She was so tall she had to duck under the ceiling fan.
He was so big they custom made shoulder pads for him.
They were so small I stepped on them without knowing.
It was so long it wouldn't fit on the flatbed truck.
There were so many the birds got tired of eating them.

really

Most of us have the same problem with using *really*, as a contrast against nothing, as we do with *so*.

The flowers were really yellow.

The sun was really bright.
The building was really tall.

We all really like to use the word *really* to emphasize how much something is. But it really doesn't tell us anything. Really.

The flowers were yellow as the brightest sunset.
The sun was bright enough to make my eyes water.
The building was taller than the tallest trees.

only

Only is a word that can trick us into thinking it has given specifics when it has not. It is still a poor contrast.

I only had a few.
It was only a couple of days.

For some people, a few means two, for others it can mean dozens. For some people a couple of days means two. For my friend, who was late paying me back the money he borrowed, it was twenty-seven. (I'm kidding.)

Again, using *only* as a quantifier in speech might work fine colloquially for emphasis, but it often works poorly in writing.

The cavalry decided to march. They only had a few horses left and they used those to carry their supplies.

Imagine my surprise when the soldiers arrived in town with twenty horses they needed to feed and stable. I feel like twenty is a large number of horses.

just

When used as a descriptor in writing, the word *just* tends to substitute for *exactly* or *only, barely, merely* or *very recently*, and it rarely adds any meaning to the description. (Which I think is odd for a word that means *exactly*.) This broad range of meanings causes this word to be overused by many writers, and overuse always diminishes the strength of a word. Couple that with the problem that, in many cases, its use is redundant, and you have the reason so many editors dislike the word.

This doesn't mean there is never a use for the word *just* as a descriptor, but it does mean you should reconsider using it each time, just to make sure you needed it.

Just has an advantage over the other words in this section in that it generally carries a stronger connotation with it that changes the feeling conveyed by the sentence, even if it is not adding any actual information.

She was just so tall.
He was just so big.
They were just so small.
It was just so long.
There were just so many.

The reader has no more information that applies to how tall, big, or small something was than they had before *just* was added, but there is a definite change in the meaning added by the word *just*, even when used without the *so*.

If that feeling is what you mean to convey, don't be afraid to use the word, but do be aware it didn't add anything to clear up any vagueness in the measurements.

This idea applies to everything else in this section. You can use the words, but reconsider and review each instance to make sure you need them.

very

Likely the biggest offending word in this section, *very* is often used as a contrast to mean *more* or *a lot* or *exceptionally*. But like all of the other examples, it gives little information.

She was very tall.
He was very big.
They were very small.
It was very long.
There were very many.

As with *just*, there may be some connotation added to the sentences, but were those examples any more informative than the same ones that used the word *so*?

Part of the problem with *very* is that it is overused and has lost much of its ability to add the connotation.

-ly words

Adverbs tend to end in *-ly*, which makes them easy to find with the search function of my writing program. That's why I have them on my **Final Checklist** as "search for –ly words."

As new writers, we tend to romance the adverbs, trying to control what the readers see in their minds as they read our stories. We try to tell the writers that the characters do things slowly, quickly, loudly, weirdly, and on and on we go, modifying every verb we can.

Writing instructors and editors often preach that we should never use adverbs (and some go so far as to add adjectives), as the use of the descriptors is a crutch that weakens the writing. One of the most obvious places for this is in dialog. That is the basis behind the idea of *show don't tell*. (Please see the sections **Descriptions** and **Use Of Verbs And Adverbs With Dialog Tags** for more on this.)

Many of the adverbs we use are redundant and don't always add to the description in the story. Sometimes they can detract from the overall value of the story. (See **Redundancy** for more.)

He quickly ducked under the sword, mightily kicking out at his opponent's knee. His foot landed solidly, and the crunch was followed by an agonized bellow.

If you consider the adverbs, and the context they are being used in, you should see how they are redundant. There is no way the protagonist would duck a sword in any way but as fast as he could, so *quickly* added nothing. In a battle for his life, why would a kick at someone's knee be anything but mighty? So *mightily* also added nothing. When our hero's foot landed, it got a good result. This result tells us that the blow must have landed *solidly*, making the adverb irrelevant.

If we take out the adverbs, these two sentences still mean the same thing, use three less words, and the action of the story speeds up, making the fight scene more intense for the reader. (See **Over Describing Action** and **Pacing** for more on this.)

He ducked under the sword, kicking out at his opponent's knee. His foot landed and the crunch was followed by an agonized bellow.

This same idea applies to adjectives (which are much harder to find as they don't usually end in –*ly*). Adding adjectives and adverbs into these two sentences creates eight extra words that don't necessarily progress the story at all.

He quickly ducked under the flashing sword, mightily kicking out at his opponent's overexposed knee. His foot landed solidly, and the satisfying crunch was immediately followed by an agonized roaring bellow.

Now that I have said so many negative things about adverbs and adjectives, please realize they are a large part of what comprises the narrative voice and lends a specific personality to your writing. As often as famous writers and editors say negative things about adverbs, they still use them. I believe they are merely trying to prevent newer writers from overusing them.

You may want your prose to sound flowery and full of adverbs and adjectives, but be aware that overuse causes fatigue in the reader. Not only literally, but also in an, "I don't want to ever read anything by Shakespeare again!" sort of way.

Readers eventually get tired of everything having a modifier.

Pacing

Pacing your story is a big deal. For some writers it comes naturally, the rest of us have to work at it. People often talk about the pacing of the story in terms of the plot, using techniques such as action scenes vs. descriptive scenes or cliffhangers and quick scene cuts, but they rarely consider the just-as-important pacing of the words the reader is reading.

Depending upon the words and the sentences the writer puts on the page, the reader will read faster or slower. This is a great thing to take advantage of. When the action is fast, the reading should be fast too. When you slow the action down, slow the reading pace down as well, to give the reader a rest.

The easiest ways to speed up the reading are to make use of shorter sentences, shorter words, and shorter paragraphs. Exciting verbs that need no adverb, such as shriek, creep, scurry, ooze, and gasp, are quick to read and easily convey ideas, allowing action scenes, or even non-action scenes to flow rapidly for the reader.

The opposite is true for slowing things down. More complicated sentence structures, metaphors, analogies, and longer paragraphs all slow down the rate at which the reader can digest the text, which naturally slows down the pacing of the story in the reader's mind. (See also **Putting Your Characters To Bed.)**

White Space

(this space intentionally left blank)

Just kidding. Sort of. That caught your eye right away though didn't it? Was it the words or the white space that caught your attention? I think it was probably both. (this space intentionally left blank) Did you notice that same sentence was repeated here, in the middle of this paragraph, before you got to it while reading? Probably not. It was buried within the rest of this text. So, it probably wasn't the words themselves that caught your attention. But blank pages don't catch your attention either. It is the combination of the two, and how you use them, that creates an effect upon the reader.

White space is very closely related to pacing. Too much or too little of it can have a seriously detrimental effect upon the story. Not because the words are any different, but because how the reader interprets the words is.

Just as we pause to take a breath after every sentence, we do the same thing mentally as we read. We take a slight pause at the end of every sentence, paragraph, scene break, and chapter. This allows us just a moment to regroup our thoughts and mental energies before continuing on. A full page of text, with few or no indentations showing new paragraphs, becomes an intimidating block of words that most people dread trying to read. Just looking at the page makes people think of indecipherable college textbooks. Reading a page like that becomes a slog with the reader looking for places to catch their breath.

Once we become proficient readers, most of us read more by the shape of a word than the actual word itself. That is how speed readers read so quickly. With this in mind, consider how we recognize the shape of the blocks of text on a page in a novel, or even on this page here. We can quickly, as soon as we turn the page, see if there will be dialog, if there will be a lot of it, and if it will be broken up. Seeing that, we anticipate what we are going to be reading, and we prepare for it.

When we see a solid page of text, we also begin to anticipate we are probably not going to like reading it, and we begin to dread it, and grow weary of it, even before we start to read. We also tend to lose our place a lot more frequently. There just aren't as many unique and identifying features for our eyes to latch onto that will help us keep track of where we are. This is why reading long pages of text, with little or no white space, can be exhausting for the reader.

You might have noticed that throughout this guide, in general, I have used quite a bit of white space. I often put an extra line between examples to set them apart from the rest of the text. This makes them stand out and tells the reader it is different. It adds a bit of importance or emphasis to the examples.

It also makes this book look more exciting and interesting than if I had just done pages of text with little whitespace. Like I just did for this section. Did you notice? Did this section feel different to you when you first saw it? How about once you started reading it? Did it seem to lack places to take a mental breath?

I feel like it did. So here is some white space to make me feel better. Hopefully it helps you, too.

Did you see that space coming up as you were reading higher up on the page? Or maybe even when still on the previous page? Were you anticipating reaching it, to see what this part said differently, or even just because you needed a break?

That is how white space works.

Stephenie Meyer famously used white space in the Twilight novel *New Moon*, leaving pages nearly blank, representing months passing with no entries in a diary. This was a rather effective use of white space that immediately caught the reader's attention and conveyed meanings without the use of much text.

Setting a sentence, a paragraph, or even a word, apart from the rest of the text surrounds it with white space. This immediately makes it different, and the reader registers it as important. For example:

It had taken months to get to this point. It had been an effort of sheer will. But now, looking at the twisted wreckage scattered across the mountainside below him, Jerry could no longer lie to himself.

Amy was dead.

Even though writers don't (usually) separate out paragraphs with white space in a novel, they do occasionally set aside one sentence as its own paragraph for emphasis. The white space around that short sentence brings more attention to it and adds weight to its importance.

The same thing happens when you end a chapter that way.

Sometimes the white space is more about what isn't said. This can focus the reader's attention on the implications of what was said. The white space both emphasizes that the reader should think about it and gives them a break in which to do so.

But be careful of using too much white space. Had I set that sentence into its own page, with nothing else around it, I suspect it would look strangely out of place, perhaps even comical, and that would ruin any effect I would have hoped to gain from it.

Single Words, Sentences, And Paragraphs

As discussed in **Pacing** and **White Space**, short words, sentences, paragraphs, and chapters can be used to create an effect. Used sparingly, shortened writing such as this can add gravitas and impact to the story. It is perfectly acceptable to write a one-word sentence, or a one sentence paragraph, or even a one paragraph chapter.

I would caution against a one-word chapter, but I am sure someone could pull that off very effectively. It just isn't likely to be me.

Like any tool in our writer's box, this is a tool that works best when it remains invisible to the reader, and the best way to ensure that is to use it sparingly and with forethought.

Redundancy

Is it ironic that I listed *repetitive word use* twice in my outline for this guide? It was listed both before and after *redundancy*. *sigh* Many of the things we write have implied meanings, but we feel the need to add on a descriptor of some sort anyway. This creates a redundancy that some people don't notice and other people are thoroughly irritated by. It's up to you to decide if you want to write this way or not.

Ralph always thought Herb was weird. Plumbers whose butt cracks didn't show were rare in the field.

The phrase *in the field* may sound right, and it may even be right, but it is superfluous and redundant. We already know we are talking about plumbers, so to mention that we are talking about where they work can be redundant. Are they rare in the field, or are they just rare in general?

Many of the phrases we routinely use in writing are redundant.

Sarah called for a cab while Will just stood there and watched.

Of course Will just stood *there*. Where else would Will stand as he watched?

Bobby chewed his food slowly as he ate.

We already know Bobby is eating, because he is chewing his food.

Mark stood up out of the chair and looked around himself.

Anytime Mark stands, it should be up. If we knew he was sitting, we probably already knew what he was sitting on. And even if we didn't, we would probably assume it was a chair unless we had been told differently. And nearly anytime he looks around, it is probably going to have to be around himself in some way.

Time to get out of the basement, Marcy thought as she stood at the bottom of the stairs leading up.

Again, these types of redundancies are a bit of a stylistic choice, but it does bother some editors and some readers, making it worth pointing out. My general goal for this guide is to inform you so that you can make your own choices about how to write. Other, less acceptable, forms of redundancy involve dialog tags.

"Please," he pleaded.
"No!" she shouted.
"Can I have that?" he asked.
"Ha!" Fred laughed.

See also **Use Of Verbs and Adverbs With Dialog Tags**.

Repetitive Word Use

Using the same words over and over again begin to make them stand out to a reader, especially if it is a word they don't know or don't like. Uncommon words require more thought on the part of the reader and take energy away from enjoying the story. Repetitive use of an uncommon word can seriously detract from a reader's enjoyment.

I've often noticed, as a writer, that when an adverb pops into my mind for a certain part of a scene, it stays with me, and I end up using it two or three times within a couple of pages. As writers we should strive not to use a word twice in one sentence or even in the same paragraph. Some words shouldn't be used more than once a page, or maybe even more than once in the entire story.

In general, this is merely a matter of not realizing how closely together we wrote the words.

Josh kicked the door. The door flew open.

The dirty room smelled like dirty laundry.

Okay, she thought. This isn't working.
"Okay," she said. "Everyone listen up!"

Sergeant Miller thumbed up the switch to call up his heads-up display.

"Just like I said," he said.

There were children whose feet were bare and there were men whose faces were grim. I saw women packing things away and people whose belongings had gone missing. There was one man whose whole house had vanished and another whose family was gone.

Sometimes we become repetitive in our sentence structure as well as our words. Not just in a paragraph, as in the last example above, but throughout our entire story, repeatedly using *and then* or *and said* so many times that the story feels stilted or strange. (See **Rhythm Of Sentences** for more on this idea.)

These kinds of repetitions are a problem for many readers. It is the same problem as with authors who insist on always using the dialog tag *said*. Once we notice it, we can't stop noticing it, and then we can't enjoy the story. (See also **Starting Sentences with Pronouns And Proper Nouns**.)

that that and had had

Have you ever found yourself writing *that that* or *had had*? Did it leave you scratching your head? This is just about the most redundant thing ever, yet we seem to often find ourselves trying to write sentences with them.

She knew that that was the wrong answer.

He decided he had had enough!

While these are grammatically correct (past perfect) they sound strange when we say them, and they look strange when we write them. I find it is always best to rewrite the sentence in such a way that you don't need to do this.

If the idea of this being grammatically correct piques your interest, search the internet for the Wikipedia page on "**James while John had had had had had had had had had a better effect on the teacher.**"

It's a fun (depending upon who you are) exercise in grammar and punctuation. Or, more accurately, why we really need it.

Starting Sentences with Pronouns And Proper Nouns

Repeatedly starting sentences with pronouns and proper nouns creates a repetitious pattern that carries over into the rest of your writing and affects the flow and pacing of your story. Sometimes authors are good about spacing out sentences that start with pronouns but then discover they still started all of their paragraphs with pronouns.

Not only is it strange and repetitive to see the left side of page covered with *I, He, She, They,* or *Bobby* (or whatever the character's name is), but always having the pronouns and proper nouns at the start of sentences creates a setup for the sentences to follow the same pattern over and over again. (See **Rhythm Of Sentences** for more on this idea.)

Rhythm Of Sentences

As mentioned in the last section, readers notice repetitive patterns in sentence structure. If they didn't, poetry wouldn't exist. But while poetry is a purposeful attempt to make rhythm an enjoyable thing, many of us writers don't think about the rhythms we are creating as we write.

Too many short sentences in a row begin to read oddly. Too many long ones become exhausting. While sentence length is a factor in this idea, it is not the only thing to keep in mind. If all of your sentences follow a simple, direct subject-verb-object pattern, the reader will notice. If all your sentences start with a conditional clause it will become awkward even more quickly. If you always, or never, create compound sentences, or if you use the same number of words in all your sentences, it will become noticeable.

Not only is repetitive sentence structure not as interesting to read, but it becomes distracting once it is noticed.

My main point in bringing this to your attention is so that you can avoid it. However, many authors also use this to their advantage. By creating a rhythm that lasts through a paragraph, or a couple of paragraphs, you can affect the feel of the writing. Sometimes this is shorter or longer sentences used to control the pacing of the writing (see **Pacing** for more on this), and sometimes it is much more elaborate.

An example could be the use of three different sentence structures in a repeating pattern for a couple of paragraphs, or repetitive syllable count in similar sentences—similar in that they may all be about the same thing or used each time something bad is about to happen. Kind of like theme music for a character in a movie. You know, like right before Jaws shows up.

There are a lot of ways to play with this idea, but the most important thing is to avoid unknowingly creating awkward rhythms that disrupt the reading experience.

Over Describing Action

The ninja's right hand flicked, and a star flashed through the air towards BadManJoe's left eye. Before the star was halfway there, the ninja flicked his left hand and then his right and then his left again.

BadManJoe dropped down on his left knee, spinning counterclockwise and sweeping his right leg out to dislodge the main lynchpin holding up the sandbags to the right of the ninja. He continued his spin and took out the lynchpin holding the sandbags to the left of the ninja as the stars sailed harmlessly over his beautifully ringleted shiny black hair.

The ninja shifted his weight to the right before realizing the sandbags were coming down. Shifting back to the left, he saw those were falling as well. He pushed off with the toes on his left foot, while kicking his right leg up over his right shoulder to throw himself into a perfectly executed one-legged backflip.

Not only does writing out every detail of the action like this slow the action to a crawl, but eventually it becomes wearying for the reader. Occasionally writing a specific, pivotal moment like this can be beneficial to a story, but for the most part it turns the writer into a choreographer. While there are a few readers out there who like that (and if you are writing to that niche go for it!), most readers just want to enjoy the story, not learn the dance steps.

The ninja's hand flicked, and a star flashed through the air towards

BadManJoe's left eye. Before the star was halfway there, the ninja flicked his hands three more times.

BadManJoe dropped, leg sweeping to dislodge the lynchpins holding the sandbags up above the ninja.

The stars sailed harmlessly over BadManJoe's head as the ninja realized the sandbags were coming down and perfectly executed a backflip to avoid them.

The second example says nearly the same thing in less than half as many words, and, arguably, does it in a more enjoyable manner.

Often readers get confused when told exactly what each body part is doing during a fight, and, when writing that way, writers become more susceptible to the third hand mistake. (See **The Third Hand** for more on this.)

This applies to more than fight scenes or action scenes. Chess moves, sultry looks in a bar, mixing liquors in a drink, or even how a character gets to work in the morning can all suffer from this problem. Some writers even have this problem in dialog, listing incessant minutiae of things the characters say to each other.

Over-describing simple actions, and repeating actions for emphasis, can backfire on a writer. Simple actions are easy for readers to fill in with their mind, and often, when you describe them in too much detail, the reader has already moved on ahead of the writing in their mind, imagining what happens next, and then the reader gets pulled back and must read about something that has already happened in their mind but is still being drawn out in description on the page. (See **Going Back To The Future** for more on this issue.)

As You Know, Bob... It's An Info Dump

The term "As you know, Bob…" is a reference to the old B-movies wherein one scientist would turn to another and say something like:

"As you know, Bob, the speed of light is 671 million miles per hour, so if we push the speed of this train to 672 million miles per hour, we should be able to arrive before the S.O.S. signal arrives. Then we can position ourselves between the receiver and the signal, blocking it with our newly invented absorball shielding technology, and no one will ever even know it was sent. Except us. Ha. Ha. Ha. I love talking to you, Bob. You're such a good listener."

This technique allows the author to give necessary information to the reader, so that the reader can understand what is going on. The problem is that it makes no sense, story wise.

People don't typically tell each other things they already know. Why would you say this to Bob when he already knows? On top of that, you know he knows, but then you tell him anyway.

This technique bothers some readers (and especially editors). It is what is known as an info dump.

An **info dump** is a place in a story where the writer suddenly dumps a bunch of information they feel the reader needs to have. Sometimes this is important to the story, sometimes it is not. It could be a quick history of the 23 Kingdoms and the linage of their royal families, or just exactly how the subatomic particle known as a quark is related to, and affected by the Higgs boson particle, and how that is used to power the... Lost you already, didn't I?

My sentence was turning into an info dump.

When a writer doesn't take the time to work information into the story naturally, and instead just "dumps" it all out, either in an exposition by a character or in the narrative, the reader's eyes tend to gloss over. Not only is it boring, but it interrupts the flow of the story.

Try to find an interesting way to work necessary information into your story and beware of pitfalls such as "As you know, Bob..." or the television turned on to the news in the bar at just exactly the right time.

Raising Questions In Your Narrative

A subtle way of filling in plot holes, or at least covering them with cellophane, is to mention them. I have heard this referred to as hanging a hat on it, putting a lampshade on it, lampshading, spotlighting, and red flagging. I am sure there are many other terms for it, but you get the idea.

The point is, if a character ponders the *why's* and *how's* of something, even if a satisfactory conclusion is never reached, the reader (often) feels the issue has been addressed, and it no longer bothers them.

This can be used for self-referential humorous effect, if you are writing a comedy or a cheesy pulp, but it doesn't have to be.

If you have finished your masterpiece and then suddenly realize that the whole thing could have been prevented if someone just turned on the lights, you can circumvent a lot of the problems merely by having a character ask:

"Why the hell didn't they just turn on the lights?"

If another character offers a bit more information, that will lend credibility to the idea the issue has been addressed, even if it will never be resolved.

"No one knows. We've searched all the logs and recordings. Something must've happened."

Yay! Problem solved in the governmental fashion. We looked into it and didn't find anything, ergo there is no problem.

Now this is an extremely simplistic example, but it can work.

Another thing raising questions does is add depth to your world and to your characters. Suppose you write a scene where your heroine needs to hide, so she goes into the back of a dry-cleaning store, walks straight through, past all of the people who work there, and out the front door.

Your beta-reader, or maybe your mom, reads this and asks you, "Why didn't anyone who works there ask her what she was doing?"

You shrug. "I don't know. I forgot anyone would care. I was writing an action scene."

An easy fix is, of course, to have someone say something, but conversely, having the character wonder, "Why isn't anyone saying anything? Does this happen to them all the time? I can't believe the old man actually smiled at me!" works just as well.

This little bit adds realism to your story. It shows that your character is aware of herself and the world she is in, not just cut and pasted into this scene and then that scene. It also added a smiling old man for depth of scenery.

This can apply to any situation where you start to second guess yourself as a storyteller. If you start to wonder "What happens if they cross the streams?" but you can't explore that idea in this particular story for some reason, like word count limits maybe, add it to your character's musings.

I wonder what would happen if we crossed the streams? Now might not be the best time to try that. It might be a bad thing. Maybe a very bad thing. I better not mention it to the others. One of those fools will try it.

It is perfectly acceptable to raise questions for the reader to consider and not answer them. Real life is full of things we'll never find out. It's good if your characters explore the world around them with thoughts that recognize this.

To a certain extent.

You don't want to use this to accidentally set up a huge expectation that will go unfulfilled. We all want to know what happens when you cross the streams, so be careful about accidentally setting up foreshadowing and failing to live up to the idea of Chekov's Gun[51].

---

[51] You should look this up for more, but the basic idea is that if you introduce a gun in the first act, it needs to be used by the third act.

Final Thoughts On Pro Tips

A few things to consider:

—Make a blank, formatted document you can open and start writing in every time you start a new story. Especially if you have a hard time dealing with formatting. This can save you minutes with every short story. That adds up! And it can help reduce the number of times you send out embarrassing mistakes.

—Make a blank template for print and e-books if you are going to be a self-publisher. This will save you a lot more than a few minutes per project. A lot more. Trust me, you don't want to have to re-learn everything every six months as you finish your latest project.

—A dictionary works even when your internet is down or you are out of cellphone range, and they are not (as) susceptible to bad definitions posted by someone who really didn't know.

—Reverse dictionaries, emotion dictionaries, and other similar tools seem like kind of a silly idea at first, but there will come a day when you are pulling your hair out screaming, "What is that word! I just had it on the tip of my tongue! ARGH!"

—Read aloud the words you have written. Saying the words out loud requires more attention and concentration and you will find mistakes you missed. Sometimes you will discover a missing word and sometimes you will discover sentences that make no sense at all. This is one of the best ways to self-edit.

—Read your story "backwards." Start at the last line, or paragraph and read each sentence, or paragraph out of the normal context. Don't read the sentence itself backwards, just read them all out of order. This will help you pay less attention to your story and more to your sentence structure. This is good for finding things like sentence fragments and misplaced modifiers.

Final Check List

One of the first things I did when I decided to become serious about writing was make myself a list of things I felt I needed to go back and check to make sure I hadn't done them. Kind of like the opposite of a to-do list. I would go down the list and remove or change as many of the things as I could. Eventually I started to become aware of them while making them, and I stopped (mostly) making those mistakes as they tried to come out of my fingers and onto the keyboard.

And that is the whole point of this book: to help you become aware of things so that you can choose whether or not to have them in your story rather than not realizing you already had them there or were missing them.

We all have our own idiosyncrasies, so you should make a list that works best for you. Don't be afraid to add new things to the list as you find them. Mine had been next to my monitor for years, until I cleaned my desk while writing this guide. I moved it, misplacing it so that I could no longer honestly say I always keep it there. I am wondering if the shredder got it. Seriously. I know I joked a lot in this guide, but my list really disappeared.

Not a big deal. I easily made a new one from the outline for this book[52]! Hopefully this book helped and you can easily make your own.

Here is what my new list looks like:

Search and destroy: (These are words I personally use too often and have to go back and remove, or that I know bog things down, so I want to make sure I really wanted them in the story.)

all of
and then
and said
as if
as though
began
beginning
calmly
finally
glanced
had
just
looked

---

[52] Which I promptly lost right before doing the 2nd edition. *sigh* Not that it really matters at this point. I can close my eyes and see the damned list. Like it is tattooed there, just inside my eyeballs.

managed
quickly
realized
really
rolled (Along with glanced and looked, this helps find eye-talk.)
seemed
slowly
so
started
suddenly
that
then
very
waive (I always typo wave into waive. I don't know why.)

Search for –ly words (Remove extra adverbs.)

Passive voice: Search for was, were, and by (Finding these reveals most places I used the passive voice.)

Run spell check 3 times (To make sure it checks everything. Sometimes it doesn't.)

Search for two spaces between sentences (I do this last. After I am done changing words and may have introduced new typos accidentally.)

Him = Whom
He = Who (Quick reference, because I can't ever remember.)

EPILOGUE

Who would've expected an epilogue in this kind of a book, huh? Well, you've probably figured out by now that I would. And why not? I tend to break all of the other rules I am supposedly teaching here, so why not this one, too?

Actually, this is a smartassed way to point out that this is in fact not an epilogue. This is an afterword. Not an afterward. (See also **Afterward vs. Afterword.**)

Epilogue: a final wrap up of a story. Like a final "Nine months later the baby was born, and they lived happily ever after" type of thing. (Also sometimes spelled *epilog*. I have heard there is a difference in meaning between the two spellings, but I have never found anything to substantiate that claim.)

Afterword: notes or comments on the story, not the story itself. Think of it based upon how it is spelled: things written after the words.

Afterward: This is an indication of time relation. "We went out to dinner afterward." As with *backward* or *toward* or any of the __*ward* words, it can have an *s* on the end or not. It's up to you but be consistent.

AFTERWORD

Congratulations! We made it to the end! It was probably harder for you to get to this section than for me, as I wrote this section pretty early in the process of creating this guide. Writing things out of order can be fun!

I wanted to take a moment and say I hope you got something out of this. I wanted it to be friendly and helpful. Maybe there were lots of things you already knew. Maybe there were a couple you hadn't thought of since third grade. Either way, I hope you realize the whole point of this, for me, was to pay it forward.

These are things I learned as I was going along, slogging through the muck, trying to get ahead. I learned many of them from other authors around me, some of whom are New York Times Bestselling Authors. It turns out many of them are also great people who will take a minute to answer questions and help an up-and-coming author, if you just ask. (And know *how* to ask! Don't ask in the bathroom at the hotel, or after you get slobbering drunk to build up your courage. Those backfire. Trust me.)

The insights collected throughout this book are all things I wish I could have had in a book, in my hand, the day I decided I was finally going to put my butt in the chair and write a novel. Having this would have moved my learning curve up by years. Literally. So many of these were mistakes I made over and over again until some kind soul finally pointed it out, or until I had seen it (and hated it) in enough other authors' stories to finally recognize it in my own.

Some people may feel my writing doesn't show I learned any of this. I won't argue. That's their opinion and they're entitled to it. Not to mention I know I don't follow a lot of the rules. The whole point is to better learn to communicate through your writing, which I feel I am constantly improving at. It took me a long time to shrug off overwhelming criticism and become comfortable with my writing style. That doesn't mean I don't make mistakes. It doesn't mean I'm not wrong. It just means that I feel the rules are there to help aid in communication, and I'm comfortable with breaking them when I feel I am communicating my ideas in an entertaining and comprehendible way.

A little side note: Many writers talk about something they call imposter syndrome. Basically, it is the thought that you (me, they, whoever is thinking this about themselves) are not good enough, that people will figure out you don't know what you are doing and finally realize you are a fraud and shouldn't be a writer. I personally know MANY bestselling and award-winning authors, whose names you would most likely recognize, who openly admit this never goes away. Or if it does, it always seems to come back.

The first time Kevin J. Anderson complimented one of my stories, I thought he was being nice. And he probably was. But I was on top of the world from the compliment. For a couple of days. Then the imposter syndrome set in. Like it always does. But Kevin must have actually seen something in my writing, because it was soon after that he asked me to co-author a novelette with him. And that did my ego some good, let me tell you. Happy dance across the living room when I got off the phone with him. Then, of course, the stress and worry about the project set in. You can see where this is going.

The third time Kevin asked me to write with him, I remember thinking that if he was going to ask a third time, I must be doing *something* right. And there is a lot of truth to that. If I sucked as a writer, if I were terrible to work with, why would he reach out to me. After all, it's not like he doesn't know any other writers.

But that doesn't stop the imposter syndrome from rearing up and filling me with doubt and anxiety even as I write these words now. So I am going to tell you what I tell myself:

It's a part of life. Get over it and move on. There are enough people who will make you feel bad about your writing, you don't need to add yourself to the list. Do your writing and move on.

You won't listen to me any more than I listen to myself, but there it is. Know that you are not alone with these feelings. The only writers I have ever met who did not seem to display any signs of imposter syndrome were writers suffering from a different problem. The one I mentioned in **TL;DR.** They were the authors who thought that when a reader "doesn't get it," it was the reader's fault, not their fault for failing to put words on the page that other people could follow.

So, take that bit of imposter syndrome that you always feel, that tiny bit that never goes away, and fold it up, put it in your pocket, and save it for times when you really feel bad about your writing. Then, pull it out, look at it, and realize it's not a bad thing. Remember that this little piece of doubt is what keeps you striving to be better. All the time. No matter what.

It is actually a key to success, and you have it, and no one can take it away from you. It's yours to use anytime, to motivate yourself, to open up new opportunities, to constantly improve yourself. And it can and does do this, if you let it.

When you become comfortable enough with your own writing, do me a favor: pay it forward. Help struggling writers see the mistakes they are making, whether it's in their writing or in their careers, and then, if you have any generosity left, and you feel like it, leave me a review on something I have written.

Thanks!

And good luck. I look forward to seeing your name in print.

ABOUT THE AUTHOR

A Colorado native, Sam Knight spent ten years in California's wine country before returning to the Rockies. When asked if he misses California, he gets a wistful look in his eyes and replies he misses the green mountains in the winter, but he is glad to be back home.

As well as having worked for at least three publishing companies, Sam has started his own publishing company, Knight Writing Press, which published the book you are now holding. He has edited numerous short stories, novels, and anthologies, and is the author of six children's books, five short story collections, three novels, and over 75 stories, including three co-authored with Kevin J. Anderson, two of which were media-tie-ins: "Wayward Pines: Aberration" (Kindle Worlds, 2014) and "Of Monsters and Men" Planet of the Apes: Tales from the Forbidden Zone (Titan, 2016).

A stay-at-home father, Sam attempts to be a full-time writer, but there are only so many hours left in a day after kids. Once upon a time, he was known to quote books the way some people quote movies, but now he claims having a family has made him forgetful, as a survival adaptation. He can be found at SamKnight.com and contacted at sam@samknight.com.

www.ingramcontent.com/pod-product-compliance
Lightning Source LLC
Chambersburg PA
CBHW020248030426
42336CB00010B/664